COMPARATIVE PERSPECTIVES ON

STRATIFICATION

Mexico, Great Britain, Japan

Edited and with Introduction by

JOSEPH A. KAHL

Washington University, Saint Louis

LITTLE, BROWN AND COMPANY   Boston

ACKNOWLEDGMENTS

The preparation of this volume benefits from happy accident and generous friends. When I was invited to organize it by Professor Alex Inkeles, the general editor of this series, I was about to take an intermission from several years of study of Mexico to spend a short time in England. As Visiting Professor at the University of Leicester, I had the benefit of stimulation and advice from my colleagues there, who guided me in a reading course on contemporary Britain. I am particularly indebted to Professor Ilya Neustadt, Eric G. Dunning and Sydney Holloway of Leicester, and Earl I. Hopper of the London School of Economics and Political Science.

At the same time that I was in England, my friend and colleague at Washington University, John W. Bennett, was in Japan, continuing his long-standing association with that country. He kindly consented to help collect the articles on Japan, and participated in the writing of the introduction to them which appears below. He in turn was ably assisted by Miss Michiko Ise of Tokyo University.

I have received a continuing education about Mexico from many sociologist friends there, including Pablo González-Casanova, Rodolfo Stavenhagen, Raúl Benítez-Zenteno, and three honorary sociologists, Lini de Vries, Francisco Garza-García and Michael Maccoby. Most recently, my tutor has been Claudio Stern, who shared the writing of the essay on Mexico which attempts to synthesize the existing materials on stratification in that country.

The preparation of this book would have been impossible without the usual loyal assistance of my secretary, Mrs. Dorothy Altheimer.

J. A. K.
Cuernavaca, Mexico

TABLE OF CONTENTS

Introduction by Joseph A. Kahl   ix

I Mexico, a Developing Society   1

  1. CLAUDIO STERN AND JOSEPH A. KAHL,
     Stratification Since the Revolution   5

  2. RODOLFO STAVENHAGEN, *Classes,
     Colonialism, and Acculturation*   31

  3. PABLO GONZÁLEZ-CASANOVA,
     Dynamics of the Class Structure   64

II Great Britain, Continuity Amidst Change   83

  4. RICHARD TITMUSS, *Goals of
     Today's Welfare State*   89

  5. DAVID LOCKWOOD, *Sources of Variation in
     Working-Class Images of Society*   98

  6. JOHN H. GOLDTHORPE, DAVID LOCKWOOD, FRANK
     BECHHOFER, AND JENNIFER PLATT, *The Affluent
     Worker and the Thesis of* Embourgeoisement:
     Some Preliminary Research Findings   115

  7. JEAN FLOUD, *Social-Class Factors
     in Educational Achievement*   137

III *Japan, Oriental Industrialism*   154

8. HERBERT PASSIN, *Education and Career*   159

9. KEN'ICHI TOMINAGA, *Occupational Mobility in Tokyo*   180

10. EZRA VOGEL, *The Salary Man*   195

11. SHIZUO MATSUSHIMA, *Labour-Management Relations*   223

Introduction

In broad outline, the stratification systems of contemporary industrial societies are strikingly similar. Although at close range they show variations, in comparison with the much greater variations among non-industrial stratification systems they stand out as a single type. A brief glance at world history illuminates the contrast.

Non-industrial societies range from small bands of hunters and gatherers, through isolated communities of subsistence farmers, to diverse types of high agrarian societies that link local areas together into large systems. As Gerhard Lenski has recently shown,[1] the hunters and gatherers lack institutionalized stratification, since there is no economic surplus that can be monopolized by a few men and passed on to their children. The only way a man can gain prestige or power is through his personal qualities, and these are ephemeral. However, the agrarian societies do produce a surplus, and this is usually concentrated in the hands of a small elite: they dominate politically and militarily, they own the land, they have high incomes, they are educated.[2] The vast mass of the people — some 90 per cent of them — are peasants who labor for mere subsistence. Once the concentration of land ownership and political

[1] Gerhard Lenski, *Power and Privilege* (New York: McGraw-Hill, 1966).

[2] A detailed comparative account of the emergence of highly-organized stratification systems in ancient Mesopotamia and pre-conquest Mexico is given by Robert Mc. Adams, *The Evolution of Urban Society* (Chicago: Aldine, 1966).

power by a minority begins with settled agriculture, it tends to increase in a linear fashion as society develops (with only minor variations according to local historical circumstances) until the top one or two per cent of the population may be receiving over fifty per cent of the total income produced.

This process of concentration illustrates the systemic property of social stratification: one thing leads to another. Power leads to property which leads to income which leads to prestige – and to a lesser degree, this works in reverse order as well.

But industrial society changes these systemic relations in fundamental ways. Productivity per worker for the first time in the history of mankind increases to the point where the mass of the population can be raised to a level considerably above subsistence (if, as Malthus correctly taught us, the birth rate is simultaneously brought under control). This is most dramatically seen in agriculture: instead of some 90 per cent of the people working as farmers, producing a surplus that allows 10 per cent to live in cities and do other kinds of work, the proportions are reversed. Today, less than 10 per cent of a population, if good land is available and modern techniques are used, can easily feed the remainder. This transformation reduces the cost of food and is reflected in average family budgets: instead of two-thirds or more of income devoted to food, a quarter or less will suffice.

Time and energy released from agriculture flow into other occupations. With the aid of machines, men produce large amounts and new varieties of material goods – from the ready-made suit of clothes that makes it hard to distinguish a factory worker from a banker, to the automobile and the television set which together break the bonds of locality. Another change is equally important: the majority of men no longer work at growing crops or making objects. They work at selling things, repairing them, keeping track of them on paper, or in educating, transporting or amusing the millions who now spend only a small portion rather than most of their waking hours at work.

If we take, therefore, the occupational distribution as the single most important index of the structure of a society, all advanced industrial societies are similar, and get more similar every year. That is not to say they are identical, even in occupational terms. France has proportionately more farmers than England; the United States has more entrepreneurs than the Soviet Union. But broadly speaking the trends are clearly toward a distribution with few farmers, as many white-collar as blue-collar workers, and increasing levels of skill throughout the system.

These occupational patterns in turn dictate a certain type of educational preparation. Universal literacy is necessary, and in the early stages of transition to industrialism, every society institutes free and compulsory primary education if it did not already exist. Furthermore, secondary and university education expand in size and change in content, becoming more directly attuned to the preparation of middle- and higher-level technicians and administrators.[3]

Income and prestige now flow from education and occupation (as they used to flow from property ownership). As the middle ranks on the educational-occupational hierarchy expand, so do the "middle classes" as judged by consumption styles and patterns of respect and deference. Eventually the urban manual workers and the farmers also share in the benefits of material prosperity and educational expansion. These changes in turn produce political changes: the franchise expands, all adults become citizens, and the complete monopolization of knowledge and power in the hands of a tiny permanent elite becomes impossible.

Thus Lenski correctly maintains that the long-term trend toward concentration in the stratification variables that began with settled agriculure and reached its peak in the high agrarian societies, reverses itself under industrialism. There are tendencies toward greater equality, toward more widespread distribution of both material goods and participation in the affairs of the mind and the state.

These trends toward equality can be measured in several ways. For instance, one can make a gross historical comparison between the high agrarian societies in which the top 2 per cent of the population used to receive more than half of all the income that was distributed, and the high industrial societies in which the same elite group now gets only about 10 per cent of the available income.[4]

Or, one can compare a range of contemporary countries at different stages of development. Gláucio A. Dillon Soares, basing his analysis on the work of Simon Kuznets, looked at the rewards flowing to the top 5 per cent of the population in various countries in 1950. It varied from 65 per cent of all income for Southern Rhodesia, through 40 per cent for Mexico and Colombia, to about 20 per cent for the United States and the countries of Western Europe.[5]

Or, one can look at time trends within a given country. In Great Britain, the top 5 per cent of families (before taxes) received 48 per cent of the income in 1880, but only 18 per cent in 1957. In the United States, the decline for the same elite group has been from about 30 per cent in 1929 to about 20 per cent in 1959.[6]

[3] Frederick Harbison and Charles A. Myers, *Education, Manpower & Economic Growth* (New York: McGraw-Hill, 1964).

[4] Lenski, *op. cit.*

[5] Gláucio A. Dillon Soares, *Economic Development & Political Radicalism* (New York: Basic Books, forthcoming). Soares' data also show that comparisons of rich and poor states within a given country do not show the same positive relation between industrial development and equality of income distribution.

[6] *Ibid.*

The concentration of property (and thus potentially of economic and political power) is much greater than the concentration of income, since in industrial society most men can earn a good living from wages and salaries even if they own nothing. For example, in the United States the wealthiest one per cent of the families were estimated to own about one-third of all the property in 1922, and one-quarter in 1953.[7] In Great Britain the top one per cent is thought to own at least one-fifth of the property.[8] In both countries, the concentration of ownership of shares of stock in corporations is greater still: over 75 per cent of the shares held by individuals in the United States are in the hands of the wealthiest one per cent of the people (although an increasing proportion of stock shares are not held by individuals but by pension funds and other "fiduciary" groups).

These figures, revealing as they are, hide some of the facts. The wealthy receive more "fringe benefits" than do the poor, and these are difficult to calculate and add to their incomes. This is true of corporation executives who have the use of a company car, or can buy stock at special prices, or who enjoy the fruits of tax-deductions based on capital-gains bookkeeping; it is also true of middle-income families who tend to take more advantage of public services, particularly schools, than do the poorest families.

Furthermore, a declining share to the very rich does not always equal an increasing share to the very poor. In the United States, in particular, the middle groups have gained the most, while the poorest may be relatively (though not absolutely) worse off than before. The main reason for this is that our welfare system and our minimum wage laws for aiding the poor are niggardly by comparison with European countries. As Michael Harrington made us all aware, some 20 per cent of Americans are being left out of the benefits of our current affluence.[9]

Finally, it is important to realize that these trends do not represent a "natural law" that is linear and everlasting. Indeed, it appears that during the early phases of industrialization inequality tends to grow; since that tendency is coupled with a low level of average income for the whole country, distress among the lower classes can be acute, and political protest is likely.[10] (It should be remembered that the communist revolutions

[7] Robert J. Lampman, *The Share of Top Wealth-Holders in National Wealth* (Princeton: Princeton University Press, 1962). See also Gabriel Kolko, *Wealth and Power in America* (New York: Praeger, 1962).

[8] John Westergaard, "The Withering Away of Class: A Contemporary Myth," in *Towards Socialism*, eds. Perry Anderson and Robin Blackburn (Ithaca, N.Y.: Cornell University Press, 1966). Another estimate puts the proportion at two-fifths; see the data of J. E. Meade, quoted by Robin Blackburn, "Inequality and Exploitation," *New Left Review*, No. 42 (March-April, 1967), p. 4.

[9] Michael Harrington, *The Other America* (Baltimore: Penguin, 1963).

[10] Soares, *op. cit.* But see the article by González-Casanova below, which indicates that deliberate government action can soften the consequences.

in Russia and China occurred during the early phases of industrial development.) Then in the later phases of industrialization, equality in income distribution increases at the same time that average levels of living go up, thus the distress of the masses is doubly relieved. This process has occurred in all the advanced industrial countries during the first half of the 20th century. To use only one illustration: the proportion of families below the "poverty line" in the United States fell from 51 per cent in 1929 to 21 per cent in 1962.[11]

In general terms, this trend toward greater equality of income has operated through two processes: (1) groups of industrial workers have forced employers to raise their wages by organizing effective labor unions, often with government help; (2) there has been a redistribution of jobs, with an expansion of middle-level positions, and a contraction of unskilled positions at the bottom of the hierarchy, and therefore more people are able to earn middle incomes. If the few who receive large profits are not included, then we can say that differentials in wages and salaries have been narrowing over the years in all the industrial countries, both capitalist and socialist.

But now a new equilibrium may have been reached, for in the last decade studies in the United States and Great Britain show no gains in equality of distribution (and even a few reverses).[12] It is probable that any further redistribution of income, at least for the benefit of the very poor, will have to come from more vigorous political action through expansion and reorganization of welfare programs, and not through automatic market processes or labor union pressures; indeed, most of the very poor who work do not belong to unions, and many are retired or unemployed.

The figures just presented indicate that mature industrial societies distribute income in a more equal fashion than do traditional high agrarian societies. The same is true for education. For example, in the United States about 80 per cent of the young people now graduate from high school; about 40 per cent begin college, and half of them graduate. When everyone is literate and more than half the people graduate from secondary school, sharp distinctions in culture and prestige among men are bound to fade; a mass market is created for ideas as well as for goods.

In Mexico, only two-thirds of the children of primary-school age are currently (1960) attending classes, and only about 13 per cent of the adolescents are studying in secondary schools. About 3 per cent attend a university.

In Great Britain (1960), primary education is universal, and so is basic

[11] Herman P. Miller, *Rich Man, Poor Man* (New York: Crowell, 1964). The criterion of poverty is a family receiving less than $3,000 in terms of the 1962 purchasing power of the dollar.
[12] *Ibid.* Also see Blackburn, *op. cit.*, and Westergaard, *op. cit.*

secondary education (until the 10th grade). After that, only about 20 per cent continue to advanced secondary. About 4 per cent attend a university on a regular basis, but another 10 per cent get some alternative form of higher education.

In Japan education is universal until the end of junior high school, or the 9th year of study. After that, further training depends upon the passing of rigorous examinations; about 60 per cent of the youth go to senior high school, and 20 per cent of the graduates (not the age cohort) enter university.

Once formal education is widespread in a society, it becomes the most important single influence on a man's occupational career. Instead of learning to work by toiling alongside his father, as did a peasant boy, a modern youth prepares for work by studying in school. Thus his "life chances" are explained to a large degree by the number of years and the type of schooling he has obtained. But what determines the length of schooling?

Here we must make a sharp shift in theoretical emphasis: from the profile or shape of the stratification hierarchy (the sizes of the strata, and the gaps between them), we turn to the process which sorts individuals and places them in various positions. This sorting can lead either to "succession," in which son follows father, or to "mobility," in which son moves to a position different in status from that of his father.

Succession is always common, since a boy in any society who grows up in a family with high status has many advantages that increase his chances of staying there. In contemporary society, his parents encourage him to get a good education, and make it easier for him to obtain quality schooling. To take two examples: In Britain, only about 2 per cent of the boys from working-class homes reach a university, but almost 20 per cent of the boys from middle-class homes get there. In the Soviet Union, only about 10 per cent of farm boys study beyond junior high school, but over 80 per cent of the sons of urban white-collar workers continue.[13]

Yet mobility is also widespread in modern society. In Britain, about a third of the men have jobs at the same level as their fathers, slightly less than a third have risen, and slightly more than a third have fallen. In the United States, somewhat more have risen and fewer fallen.

It has long been theorized that rates of mobility should be positively correlated with the degree of industrialization. It seems logical to assume that a society which constantly up-grades its occupational structure, and makes high-level jobs open to wide sectors of the population through state-subsidized education, would be likely to induce a lot of movement freeing sons from the restraints of their fathers' statuses. Yet precise com-

[13] The figure for Britain is from the article by Jean Floud in this volume; that for the Soviet Union is based on a sample survey quoted on page 41 of the volume edited by Smelser and Lipset, cited in the following note.

parison of mobility rates has proven to be far more difficult than anticipated. The evidence is clear that industrial societies have a lot of
mobility, but how much more than high agrarian societies remains a moot
point, as does the comparison of rates among contemporary industrial
countries.[14] For our present purposes, we shall concentrate mainly on
the processes through which societies select individuals for various roles,
that is, the manner in which familial, educational and occupational
institutions are linked together, rather than study rates of mobility in
detail.

There are basic trends toward similarity among industrial societies;
but will they necessarily become all alike? Obviously not. Their similarities in broad structure, their homogeneity compared to non-industrial
societies, need not imply that they are or will be identical. They have
reached their present condition through varying paths of history, and the
residues of their different trajectories continue to influence present action.
They have borrowed much of their technology, and indeed, many of the
social forms of organizing and applying techniques, from one another —
but there exist two models to follow, capitalist and socialist, which overlap in some ways but diverge in others. The occupational and educational
distributions of the two types of system are quite similar, but the ideological commitments that combine with those distributions to shape
political realities are of course dissimilar — though many observers note
some paths of convergence in ideologies as well, since the present policies
of the U.S. are far from the laissez-faire capitalism of William Mc-
Kinley, and those of the U.S.S.R. (and even more, Yugoslavia) are far
from the original prescriptions of Marx and Lenin.[15]

To make detailed studies of stratification in present-day industrial societies, it is necessary to take advantage of modern sociological research
techniques. Unfortunately, most applications of these techniques have
been confined to one country at a time, so the reader interested in com-

[14] The main sources of information are: S. M. Lipset and R. Bendix, *Social
Mobility in Industrial Society* (Berkeley and Los Angeles: University of California
Press, 1959). S. M. Miller, "Comparative Social Mobility," *Current Sociology*,
IX (1960), No. 1. Thomas Fox and S. M. Miller, "Occupational Stratification
and Mobility," *Studies in Comparative International Development*, I (1965)
No. 1. N. J. Smelser and S. M. Lipset, eds., *Social Structure and Mobility in
Economic Development* (Chicago: Aldine, 1966).

[15] For an enlightening debate on the degree of convergence, see John H. Gold-
thorpe, "Social Stratification in Industrial Societies," in *The Development of
Industrial Society*, ed. Paul Halmos (Sociological Review Monograph No. 8,
1964); E. G. Dunning and E. I. Hopper, "Industrialization & The Problem of
Convergence: A Critical Note," *Sociological Review*, XIV (July, 1966) No. 2;
and Goldthorpe's "Reply," *Ibid*. See also two books: Ralf Dahrendorf, *Class and
Class Conflict in Industrial Society* (Stanford: Stanford University Press, 1959);
Stanislaw Ossowski, *Class Structure in the Social Consciousness* (New York: Free
Press, 1963).

parative generalizations must supply the theoretical and historical perspective that permits conclusions about degrees of similarity and difference. One procedure is to cast as wide a net as possible, and catch examples from many countries. This has been well done in a massive collection edited by Bendix and Lipset.[16] But in a short volume such as this one, it seems best to concentrate on very few countries, so that a set of overlapping articles about each society can entice toward deeper understanding.

Since this volume has been prepared mainly for the American college undergraduate who is studying about his own society and seeks a comparative perspective, it assumes that detailed knowledge of stratification in the United States is being gathered from other sources. It is here that the comparative perspective is offered.

We have chosen three societies upon which to focus. First, we discuss Mexico. It is close by, and many readers will have visited it. It is entering industrial life with great speed — indeed, it has had a rate of steady development, especially since 1940, that is among the highest in the contemporary world. It is just at that point of transition which makes it a magnificent laboratory, enabling us to see history being made before our eyes. Many forms of pre-industrial life continue with vigor, at the same time that new demands impinge upon and re-shape all phases of society. By moving from one part of the country to another, one moves from the 16th to the 20th century. Often in the mind of one man can be found traces of both styles of civilization.

Next, Great Britain. First country of the world to industrialize, first to become predominantly urban, she now faces deep crisis. The empire is gone, and her pattern of international trade is under pressure from new competitors. She attempts to reform to become more efficient, and yet keeps finding that tradition dies hard. At the moment, she seems to have an even balance between the forces of continuity and those of change: the Conservative and Labour parties alternate in power, and within each party there are divisions reflecting forces of tradition and forces of reform. Her biggest debate about stratification centers on the role of education. In the past, it was designed to reinforce the style and strength of the elite: to produce polished gentlemen from the old families, and admit a few promising youths from lesser stock at an age young enough to permit complete socialization into the ways of their superiors. But in 1944 revamping took place, the culmination of changes which had begun earlier but moved slowly. Education (along with medical care) became equalitarian in philosophy — all men and women were to have equal access to schooling, and be trained up to the limit of their innate capacities. But the realities of stratification have in large measure defeated the reforms,

[16] Reinhard Bendix and Seymour Martin Lipset, eds., *Class, Status and Power*, (New York: Free Press, 2d ed., 1966).

as we shall see in detail through the studies of several English social scientists.

Finally, Japan. For American eyes, it is the most exotic and interesting contrast to the United States.[17] Japan began her modernization at the end of the 19th century under a deliberate policy of strengthening the nation against the inroads of the Europeans who were at that time carving up China and threatening to do the same to Japan. A dissident group within the old elite seized power, and by authoritarian measures, always directed and controlled from the top, produced a rapid industrialization. This phase reached its peak — and overstepped it — during World War II. After the war a new phase began, built from defeat and energized by a more democratic and equalitarian philosophy that reflected the will of the occupying power, as well as the release of long-suppressed latent forces within Japan. In a very few years, one of the miracles of the contemporary world occurred. Japan not only recovered, she progressed at breathtaking speed. The industrial revolution was completed; the farms were turned over to those who labored on them, and were modernized in technique; Tokyo grew to become the world's largest city; the birth rate was brought under control; and the new working and middle classes moved into the era of mass consumption. Many features of the old authoritarian society were cast aside; women gained a measure of equality, parliamentary democracy prevailed, and even the Emperor became but a human symbol of national identity instead of a God. And yet from a distance Japan still appears to Americans to be quaint and oriental and different. She continues many traditional ways of life that seem far from industrial modes, and indeed uses the old social forms to solve new problems. Surely Japan is the test case: how far does industrialism lead a society toward ecumenical patterns of stratification?

Through study of these three societies the American reader can enlighten himself not only about other ways of life but also about his own. By comparison, he will begin to understand how some aspects of American life reflect particular traditions, and others are adaptations to the universal requirements of industrial civilization. He will begin to appreciate the interplay between general structural pressures and unique ideological goals, to dissect the flow of history into its automatic imperatives and its areas of choice that allow men and nations to express their own purposes. He will begin to understand that in some ways a middle-class man in St. Louis is more like a middle-class man in Tokyo or London or Mexico City than he is like a lower-class man in his own city. The reader will find here similarity amidst diversity, and is invited to ponder the implications.

[17] Except, perhaps, for the Soviet Union. Two excellent studies of Soviet stratification can be found in the Bendix and Lipset volume, already cited: Alex Inkeles, "Social Stratification & Mobility in the Soviet Union," and Robert A. Feldmesser, "Toward the Classless Society?"

COMPARATIVE PERSPECTIVES ON

STRATIFICATION

Mexico, Great Britain, Japan

I

Mexico
A Developing Society

Until 1910, Mexico was a relatively stagnant society which had been ruled for a quarter of a century by an efficient military dictator, Porfirio Díaz. During his regime, internal peace was established and maintained, a new experience for Mexico, and a start was made toward modern industry by the construction of railroads, textile mills, and oil wells. These were built mostly by foreign capital and directed by foreign managers and engineers. There were some jobs for local people, and some taxes to the government, but the impact on the old society was not great. About 80 per cent of the people continued as peasants laboring for mere subsistence; most of them lived as semi-serfs on large plantations or *haciendas*. The rulers of the country were absentee landlords, politicians, and military men, in collaboration with foreign capitalists. The profits from the new industries mostly flowed abroad, and the economy was typically "colonial" in form despite a century of political independence.

Then the old order collapsed in revolution. There followed a decade of terrible turbulence in which the population fell by almost half a million (from a base of 15 million) as a result of civil war, disease and malnutrition. Many foreigners were driven out, and many local landlords were forced from their *haciendas*. The political power of the Catholic Church was broken. The old symbols were reversed: the glorious Spanish

conqueror, Cortés, was turned into a plundering despoiler of the true
Mexican people, and the Aztec king, Cuauhtémoc, was elevated to the
role of tragic hero. Diego Rivera painted the new symbols on the public
walls, and thereby joined in the proclamation that Indian traditions were
henceforth to be admired, and the Indian peasant was to be the bene-
ficiary of a new way of life constructed out of old social forms combined
with modern techniques. Nationalism was to prevail over foreign exploitation, and socialism was to benefit the masses. These symbols continue to this day as images of the future, but many compromises have
been made with practical realities as the years have passed by.

After the revolutionary decade, a new group of military chiefs emerged.
The two most famous and colorful leaders had been eliminated during
the years of turmoil: Pancho Villa and Emiliano Zapata. The strongest
survivors were Alvaro Obregón, who ruled during the early twenties, and
Plutarco Elías Calles, who succeeded him in the late twenties and early
thirties. These were pragmatic men who above all sought to maintain
themselves in power, so they formed amalgams of various pressure groups,
bending their policies to accommodate radical intellectuals, organized
workers and peasants, ambitious military careerists, bureaucratic administrators, and new businessmen.

The early years were ones of reconstruction. Some land was distributed
to the peasants in those areas where they were strong enough to demand
it. Roads were built to open up isolated regions, and irrigation dams
constructed to increase food production. The bases were established of
an entirely new system of free public education from kindergarten to
university. A bureaucracy was slowly formed which could carry out these
tasks with local instead of foreign technicians. There was a heady atmosphere of intellectual and social creativity, but it took almost a
decade before economic production had climbed back to its pre-revolutionary level.

A single dominant political party was formed by Calles which united
generals and civilians as the official heirs of the Revolution. It continues
to this day as the organ which merges all major interests into a structure
which settles disputes by internal negotiation and compromise. There
has been no successful *coup* against the ruling party since the original
Revolution. Elections are held every six years; the official candidate always
wins, and the previous President gracefully retires from office. The system
maintains order, but also has introduced flexibility, since younger men
continually rise to the top and bring new skills and new ideas at the
same time that they reiterate old ideological slogans. The Mexican Revolution seems to be the only one of modern times in which the original
strong men were retired from office; since Obregón was murdered and
Calles failed to perpetuate himself in power, it has been clear that no
Stalin, Franco or Mao Tse-tung would be allowed to emerge. This has

a double advantage: new ideas come to the fore, and energetic younger men are co-opted into the system and promoted to positions of responsibility rather than left outside as frustrated rebels. The President is now a civilian politician, and his top aides are men in their forties and fifties. By contrast, at the end of the Díaz regime the dictator was still surrounded by his earlier collaborators, and their average age was over seventy.

Since the Revolution settled down and "institutionalized" itself, there have been two major shifts in policy. General Lázaro Cárdenas succeeded to the Presidency in 1934 and moved policy to the Left. He greatly increased the distribution of land to the peasants: the population living on *haciendas* dropped to about 800,000 by 1940 (it had been about 3 million before the Revolution); about half of the rural families gained control of the land they worked. In industry, Cárdenas usually favored workers against owners in strikes, especially when the owners were foreigners. This policy led to an impasse in the oil industry in 1938 which was solved by nationalization.

In 1946 Miguel Alemán became President. He moved policy toward the Right, and favored forced-draft industrialization. Certain forms of foreign capital were invited back, especially in manufacturing; Mexican firms were given high tariff protection; and government money was made available to new industries. Actually, the years of World War II had started the push toward industrial development, since local manufacturers had a golden opportunity to produce goods that had become scarce on the world market; the policies of Alemán continued the boom. Ever since, the stress has been more on increasing production than on redistributing wealth and income. There has been a growth in the Gross National Product of about 6 per cent a year, maintained since 1940.

Much of Mexico's dynamism and optimism stems from this steady economic growth in agriculture and industry. But increase of production has not solved all problems. One unanticipated trend has been a "population explosion"; the current annual increase in population is 3.5 per cent, among the highest in the world, and this cuts the *per capita* increase in income to less than half of the gross figure. Consequently, at the same time that average income, average education, and the average level of consumption keep going up, so does the absolute number of poor people, the "marginals" who do not participate in progress. They live in great numbers in the countryside, but in recent years are beginning to shift to the cities, which grow in population faster than they can provide jobs and schools and decent houses.

Mexico's progress and her problems can be measured by transformations in the system of social stratification. The main existing studies of this process are synthesized in the article which follows by Stern and Kahl. Using the occupational structure as their key index, they show

how profoundly the society has changed since the Revolution. They depict the movement of people from farm to city, from peasant labor to industrial and commercial jobs, and they show the concomitant shifts in education, in income, in style of life. They also hint at some of the implications of the stratification system for the modes of political action.

The details of stratification in the rural scene are examined by Rodolfo Stavenhagen. He shows the interplay between ethnicity, class and status, and demonstrates that the Revolution still has a long way to go before it bestows full participant citizenship upon the Indian peasants of the isolated regions. His article is particularly noteworthy for its ability to take previously published ethnographic materials and reanalyze them from a new and more revealing theoretical framework, one which emphasizes class and stratification.

Pablo González-Casanova, using mainly the data of the 1960 census, describes the current stratification profile of the country. Then he asks an important question: given the great inequality which exists, why is there so little political protest? Why does a Second Revolution not appear to fulfill the high promises of the First? His answers reveal the meanings of Mexican politics, and suggest new insights about old theories of the relation between social class and political behavior.

For the student of comparative stratification, Mexico is a particularly revealing case. The very rapidity of change, the fast pace of the move from traditional agriculture to modern industry, makes it easier to perceive some of the processes involved. Furthermore, her mixed system, which combines many features of socialist planning and government investment with a vigorous sector of private capitalism, puts the lie to ideological purists from both sides. She has created a unique blend based on her own design. The Revolution was a success in that it destroyed an old order that perpetuated social injustice and prevented rapid economic growth. And yet the Revolution fails to bring knowledge and food and hope to all the people, despite over fifty years of effort and many triumphs. Perhaps the redeeming fact of the current system is that its political leaders are aware of its deficiencies, and Mexican intellectuals and social scientists continually analyze and expose the country's social problems. The sympathetic visitor to Mexico notes a sense of purpose and a pragmatic flexibility of procedure that augur well for the future.

1   CLAUDIO STERN AND JOSEPH A. KAHL

Stratification Since the Revolution

The economic, political and social changes which flowed from the Mexican Revolution produced a transformation in the system of stratification. Our purpose here is to summarize and integrate the available studies of this transformation, relying mainly on those which use quantitative indicators. We do not deal extensively with the structure of power emerging from "classes" in the European sense of that term, but rather emphasize the distribution of status characteristics among the population which produce "strata" of families in the form of a hierarchy.

Published materials on this subject are scattered and partial. The most comprehensive attempt at integration is over fifteen years old (Iturriaga, 1951 — see bibliography below). Some more recent essays have been published, and will be referred to in this article; they rarely deal with the whole system, and often are not clear about their methodological procedures, so the reader upon finding inconsistencies does not know if they are a consequence of the raw data or the treatment of the data by the authors. By discussing some of the methodological issues, we hope to clarify the situation as a guide for further research. We would also hope to stimulate more studies of local and regional variations, and of the interconnections between the statistical indicators of status position and the qualitative description of life styles (such as Lewis, 1951; Whiteford, 1964). Most of all, we need more studies of the forces which produce change (such as Wolf, 1959; González-Casanova, 1967; Stavenhagen, this volume).

THE SETTING BEFORE THE REVOLUTION

Before analyzing the rapid changes of the last two generations, it is necessary to sketch in the background of the social system before the Revolution — a representative of the type of high agrarian society in which power and land are concentrated in the hands of a few families. There was effective control through dictatorship; although many of the

This article has been prepared especially for inclusion in the present volume.

Claudio Stern received the degree of "Licenciado en Ciencias Sociales" from the National University of Mexico in 1966, and is currently a candidate for the doctorate in Sociology at Washington University, St. Louis.

regions had high degrees of autonomy and self-sufficiency, there was a single national system.

The population was about 15 millions, four-fifths of whom lived in rural zones. Most of these people were illiterate peasants, more than half of whom were tied to the large estates or *haciendas* as workers or share-croppers, often in a form of serfdom based on debt-peonage. Few of the landowners lived on their estates; most of them consumed their profits in Mexico City or other capitals of the world.

The concentration of landownership at this period is well known: according to Stavenhagen (1966), one per cent of the population owned 97 per cent of the total land, while 96 per cent of the people owned only one per cent of the land. Other figures (Silva Herzog, 1959) show that eleven thousand *hacendados* controlled 57 per cent of the national territory; many of them were foreigners. Many *haciendas* covered thousands and some even millions of hectares.[1]

As Stavenhagen (1966, p. 465) points out: "the *hacienda* was not only a large landholding system but above all it was a social system, a universe within which certain kinds of social and economic relationships took place. The greater part of the population lived within the limits of the *haciendas* and in fact lacked the most elementary civic rights." The landowner or his agent controlled the local police and courts; and there was no other employer within easy reach. Erasmus (1961, pp. 210-12) makes the situation quite vivid:

> All the haciendas operated stores (*tiendas de raya*) where the workers could get food and clothing on credit. . . . Once in debt a man was obliged to work as directed until he had paid his debt in full. . . . With wages of eight pesos a month the prospect of repaying debts was hopeless once a man owed more than a hundred pesos. . . . The worker could appeal to no higher authority than his patron, for all local government was controlled by the hacendados.

The system contained little motivation or opportunity for mobility and change. The landowners were not interested in steadily increasing the productivity of their land by reinvesting profits, but only in obtaining enough surplus for their urban living; and the peasants were bound to the *hacienda* and had little or no contact with the outside world. Opportunities for education were restricted to the privileged sectors of the urban minority, and there was a conscious effort to impede any cultural contact which could heighten the aspirations of the peasants. At the turn of the century more than three-fourths of the Mexican population could not read or write.

Between the tiny elite and the vast mass of the peasants were small intermediary strata. The rural structure was dominated by the *hacenda-*

[1] One hectare equals 2.47 acres.

dos or large landowners, who constituted less than one per cent of the rural population; there was a group of small landowners that added up to another 7 per cent; about 3 per cent were artisans; about 9 per cent were traders or village service workers; and the remaining 80 per cent were landless peasants (Iturriaga, 1951).[2] These estimates are based on census reports of landownership and occupation; they correspond roughly with the inferences we would draw from the figures (also taken from the census) on illiteracy.

Though the country was predominantly agricultural, some industry existed, and it received a strong impulse during the last quarter of the 19th century. Foreign investment was welcomed by the administration of Porfirio Díaz. English and American capital went into the oil, railroad and mining industries, and French capital into textiles. However, these industries did not spread and produce fundamental changes in the system as a whole.

The few data available suggest that the urban strata were divided somewhat as follows (Iturriaga, 1951): an upper class of businessmen, financiers and politicians, one per cent; independent middle class of merchants and professionals, 15 per cent; salaried middle class, 8 per cent; petty traders and street vendors, 10 per cent; artisans, 25 per cent; industrial workers, 13 per cent; and laborers, 28 per cent.

With the rural and urban sectors considered separately, according to Iturriaga the occupational groups could be categorized as follows:

	Rural	Urban
Upper class	1%	1%
Middle class	2	23
Popular class	97	76
	100%	100%

Combining the rural and urban distributions, he got the figures shown in Table 1. Iturriaga's break-down is given in parallel form to that of González-Cosío, who appears to have used the same census data but organized it in a slightly different manner.

From the publications it is not possible to determine precisely the criteria utilized for defining each class, although the census data on occupations appear to be the basic source. There are some important differences between the two authors, especially concerning the size of the upper class, and the proportion of the middle class living in urban compared to rural areas. However, both sets of figures are similar in portraying the broad shape of the stratification pyramid: a tiny upper

[2] Thus, of those who were actually agricultural workers, about 11 per cent owned some land, and 89 per cent were landless. Figures for 1960 are given below.

TABLE 1. PRE-REVOLUTIONARY CLASS PROFILE

	1895 Iturriaga	1900 González-Cosío
Upper class:		
living in urban areas	0.39%	0.2%
living in rural areas	1.05	0.4
Sub-total	1.44	0.6
Middle class:		
living in urban areas	6.12	1.7
living in rural areas	1.66	6.6
Sub-total	7.78	8.3
Popular class:		
living in urban areas	14.17	16.3
living in rural areas	76.61	74.8
Sub-total	90.78	91.1
Total population	100.00%	100.0%

Sources: J. E. Iturriaga (1951), p. 28, and González-Cosío (1961), p. 55.

class, a relatively small middle class, and a very broad "popular" or lower class, mainly rural.

THE FORCES OF CHANGE

There have been important changes in the Mexican social and economic structure during the last half century. The Revolution of 1910 destroyed the old political order — the Dictator fled, the way was opened for gradually stripping the *hacendados* of power, a new army took control, and groups of industrialists, peasants and urban workers emerged as political forces. It took almost two decades for this system to organize itself; then in the 1930's it used its new power to redistribute part of the land to the peasants; it nationalized the oil industry and the railroads; it began a massive building program, constructing irrigation and power dams, and roads to open up the countryside; it established a system of popular education from kindergarten to university; it created a public health program; it nurtured enthusiasm among the people. During this period, emphasis was more on redistributing than on increasing the economic product.

After 1940 the emphasis had shifted to industrialization, and since that time, a steady growth in the total economic product of about six per cent a year has been maintained. The industrial expansion has used both foreign and domestic capital (though much more of the latter than the former), and both public and private forms of organization.

All of the above developments were intertwined, and produced two important social consequences: a major increase in the rate of population growth, combined with a redistribution of the population from stagnant to dynamic regions of the country, and from farm to city. Thus the direct impact of economic development upon individuals was that it enticed or forced them to change jobs (Germán-Parra, 1954; Jaffe, 1959; Kahl, 1960). The occupational structure was reshaped, and therefore a new stratification profile emerged. We must think about these interdependent changes all at once, but can describe them only one at a time. The place to begin is with agrarian reform.

Distribution of Land

The Revolutionary government created a new type of landholding, the *ejido*, although its ideological roots go back to early forms of both preconquest Indian and Spanish collective land systems. At first, communities (mainly Indian) who could claim that *haciendas* had swallowed up lands that traditionally were theirs could request restitution. Later, any group of peasants could claim the land they were working; the *hacendado* could keep a section for himself (usually 100 hectares of irrigated land) and the rest was subject to expropriation for the peasants. Some attempts were made at the collective tilling of farms, but they mostly failed. The bulk of the land was distributed in a form that technically made it community property which could not be sold or mortgaged, but in fact small plots were given to be worked, more or less in perpetuity, by the individual families who belonged to the *ejido* (Whetten, 1948; Flores, 1961).

More than 45 million hectares of land, representing almost half the current cropland in the country, have been distributed to about 1½ million families in the form of *ejidos* over the years since the Revolution. The current situation is difficult to describe exactly, since many men fall into more than one category: they may have an *ejido* plot and also a bit of private property, and they may also work on occasion as day laborers on someone else's land. But we can follow Stavenhagen (1966), who gives the 1960 census data for all agricultural workers (often including more than one per family):

Ejidatarios	25%
Private landowners	22
Landless workers	53
	100% (6 million)

The private owners can be further subdivided. Fifteen per cent of all agricultural workers own very small plots of less than 5 hectares, insufficient to support a family; 3.5 per cent own family-sized farms of 5 to 25 hectares; 2.7 per cent have medium farms of 25 to 200 hectares; and 0.8 per cent (about 48,000) own large farms over 200 hectares — adding up to the 22 per cent who are private owners. They control 57 per cent of the cultivable land; the rest is in *ejidos*.

Thus the reform has reduced the proportion of the landless among the agricultural workers from some 89 per cent down to about 53 per cent. Given the increase of 59 per cent in the rural population since the Revolution (1910 to 1960), that is a major accomplishment, yet rural landlessness remains acute. Many adult sons of *ejidatarios* or petty landowners are forced to the cities to look for work, while others stay in the villages as underemployed day laborers or unneeded family workers.

Large landowning continues to some degree; in fact, farms over 200 hectares represent 24 per cent of the total cultivable land. Many new large farms have been created, often by men with political power, in areas that have been opened up with irrigation. However, most large farms today are not like the old *haciendas*. If they are not cattle ranches in dry areas where vast amounts of land are needed to support the herds, they tend to be modern, mechanized farms producing for the urban and foreign markets. They are highly productive, pay wages above mere subsistence, and do not involve the complete and isolated social system that was so characteristic of the *hacienda*. And the relative political power of the owners is but a shadow of that once possessed by the *hacendados*.

Population Growth, Urbanization, Internal Migration

The land reforms freed the peasants from debt peonage, and made it much easier for them to move about looking for work. The improvements in diet that came from control over their own crops by farm workers, together with the organization of new public health services, rapidly reduced the death rate (especially infant mortality). The birth rate remained stable and high. The result was a steadily increasing pace of population growth, to the point that the distribution of land in a given area could reduce landlessness for only a generation's time: after that there would be more sons than plots. The population more than doubled from 1910 to 1960, reaching almost 35 million, and the present rate of growth of about 3.5 per cent a year will produce another doubling in 21 years.[3]

Since industry was developing, the excess population drifted toward the cities. The proportion of the population living in urban places (over 2,500 inhabitants) increased from 29 to 51 per cent between 1910 and 1960. The distribution of the urban population by size of city changed significantly in these decades, since there was increasing concentration in the larger cities. The proportion of the total population living in cities with 100,000 or more inhabitants went from 5 to 24 per cent. Mexico

---

[3] Before the Revolution, it took about four centuries for the population to double, a rate which permitted a stagnant society to maintain a sort of equilibrium.

City grew from 721,000 to almost 5 million inhabitants (Browning, 1962). At the present time, the rural population is growing at the rate of 1.6 per cent a year, and the urban population at the rate of 5.9 per cent a year.

Migration has taken place not only from rural to urban areas, but simultaneously from the less developed to the more highly developed regions of the country. The Federal District (Mexico City) and some of the Northern states have gained substantial amounts of population, whereas the poorer states in the Center and the South have relatively declined. In 1950 the census showed that the proportion born in other states was 46.4 per cent in the Federal District (which had in this way gained more than 1.3 million individuals), 63.4 per cent for Baja California Norte, 31.6 per cent for Tamaulipas, and 18.6 per cent for Nuevo León. By contrast, in the poorer states less than 6 per cent of the population had been born elsewhere (Myers, 1965, p. 69; Benítez-Zenteno, 1961, Ch. 2; Stern, 1966, Ch. 3).

Literacy and Education

We have seen that prior to the Revolution even the most basic education, knowing how to read and write, was a privilege granted to a very small minority of the population. Mainly as a result of publicly-financed programs, this situation has changed drastically in the last fifty years. Literacy has increased from 25 to 66 per cent of the adult population; the proportion of the children 6 to 14 years old attending school has grown from about 30 to 63 per cent. Yet the steady growth of total population means that more adults in absolute numbers are illiterate now than before the Revolution, and more children are lacking a place in school than was the case in 1910. (González-Casanova, 1967, p. 232).

Primary-school pupils have increased from less than a million to more than 5 million. Changes at the middle levels of education have also been substantial: at the turn of the century the country had only 76 secondary and preparatory schools (confined to the big cities, particularly Mexico City) with 8,173 students, approximately 1 per cent of the relevant age group; by 1960 there were over 550 schools at this level, and the population receiving education in them was approximately 305,000, which constituted 12.7 per cent of the appropriate age group. In Mexico City, over a third of the youth attended secondary schools (Cline, 1962, p. 203; Myers, 1965, pp. 92-93).

Higher education was elitist in the pre-revolutionary era. There were a few independent professional schools, remnants of the famous Royal and Pontifical University of New Spain, founded in 1551 and closed at the time of Mexican independence in 1810. Enrollment in the professional schools probably amounted to little more than 1,500 students. According to Myers (1965, p. 112) there were about 12,000 persons in the country with some university training at the turn of the century; many of them had studied abroad. In 1960 the census showed more than 200,000 adults with some higher education (that is, 12 or more years of schooling); and almost three per cent of the appropriate age group was enrolled in a university, over 80,000 students.

Industrial and Agricultural Expansion

Since 1940, government policy has emphasized economic growth through rapid industrialization. Actually, developments in industry help those in agriculture, since industry produces fertilizers and machines for the farms, and absorbs some of the excess labor displaced from them by modernization. According to Vernon (1963), the gross national product increased 95 per cent in the 1950's, and 74 per cent in the following decade. Given the population growth, that meant an annual *per capita* improvement of 2.9 per cent in the 1950's, and 2.3 per cent in the next decade. Agricultural output went up 82 per cent in the first of these two decades, and 67 per cent in the second; manufacturing went up 129 and 90 per cent respectively. Since the labor force in manufacturing was growing more rapidly than that in agriculture, the figures suggest that the farms may have increased output per man as much as the factories. But since a factory worker produces and earns more than a farm worker, the shift toward industry improved the productivity and income of the country.

Shifts in Occupational Structure

The human impact of the economic development can be measured by changes in the occupational distribution. Whereas almost half the population was engaged in non-agricultural activities by 1960, that proportion had been only one quarter in 1910.[4] The distribution by sector was as follows (González-Cosío, 1961):

	1910	1960
Primary sector (agriculture, fishing, forestry)	72%	54%
Secondary sector (manufacturing, mining, construction, electricity)	13	18
Tertiary sector (commerce, services, transportation)	15	28
Total	100%	100%

Changes *within* these broad sectors of the economy have also been important. In 1910 only 30 per cent of the population in the manufacturing sector worked in factories — most of the rest being independent

[4] Recent calculations at El Colegio de México give different proportions for 1910, showing only 61% in agriculture; see Solís, 1967.

artisans — but by 1960 the proportion had grown to 64 per cent. Obviously, a factory worker is more productive than an artisan (though he sometimes enjoys less prestige in the community). A similar trend occurred with regard to occupations in the tertiary sector: the great majority of the population in this sector was autonomous or self-employed five decades ago; by 1960 the proportion dependent on salaries was much greater than the autonomous one (Iturriaga, 1951, pp. 41 and 68-73; Cardoso and Reyna, 1966, Table 13, p. 20).

Though precise statistics are not available, the data suggest that the proportion of the population engaged in non-manual occupations has grown substantially with respect to that employed in manual occupations.

A Case Study of Change

The research of Erasmus (1961) gives a good example of how rapid change in a local area affects the stratification order. He describes a zone in the state of Sonora where irrigation, roads, and land reform have in recent years stimulated pronounced economic development. In the zone are three towns, ranging from 5,000 to 40,000 in population. The townspeople recognize three social strata, which they actually label as the first, second, and third class of people. The first class are wealthy business and professional men, and are clearly symbolized by membership in the best local clubs. Some of these men are descendants of local *hacendados*; others have moved to the region as educated professionals, or administrators in private or government agencies; others have become wealthy and moved up the local social scale. Erasmus writes (page 196):

> Although people in the upper classes give considerable attention to family background, the "good" families have had to share the dominant position in the class hierarchy with the newer arrivals. . . . Population growth has been too rapid to permit any entrenched group to dominate the class system. . . . The revolution and the agrarian reforms weakened, and in some cases destroyed, the economic advantage previously held by the hacienda families.

Erasmus studied wealthy men in the three towns, and found that a little over a third were descendants of "good" families, about a third were migrants from other parts of the country (mostly university-educated professionals and administrators), and the remainder had moved up within the region itself. He reports that despite a lot of social exclusiveness in their private lives, they stressed the theory of equality of opportunity, and believed that all men should have the chance to advance through ability and hard work. He adds (page 242):

> The preoccupation with acquiring consumer goods is increased by the very fact that they are the principal symbols of status. The

occupational structure of this farming area is so relatively undiffer-
entiated as yet that it provides no clearcut measure of class. More
important than whether a man is a farmer, merchant or manager
is how big, successful or important he is within these categories.
. . . Much of buying in the towns, especially in the middle (or
second) class, is done by or for the young unmarried women in the
family. Time and time again one encounters families of very modest
means — those of schoolteachers, for example — who are remodel-
ing their houses and buying new living-room furniture, refrigerators,
and big gas ranges. And invariably when one asks the reason for
all this spending one hears, "There are young ladies in the house."
. . . Girlfriends regularly visit each other, often in groups, and
are extremely conscious and critical of each other's living conditions.

This attention to invidious comparisons was related to courtship ambitions, and to the status-consciousness and status-insecurity of rising
families. The pattern is in sharp contrast to the equalitarianism that
traditionally existed in the Indian communities nearby, where wealth
was constantly redistributed to all members through the fiesta system,
and nobody tried to climb above his neighbors. But even there Erasmus
found that the new norms of conspicuous production and conspicuous
consumption were eroding the traditional ways.

Summary

The Revolution opened up the society by destroying the rigidity of the
old order. The agrarian reform loosened the ties of peasants to the land;
educational progress made it possible for many peasants to turn themselves into industrial workers; government investments in "infrastructure"
and basic industries, coupled with increasing private investments, created
new jobs in more productive sectors, and modernized a part of agriculture. The population began to grow rapidly, and to move to more advanced regions of the country and to the expanding cities.

This constant shifting from poorer to richer jobs is the key to the
changes in the shape of the stratification profile; it produced a relative
movement toward the middle strata, and therefore an increase in the
average level of living. However, we must keep some cautions in mind.
The average levels of education, occupation and income have gone up,
but many (indeed, in absolute numbers, more) people continue to live
a "marginal" existence of extreme poverty than was the case before.
Most of them are peasants in the backward regions; nevertheless, some
are urbanites, people who have drifted to the cities faster than job opportunities have been created (Lewis, 1959). Indeed, in the coming
years the problem of the marginal population will become increasingly
an urban problem.

On the average, manual workers experience an improvement in their level of living when they move to the city, even if they live poorly by urban standards. They get a better house, a better job, and enjoy better services of health and education. Thus an average urban manual worker is objectively, and feels subjectively, better off than his rural cousin (González-Casanova, this volume; Lewis, 1952; Butterworth, 1962). But if urban underemployment grows, then this statement will no longer apply to significant parts of the city population. Furthermore, as people adjust to the city they begin to compare themselves with those around them rather than those they left behind on the land; their aspirations go up. The potential for protest is increasing in the cities.

The expansion of the middle classes is primarily an urban phenomenon. The secondary schools and the white-collar jobs are found mainly in cities. Therefore, it is the development of industry, commerce and government in the cities that is the base for the growth of the middle-class way of life.

The rural scene has also changed significantly as a result of the agrarian reform: instead of the highly polarized structure with little differentiation characteristic of the pre-revolutionary epoch, the present panorama presents far greater diversification. Beside the farm laborers, new social strata have appeared, ranging from *ejidatarios,* to craftsmen and tradesmen, local government officials, and some middle-level professionals, technicians and businessmen.

THE CONTEMPORARY STRATIFICATION PROFILE

A system of social stratification is produced by the interdependence of a few key factors: the so-called "objective" variables of wealth, occupation, education, and income; and the "subjective" factors of value-orientations, class-consciousness, style of life, and prestige ranking. Connecting objective to subjective factors are the interpersonal networks that unite families of similar level into organized cliques and communities; within them, public opinion gets formed and standardized. Since research on stratification is just beginning in Mexico, we are lacking basic information on many of these variables, and more particularly, on the ways they intertwine and influence one another.

Continuing Rural-Urban and Regional Differences

Mexico in the second half of the twentieth century is still "a land of contrasts"; urbanization, industrialization, and modernization have not reached or benefited a significant proportion of the population; the distribution of material goods and cultural opportunities is highly unequal; regional inequalities are extremely great.

Some data may help to make this more explicit:

In 1960 the metropolitan area of Mexico City and the seven northern states, comprising about 30 per cent of the total population of the nation,

16 CLAUDIO STERN AND JOSEPH A. KAHL

produced more than 75 per cent of the industrial output; industrial production *per capita* ranged from 1,000 to 3,420 pesos in the seven more industrialized states in 1955, and from 45 to 150 pesos in the less industrialized ones (the average for the nation as a whole was 950 pesos). All other indicators one wishes to compute, from literacy to income *per capita*, follow these regional variations (Yates, 1962). To take another example: 82.6 per cent of the national enrollment in higher education in 1960 was concentrated in two zones, the Federal District and the state of Nuevo León.

Or, one can merely dichotomize the population into rural and urban sectors, which in 1960 divided the population into approximately two equal halves: annual income *per capita* for the rural sector in 1960 was 1,500 pesos, compared to 6,300 pesos in the urban sector; and whereas only 8 per cent of the rural families had an income of more than 1,000 pesos a month (80 dollars), in the urban sector the proportion was 35 per cent.

Shape of Profile

In describing the pre-revolutionary situation, we quoted above two authors who attempted to synthesize basic information into a picture of the stratification profile; in Table 2 we give their parallel portraits of the more recent scene.

TABLE 2. CLASS PROFILE IN RECENT YEARS

	1940 Iturriaga	1960 González-Cosío
Upper class:		
living in urban areas	0.57%	0.4%
living in rural areas	0.48	0.1
Sub-total	1.05	0.5
Middle class:		
living in urban areas	12.12	7.2
living in rural areas	3.75	9.9
Sub-total	15.87	17.1
Popular class:		
living in urban areas	22.40	32.3
living in rural areas	60.68	50.1
Sub-total	83.08	82.4
Total population	100.00%	100.0%

Sources: Iturriaga (1951), p. 29; González-Cosío (1961), p. 55.

Neither author is explicit about his procedures, although both have enough confidence to carry the results to one or two decimal places! González-Cosío says that he combined information about "income, expenses, type of occupation, and the population censuses" — but fails to give the recipe for putting them together. One author refers to 1940, the other to 1960. Yet in general, they show agreement. The main differences are these: González-Cosío, by comparison to Iturriaga, indicates a smaller upper class (especially rural); they both give similar figures for the over-all size of the middle class, but González-Cosío places a much smaller proportion of it in the cities.

Comparing time trends from the turn of the century to more recent years, one notes that both authors report a slight decline in the upper class, along with a shift toward urban preponderance; both show a doubling of the middle class (González-Cosío reports more of an urban shift, whereas Iturriaga had a greater urban emphasis to begin with): both show the same decline in the popular class (González-Cosío puts more of it in the cities).

González-Casanova, in the article which appears in this volume, treats each stratification variable separately, except for cross-classification by rural-urban residence, but his tables are particularly useful because they give sufficient detail to allow the reader to decide for himself where to draw the line between classes or strata. Trying to identify the middle and upper classes together, he shows that 13.4 per cent of the population live in homes with 4 or more rooms; 6.7 per cent have both radio and television; that 6.6 per cent of the adults over age thirty have secondary or advanced education; that about 14 per cent are either employers or non-manual employees; that 10.4 per cent of the economically active population receive incomes of over 1,000 pesos a month (80 dollars U.S.) — figures based on the 1960 census, plus a subsequent government study of income distribution.

Our own conclusion is that Iturriaga and González-Cosío are obviously including in their "middle-class" grouping a lot of men who are small farmers, skilled manual workers, artisans, petty traders and minor clerks who live at a humble level; in other words, the authors use a "loose" rather than a "tight" definition. These people live in a lower-middle class fashion by contemporary Mexican standards, but not by European or North American standards.

Other estimates of the stratification profile for different years are given in Table 3.

In order to deepen the analysis, let us turn to a more detailed examination of several of the stratification variables.

Occupational Strata

The Mexican census questionnaire has three items directly related to occupation: main declared occupation, sector of the economy in which occupied, and position in work. However, the summary tables published by the census do not allow a clear classification of occupations accord-

TABLE 3. COMPARISON OF PROFILES OF CLASS STRUCTURE

Author	Date of data	Source	Criteria utilized	Population covered	Percentage in each class			
					Upper	Middle	Popular	Total
Iturriaga (1951)	1940	Census	Broad occupational categories	National	1.05	15.87	83.08	100.00
Lewis (1951)	late 1940's	Interviews	Ranking of families according to wealth	Tepoztlán (4 to 5 thousand)	4.4	13.9	81.5	99.8
González-Cosío (1961)	1950	Census	Broad occupational categories and income groups	National	0.5	15.5	84.0	100.0
Cline (1962)	1950	Census & survey	Combination of occupational and income groups	National	2.4	20.3	77.0	99.7
Cline (1962)	1950	Census & survey	Combination of occupational and income groups	Federal District	8.9	29.4	61.7	100.0
Navarrete (1960)	1950	Census & survey	Income	National	5.0	25.0	70.0	100.0
Scott (1959)	1950's	Census	Combination of ethnic, occupational and income levels	National	1.4	12.5	85.9	99.8
Erasmus (1961)	late 1950's	Interviews, questionnaires, estimates	Rough estimate, based on occupation, income, consumption, housing	Northwest region, towns from 5 to 40,000	1-2	20-30	70+	—
Navarrete (1960)	1957	Sample survey	Income	National	5.0	30.0	65.0	100.0
Cline (1962)	1960	Census & survey	Occupational and income categories	National	6.5	33.5	60.0	100.0
González-Cosío (1961)	1960	Census	Broad occupational categories & income groups	National	0.5	17.1	82.4	100.0

ing to a scale of socio-economic status. For instance, all agricultural workers are grouped together, whether they be owners, technicians or day laborers. The category of "personal service workers" includes people ranging from maids through barbers to hospital attendants. Thus, the categories confound two quite separate principles of classification: sector of the economy, and socio-economic level of the job. However, we must use what the government, in its own private wisdom, decides to give us. The basic data are shown in Table 4. The contrast between the Federal District and the Republic as a whole is clear: the former has a much bigger "middle class" of professional and office workers. It also has more women in the paid labor force.

TABLE 4. DISTRIBUTION OF LABOR FORCE, 1960

	Mexico	Federal District
Professionals, technicians	3.6%	8.0%
Executives (except agriculture)	0.8	2.4
Office workers	6.1	16.6
Salespeople	9.0	15.4
Manual workers:		
(a) in mining and petroleum	1.0	0.3
(b) in production of goods and services	18.9	37.6
Personal service workers	7.0	17.3
All agricultural workers	53.6	2.3
Total	100.0%	99.9%
Percentage female	18%	30%

Source: 1960 Census, *Resumen General*, Table 25.

González-Cosío presents a table, based on a government sample survey directed by Ana María Flores, in which the population in the different sectors of activity is cross-classified by "social class." There is no statement as to the criterion utilized in dividing the population into classes; most probably they utilized income. Note that the middle class here represents 31 per cent of the total, a very generous estimate. Summarizing the data to show the way each social class is divided by sector of activity, we obtain the material in Table 5.

TABLE 5. SOCIAL CLASSES BY SECTORS, 1956

	Social Classes		
Sectors	*Upper*	*Middle*	*Popular*
Primary	11.3%	12.1%	47.9%
Secondary	24.8	5.4	29.4
Tertiary	63.9	82.5	22.7
Total active population	100.0%	100.0%	100.0%

Source: González-Cosío, 1961, p. 66, rearranged and summarized. The sectors are defined above on page 12.

The same raw data can be summarized to show how each sector of activity is divided into social classes by reversing the direction in which the percentages are calculated (Table 6).

TABLE 6. SECTORS BY SOCIAL CLASSES, 1956

	Social Classes			
Sectors	Upper	Middle	Popular	Total
Primary	0.2%	10.3	89.5	100.0%
Secondary	0.1	8.1	91.8	100.0%
Tertiary	1.0	60.0	39.0	100.0%
Total	0.7	31.1	68.2	100.0%

Note: Breaking down the tertiary sector, most of the population in commercial activities belongs to the middle class (99.5%), most of that in transportation to the popular class (81.0%). With regard to the population in services, the split between the middle and popular class is about even.

The upper and middle classes are predominantly concentrated in the tertiary sector, that is, active in the distribution of goods and services. Indeed, the middle class draws very little from the primary sector, which is to be expected, and even less from the secondary sector, which is somewhat surprising, especially when we remember that almost one-third of the labor force is here included in the middle class.

The fact that a substantial minority of those working in tertiary activities (39.0 per cent) and a large majority (91.8 per cent) of those working in secondary activities fall into the popular class throws some doubt upon the common assumption that movements out of agriculture into industry and urban services are automatically movements up the social scale. Possibly these movements often constitute a form of horizontal rather than vertical mobility. One fact behind the usual assumption is that average *per capita* productivity is much higher in secondary and tertiary activities than in primary ones. However, the distribution of that productivity in the form of income is highly unequal, and therefore does not always benefit the ordinary factory or service worker. Here we have a striking example of the danger of using statistical averages (without data on distribution) to create mental images of "typical" human beings.

González-Casanova (this volume) provides another classification, using 1960 census data; he divides the economically active population as follows:

Children 8-11 years of age, working for pay	0.7%
Non-paid family workers	1.0
Manual laborers	50.5

Self-employed	33.9
Non-manual employees	13.1
Employers	0.8
	100.0%

As he himself points out, this classification is not detailed enough. The manual workers are not subdivided by level of skill, and the self-employed include people ranging from street-vendor to *rentier*.

Income

Data on income distribution are available from the census, and from a few sample surveys that have been made in recent years. The results are given in terms of numerical categories (such as "between 2,000 and 3,000 pesos per month") which must be arbitrarily translated into social strata (such as "middle class") by the analyst. We shall use whatever categories were chosen by the authors themselves, without imposing our own views on them.

Most of the authors comment on the unreliability of income data. Whether the person asking for information is the regular decennial census taker, or someone doing a special sample survey, he is likely to receive distorted answers from the respondents. Upper-class persons, in particular, tend to understate their incomes. After all, the inquirer might report to the tax collector, so caution is in order.

Table 7, elaborated by Navarrete from census and sample survey data, compares income distributions in 1950 and 1957; the table also shows the proportion of the total income which was received by each group of families. The proportion of the total income going to the richest 5 per cent of families decreased slightly; the percentage of families in the "well-to-do" group, and thus the proportion of the total income going to this group, increased markedly; and the percentage of families in the bottom group declined.

TABLE 7. INCOME DISTRIBUTION, 1950 AND 1957

Social class	Percent of families		Percent of income	
	1950	1957	1950	1957
Lower class	70	65	31	25
Middle class	18	19	17	18
"Well-to-do" class	7	11	12	20
"Rich" class	5	5	40	37

Source: Navarrete, 1960, p. 89.

González-Cosío summarizes data of a survey for 1956, directed by Ana María Flores for the Dirección General de Estadística of the Federal Government. It adds further information on consumption and savings; see Table 8.

TABLE 8. FAMILY INCOME AND EXPENSES BY SOCIAL CLASSES, 1956

	Upper class	Middle class	Popular class
Monthly averages:			
Income	5,496 pesos	1,837 pesos	542 pesos
Savings	1,874 (34%)	332 (18%)	13 (2%)
Percentages:			
Of the number of families	2.3	13.8	83.9
Of the total monthly income	15.4	30.3	54.3
Of the total monthly expenditures	11.5	28.3	60.2
Of the total monthly savings	43.3	45.5	11.2

Source: Summarized from González-Cosío, 1961, p. 68.

The categories used by Flores are different from those of Navarrete, yet the over-all picture is similar. The top 16 per cent of the families received about half of the total income of the country (Flores says 46 per cent, Navarrete says 57 per cent). Incidentally, these families were able to accumulate almost 90 per cent of all the private savings that were made. This is the root of one of the policy problems that has vexed government planners for many years: if income were more equally distributed, in the sense of giving more to the popular class, they would be likely to consume it all, and the family savings that are so useful for economic investment and growth would be diminished. Incidentally, the middle class does not spend all of its income on conspicuous consumption, as hinted above by Erasmus, since the data indicate that they save 18 per cent of it.[5]

Consumption Patterns

A few data on consumption patterns by different social classes are available. Table 9 summarizes the findings of the 1956 survey of Ana María Flores.

As is always the case, we find here that the proportion of family expenditures devoted to food goes down as income goes up. That leaves more money available for housing and furnishings, and for education, travel, entertainment, and so on. In other words, the poorer strata have less choice: they must spend most of their income for food and basic housing and clothing, and have little left for other things.

An aspect of the Mexican style of life is shown by the substantial amount spent for servants, even among the popular class.

Convergence of Different Indicators

Few systematic cross-tabulations are available of the key indicators of stratification, such as occupation, education and income. The over-all

[5] Additional survey data on income distribution are given in Tables 10 and 11, below, and in González-Casanova, this volume.

TABLE 9. DISTRIBUTION OF FAMILY EXPENSES
BY SOCIAL CLASSES, 1956

	Upper class	Middle class	Popular class
Food	32.3%	44.0%	53.3%
Clothing	9.2	12.4	12.6
Rent, electricity	12.5	10.1	6.1
Furniture	18.6	8.7	5.5
School expenses	5.8	3.1	2.0
Fuel	3.1	2.5	2.3
Medical expenses	1.3	2.6	3.6
Entertainment	4.4	3.9	3.3
Transport	1.0	2.1	2.9
Taxes	2.4	2.2	1.7
Servants	9.4	8.4	6.7
	100.0%	100.0%	100.0%

Source: González-Cosío, 1961, p. 62.
Note: Savings were not taken into account; proportions would change if computed from total income, including savings.

judgments of the shape of the stratification profile given above are impressionistic, mainly using occupation and then correcting a bit from additional information about income.

González-Casanova (this volume) gives one example of how interesting such cross-tabulations can be. He shows that the income of families is directly related to the proportion of children attending school, thus illustrating one of the mechanisms of perpetuation of the stratification system.[6]

Since available data do not permit extensive cross-tabulations, the next best procedure is to show parallel ranks on important indicators, thus giving some idea of how their distributions compare with one another. In Table 10 we have placed broad categories of occupation, education and income in parallel columns. In Table 11, similar distributions are given for the Federal District. From the tables we learn that the middle class, whether defined by occupation or by education or by income, is much bigger in the capital than in the country as a whole. Furthermore, we note that, for the entire nation, a professional or executive job is likely to be filled by a man with some university training (or at least "preparatory" education in the 10th and 11th grades), and to involve a monthly family income of over 6,000 pesos ($480 dollars); between 2 and 4 per cent of the workers are at this level.[7] Below them come a

[6] He is currently analyzing a sample survey of Mexico City with many indicators of status; its publication in the near future will add to our knowledge of the interrelations among indicators.

[7] In the Mexican system, the first six grades are primary; the next three are secondary; the next two (recently increased to three) are college preparatory, followed by four or five years of professional training at the university level.

TABLE 10. MEASURES OF SOCIAL CLASSES, MEXICO, CA. 1960

Occupation	Per Cent	Years of Schooling	Per Cent	Minimum Monthly Income, Pesos	Per Cent
Professionals, Technicians, Executives	4	12+	2	6,001	3
Office Workers	6	7–11	4	3,001	6
Sales Workers	9	6	10	1,500	15
Manual Workers, except agriculture	20	1–5	38	1,001	11
Personal Service Workers	7	—	—	601	22
Agriculture	54	0	46	1	43
	100%		100%		100%

Note: Income figures are for families, and refer to 1963; education refers to adults 30 years of age and older.

Sources: 1960 Census, *Resumen General*, for occupation and education; Banco de México, 1966, for income. The rate of exchange was 12.50 pesos per dollar.

TABLE 11. MEASURES OF SOCIAL CLASSES,
FEDERAL DISTRICT, CA. 1960

Occupation	Per Cent	Years of Schooling	Per Cent	Minimum Monthly Income, Pesos	Per Cent
Professionals, Technicians, Executives	10	12+	7	6,001	12
Office Workers	17	7–11	12	3,001	14
Sales Workers	16	6	23	1,501	24
Manual Workers, including agriculture	40	1–5	36	601	38
Personal Service Workers	17	0	22	1	12
Total	100%		100%		100%

Sources: Same as Table 10.

larger group of 15 to 20 per cent of the total who have finished primary school and perhaps some secondary, hold jobs in offices or stores, and receive family income between 1,500 and 6,000 pesos a month. They are followed by non-agricultural manual workers who have partial primary education and receive incomes of a bit more than 600 pesos a month. At the bottom are agricultural workers who are mostly illiterate (this would be less true of the younger ones) and have very low incomes. Since these indicators are not cross-classified but merely shown in parallel ranks, we fail to catch the full complexity of the situation; for example, there will be some agricultural workers with more education and/or more income than some factory workers. But the picture is a realistic one "on the average."

Turning from census statistics to sample surveys, we note a study by Kahl (1965 and 1968). Using non-representative samples, he interviewed over 700 men in Mexico City and in some small towns in the state of Hidalgo. The way in which occupational and educational levels predicted identification is shown in Table 12. Identification was measured by asking the respondent to choose from a list of labels the one which best described himself. The results clearly indicated that "objective" position (occupation, education) was reflected in the mental images carried by the men. Perhaps a clue to the tendency among Mexicans for a wide definition of the middle class can be drawn from the table: most white-collar workers, even those without secondary education, and most men with secondary education, even if they were blue-collar workers, considered themselves middle class.

TABLE 12. SOCIAL CLASS IDENTIFICATION

	IDENTIFICATION			
	Per cent Middle or Upper	*Per cent Working or Below*	*T o t a l*	
			%	N
All White-Collar Workers				
With some secondary education or more	90	10	100	224
With primary education only	77	23	100	64
All Blue-Collar Workers				
With some secondary education or more	69	31	100	108
With primary education only	33	67	100	344
All Respondents	59	41	100	740

Kahl found that rankings on occupation correlated with other stratification variables as follows:

Education	.67
Income	.60
Identification	.52

Indeed, these four variables were all reflections of a single underlying dimension of socio-economic status, as shown by their high loadings on a principle axis factor which accounted for 66 per cent of the variance of the separate indicators. There were no important differences in the results from the capital city and the small towns.

Other evidence in the study showed that men who were middle class were more likely than men who were working class (whether one used objective or subjective definitions) to have certain core values which indicated a "modern" outlook on the world. They included: activism, weak integration with relatives, a preference for urban life, individualism, a perception of the system as being open rather than tightly stratified, and a high interest in the mass media. The correlation between a measure of socio-economic status (occupation, education and identification) and a measure of modernism in values was .56. The further connections between status, modernism and certain other attitudes, such as ambitions for children and ideas about preferred size of family, were explored in the research.

The data included a correlation coefficient of .50 between the occupations of respondents and those of their fathers, which was the same as the coefficient for a similar sample of Brazilians, but higher than usually observed in the United States. Again, no important differences emerged between small towns and the metropolis.

THE SOCIAL CLASS SYSTEM

The study of stratification involves more than the construction of statistical tables which show the distributions of indicators of status. It demands an analysis of the way these variables influence one another to form social networks of linked individuals whose styles of life, value orientations and political actions tend to converge; it requires empirical investigation of rates and processes of succession and mobility in order to show how the system perpetuates itself through the generations; and it needs historical study to show how the stratification variables and their patterns of mutual dependence change through time.

In Mexico there has been little detailed research on these questions. We have no study of recruitment into the current elite groups (How many from the old upper class? How many from the Revolutionary military chiefs? How many from the bureaucratic ladders in politics and industry?) We have speculation rather than evidence on the political influence of foreign capitalists. We have no national survey that delves into the core values and basic aspirations of the various social classes, indicating regional and rural-urban variations.[8] We have no adequate research on the images that the various classes have of themselves and of others, or of the degree of exclusiveness of each group in its social networks. Indeed, we know far more in detail about the social structures of many isolated Indian communities than we do about the cities of modern Mexico.

The impressions of most observers, both Mexican and foreign, converge on a description of the system as being relatively open. The dominant

[8] Some partial data are available in Almond and Verba, 1963.

political party has made it a practice to co-opt into its ranks rising young leaders from all strata of society, and the rapid rate of growth of business enterprises and the government bureaucracy implies widespread recruitment of new men for executive and technical positions. Yet the details are in doubt: Brandenburg (1965) stresses the continuing power role of the small and exclusive group of men surrounding the President; Scott (1959) emphasizes the formal structure of the official political party as the integrating mechanism, with its branches throughout society; González-Casanova (1967) writes of the processes through which the civilian leaders circumscribed the military, and maintains that both Marxist and structural-functional analyses lead to similar conclusions about the stability and viability of the present system.

And yet we also know that the school system is such that sons of workers and farmers have little chance of rising all the way to the university. In the early fifties, the students at the National University in Mexico City came from these family backgrounds (*Primer Censo Universitario*, 1953):

Businessmen, storekeepers	30%
White-collar workers	21
Professional & technical	28
Military	4
Manual workers & artisans	11
Farmers	6
	100%

Thus the 84 per cent of manual worker and farmer fathers in the country in 1950 (or the 61 per cent of them in Mexico City) supplied only 17 per cent of the sons and daughters at the University.

There is one study of a small modern Mexican city which attempts to describe its social hierarchy as a total system, that of Whiteford (1964). He gives an ethnographic report on Querétaro, and points out its special features by indicating contrasts with Popayán, Colombia, a city of similar size but with a much more traditional social structure. Whiteford writes that although a few descendants of old *hacendado* families continued to live in the upper class of Querétaro, they were inconspicuous and not dominant. Indeed, he insists (page 33):

> Querétaro was basically a Middle Class city. In spite of the impressive vestiges of the city's colonial grandeur the typical Querétano might have been said to be the modest shopkeeper, the bank clerk, the photographer, journalist, lawyer, teacher, or engineer who had attained at least secondary education, lived in a fair-sized house with comfortable furnishings, and enjoyed a quiet, rather uneventful life with his large, well-dressed family. . . . They possessed a kind of solidarity and occasionally expressed a critical superiority toward the members of the Upper Class which was largely lacking in Popayán.

Like Popayán, Querétaro possessed a large Lower Class population. The traditional Latin prejudice against working with the hands persisted and, as such work must always be done, the ditch diggers, agricultural field laborers, street and market vendors, masons, blacksmiths, mechanics, and police were, without hesitation, regarded as Lower Class. . . . The men commonly wore large straw hats, and both sexes seemed always to carry a basket, a sack, children, or something else in their hands. Patches, *huaraches* (sandals), braids, large hats and aprons were diagnostic features of the dress of the Lower Class, and anyone who regarded himself as above this category exerted every effort to avoid them.

Whiteford discusses the substantial mobility that took place in Querétaro. Agricultural workers and common laborers in the city sometimes learned trades and began to earn much higher incomes; they sent their sons to school, and the second generation climbed into the upper ranks of the working class and often into the lower ranks of the middle class. Ambitious middle-class men got involved in the many new business opportunities that came from government construction and from the opening up of the new highway which put the city on a main line of transportation into Mexico City. They got rich and developed a self-confidence which carried them close to the upper class, although they usually were not accepted socially. But their sons, who went to university, learned the graces which opened private doors. This constant circulation among the classes created a much more dynamic spirit than existed in Popayán, where the old upper class continued its power and seemed to dominate the entire mentality of the city.

Whiteford gives sufficient detail to enable the reader to see how the stratification variables affect one another in systemic form; he describes the relations among education, occupation, income, social interaction, prestige and power. However, he does so ethnographically, impressionistically. Quantitative support is lacking, thus a fully satisfying account of the class structure of a modern Mexican community, to say nothing of the nation as a whole, is still a project for future research.

BIBLIOGRAPHY

Almond, Gabriel A. and Verba, Sidney, *The Civic Culture* (Princeton, N.J.: Princeton University Press, 1963).
Banco de México, *Encuesta sobre ingresos y gastos familiares en México, 1963* (México, D.F.: Banco de México, 1966). Partly summarized in Solís, 1967.
Benítez-Zenteno, Raúl, *Análisis demográfico de México*, (México, D.F.: Instituto de Investigaciones Sociales, Universidad Nacional Autónoma de México, 1961).
Brandenburg, Frank R., *The Making of Modern Mexico* (Englewood Cliffs, N.J.: Prentice-Hall, 1965).

Browning, Harley L., *Urbanization in Mexico* (Berkeley, Calif.: Ph.D. Thesis, University of California, 1962).

Butterworth, Douglas, "A Study of Urbanization Among Mixtec Migrants to Mexico City," *América Indígena*, XXII (July 1962) 257–74.

Cardoso, Fernando Henrique and Reyna, José Luis, "Industrialización, estructura ocupacional y estratificación social en América Latina" (Santiago de Chile: documento del Instituto Latinoamericano de Planificación Económica y Social, 1966).

Cline, Howard F., *Mexico: Revolution to Evolution*, 1940-1960 (New York: Oxford University Press, 1962).

Erasmus, Charles J., *Man Takes Control* (Minneapolis, Minn.: University of Minnesota Press, 1961).

Flores, Edmundo, *Tratado de economía agrícola* (México, D.F.: Fondo de Cultura Económica, 1961).

Germán-Parra, Manuel, *La industrialización de México* (México, D.F.: Imprenta Universitaria, 1954).

González-Casanova, Pablo, *La democrácia en México* (México, D.F.. Era, 2a edición, 1967).

González-Cosío, Arturo, "Clases y estratos sociales," en *México: cincuenta años de revolución*, Tomo II (México, D.F.: Fondo de Cultura Económica, 1961).

Iturriaga, José E., *La estructura social y cultural de México* (México, D.F.: Fondo de Cultura Económica, 1951).

Jaffe, A. J., *People, Jobs and Economic Development* (New York: Free Press, 1959).

Kahl, Joseph A., "Three Types of Mexican Industrial Workers," *Economic Development and Cultural Change*, VIII (January 1960) 164-69; in Spanish, *Ciencias Políticas y Sociales*, V (abril-junio de 1959) 193-201.

Kahl, Joseph A., "Social Stratification and Values in Metropoli and Provinces: Brazil and Mexico," *América Latina*, VIII (jan-mar de 1965) 23-35; in Spanish, *Ciencias Políticas y Sociales*, X (jul-sept de 1964) 425-39.

Kahl, Joseph A., *The Measurement of Modernism: A Study of Values in Brazil and Mexico* (Austin, Tex.: University of Texas Press, 1968); in Spanish, México, D.F.: Instituto de Investigaciones Sociales, Universidad Nacional Autónoma de México, 1968

Lewis, Oscar, *Life in a Mexican Village: Tepoztlán Restudied* (Urbana, Ill.: University of Illinois Press, 1951).

Lewis, Oscar, "Urbanization without Breakdown," *Scientific Monthly*, LXXV (July 1952) 31-41; in Spanish, *América Indígena*, XVII (julio de 1957) 232-46.

Lewis, Oscar, *Five Families* (New York: Basic Books, 1959); in Spanish as *Antropología de la pobreza: cinco familias* (México, D.F.: Fondo de Cultura Económica, 1961).

Myers, Charles N., *Education and National Development in Mexico* (Princeton, N.J.: Industrial Relations Section, Department of Economics, Princeton University, 1965).

Navarrete, Ifigenia Martínez de, *La distribución del ingreso y el desarrollo económico de México* (México, D.F.: Instituto de Investigaciones Económicas, Universidad Nacional Autónoma de México, 1960).

Secretaría de Industria y Comercio, Dirección General de Estadística, *VII Censo General de Población, 1960: Resumen General* (México, D.F.)

Scott, Robert E., *Mexican Government in Transition* (Urbana, Ill.: University of Illinois Press, 1959).

Silva-Herzog, Jesús, *El agrarismo mexicano y la reforma agraria* (México, D.F.: Fondo de Cultura Económica, 1959).

Solís, Leopoldo M., "Hacia un análisis general a largo plazo del desarrollo económico de México," *Demografía y Economía*, I (1967), No. 1.

Stavenhagen, Rodolfo, "Social Aspects of Mexican Agrarian Structure," *Social Research*, XXXIII (Autumn 1966) 463-85.

Stern, Claudio, *Las regiones de México y sus niveles de desarrollo socioeconómico* (México, D.F.: tesis profesional, Escuela Nacional de Ciencias Políticas y Sociales, Universidad Nacional Autónoma de México, 1966).

Universidad Nacional Autónoma de México, *Primer Censo Universitario* (México, D.F.: 1953).

Vernon, Raymond, *The Dilemma of Mexico's Development* (Cambridge, Mass.: Harvard University Press, 1963).

Whetten, Nathan, *Rural Mexico* (Chicago: University of Chicago Press, 1948).

Whiteford, Andrew H., *Two Cities of Latin America: A Comparative Description of Classes* (New York: Doubleday Anchor Book, 1964).

Wolf, Eric R., *Sons of the Shaking Earth* (Chicago: University of Chicago Press, 1959).

Yates, Lamartine, *El desarrollo regional de México* (México, D.F.: Banco de México, 1962).

Classes, Colonialism, and Acculturation

The purpose of this article is to analyze a system of ethnic relations in the state of Chiapas in southeastern Mexico and in the adjoining areas of Guatemala. It is not my intention to add new data presently unknown to experts in the area. My purpose is both more modest and more ambitious. It is that of reorganizing known data into a scheme of interpretation differing from those which are currently used in anthropology, and which I believe to be more fruitful for the purpose of clarifying some historical and structural problems in the formation of the national societies of Mexico and Guatemala.

The highland region of Chiapas (Mexico) and Guatemala is inhabited by Indians of Maya stock, and has the peculiarity that each local community constitutes a cultural and social unit which is distinguished from other similar communities; and whose limits, furthermore, coincide with those of modern political-administrative units called municipalities or municipal agencies. Thus, the Indian population of every municipality (or municipal agency) can be distinguished from others through their clothing, dialect, and participation in a religious and political structure of their own. This usually involves economic specialization as well; and also a developed feeling of identity with other members of the community, reinforced by a somewhat generalized endogamous system. Aside from being an administrative unit integrated in Mexican and Guatemalan national political structures, the municipality represents in this region a bounded social universe for the Indian population, which has been called

This article is reprinted with permission of the Editor, from Volume I, Number 6, 1965, of *Studies in Comparative International Development* (translated by Danielle Horowitz). Revised by the author for inclusion in this volume. (Originally published in Spanish in *América Latina*, Volume 6, Number 4, 1963.)

Rodolfo Stavenhagen, educated in anthropology in Mexico and sociology at the University of Paris, is currently engaged in a long-term study of the social and economic structure of contemporary rural society, under auspices of the Center for Agrarian Research; he is also on the faculty of the National University of Mexico.

"tribe" by some ethnologists, and which others have even termed the germ of a "nation."[1]

INDIANS AND LADINOS

In the entire region and in almost all of the local communities there co-exist two kinds of populations, two different "societies": Indians and Ladinos. The problem of the relationships between these two ethnic groups[2] has been undertaken in different ways by anthropologists. Only a few of them, nonetheless, have attempted an interpretative analysis within the sphere of the global society.[3] In these pages I intend to offer some elements for such an analysis.

It is a well-known fact that biological factors do not account for the differences between the two populations; we are not dealing with two races in the genetic sense of the term. It is true, of course, that in a general way the so-called Indian population answers to biologic traits corresponding to the Amerinds and equally, that the so-called Ladino population shows the biologic traits of the Caucasoids. But even though Ladinos tend to identify with whites, in fact they are generally *mestizo* (racially mixed); it is social and cultural factors which distinguish one population from the other.

For a long time it was common to draw up a list of identifiable cultural elements in order to separate these two groups: language, clothing, agricultural technology, food, religious beliefs, etc. The advantages of such a list are that it allows an easy quantification of Indian and Ladino populations, and that census returns which include some of these elements — principally the language — can be profitably used. Thus, using these in-

---

[1] Sol Tax, "The Municipios of the Midwestern Highlands of Guatemala," *American Anthropologist*, Vol. 39, 1937; Henning Siverts, "Social and Cultural Changes in a Tzeltal (Mayan) Municipio, Chiapas, Mexico," *Proceedings of the 32nd International Congress of Americanists*, Copenhagen, 1956.

[2] By *ethnic group* we mean a social group whose members participate in the same culture, who may sometimes be characterized in biological or racial terms, who are conscious of belonging to such a group and who participate in a system of relations with other similar groups. An ethnic group may be, depending upon circumstances, tribe, race, nationality, minority, caste, cultural component, etc., according to the meaning given to these terms by different authors.

[3] The global society is the widest operational social unit within which the studied relations take place and which is not a part of the immediate experience of the actors in the social system. It includes the community, the municipality, the region, the ethnic group, etc., and their diverse systems of interrelation. It is sociologically structured. The global society has been termed a macroscopic group embracing functional groupings, social classes and conflicting hierarchies. Generally, in this essay, it is identical to the nation (or to the Colony), but it sometimes also refers to the wider economic system, in which the nation participates. See Georges Gurvitch, *La Vocation Actuelle de la Sociologie*, Paris, 1950, p. 301, *passim*.

dices, Whetten was able to speak of the "indo-colonial" population of Mexico.[4] Confronted with the obvious insufficiency of this procedure in terms of a deeper analysis, it came to be recognized that these cultural elements were integrated within cultural complexes. Alfonso Caso used as his point of departure the fact that Indian populations live in communities which can be easily distinguished from one another, and he thus offered the following definition: "an Indian is he who feels he belongs to an Indian community, and an Indian community is that in which there exists a predominance of non-European somatic elements, where language is preferentially Indian, possessing within its material and spiritual culture a strong proportion of Indian elements and finally, having a social feeling of being an isolated community within surrounding ones, distinguishing it from white and mestizo villages."[5] This definition no longer considers the Indian as an isolated individual, but as a member of a well-defined social group. The author, however, limits the condition of being Indian to a subjective feeling, and introduces racial considerations when distinguishing the Indian community from "white and mestizo" ones. We do not find in this definition the necessary elements for an analysis of the relationships between Indians and Ladinos; on the contrary, Caso's definition stresses the idea that we are dealing with two autonomous cultural worlds whose co-existence is almost a matter of chance.

The importance attributed by ethnologists to cultural elements of Indian populations has long concealed the nature of the socio-economic structures into which these populations are integrated. Sol Tax, for instance, while studying an Indian economy in Guatemala, chooses a community in which one third of the population is Ladino. Yet Tax describes only the Indian aspect and leaves aside the mestizo population as though the community's economy were not a complex and integrated whole. When he describes the inevitable interaction taking place between Indians and Ladinos, he does so as though he were dealing with the external relations of Indian society.[6] Siverts, when speaking about monetary exchanges between Indians and Ladinos, even uses the term "foreign trade."[7]

Certain recent ethnological studies, and primarily the needs of Indianist activity in Mexico, have shown the weaknesses of an approach based exclusively upon analysis of cultural factors, which does not take into account historical evolution. Eric Wolf has recently declared that

[4] Nathan Whetten, *Rural Mexico*, Chicago, 1948.
[5] Alfonso Caso, "Definición del indio y lo indio," *América Indígena*, Vol. VIII, No. 5, 1948.
[6] Sol Tax, *Penny Capitalism, A Guatemala Indian Economy*, Washington, 1953.
[7] Siverts, *loc. cit.*, p. 183.

"Indianhood does not consist of a list of discrete social traits; it resides in the quality of social relations found in communities of a certain kind, and in the self-image of individuals who identify with these communities. Because these communities originate at a certain point in time, wax strong, lose their grip or maintain it in the face of assault or pressure from the larger society, Indianhood is also a distinctive historical process."[8] Thus, it is no longer the cultural *patterns* but the community *structure*, the relationships between its different parts, which are significant. Indianhood is to be found in those closed "corporate" communities, whose members are bound by certain rights and duties, having their own forms of social control, particular political and religious hierarchies, etc. According to Wolf, these corporate units are the result of Spanish colonial policy, having suffered successive transformations under the impact of external influences. Wolf sees these units, which are neither totally isolated nor completely self-sufficient, as taking part in wider economic and political power structures. The Indian communities are related to national institutions and are composed of various kinds of social groups oriented toward both the community and the nation. These groups perform roles as political "power brokers" between traditional and national structures.[9]

Wolf's analysis of the Indian supplies historical depth and structural orientation which are not usually found among specialists in cultural anthropology. However, while he clearly recognizes the existence of the corporate community's external relations, he sees these communities as responding mechanically to impulses coming from national and regional sources of power. Wolf does not speak about the inter-relationships between Indians and Ladinos. Tax and Redfield also admit the existence of external relations, with the difference that for them, the controls imposed upon the population from outside the local community "have their origin in natural law"![10]

Indianist action in Mexico has led ethnologists to restate the problem in different terms. There has been a shift from the sphere of the Indian community to that of the intercultural region where Indians and mestizos co-exist. It consists of *an urban complex mainly inhabited by a Ladino population surrounded by Indian communities which are its economic and political satellites.*[11] This new focus allows a better analysis of socio-

[8] Eric Wolf, "The Indian in Mexican Society," *Alpha Kappa Delta*, Vol. XXX, No. 1, 1960.
[9] Eric Wolf, "Aspects of Group Relations in a Complex Society: Mexico," *American Anthropologist*, Vol. LVIII, 1956.
[10] Robert Redfield and Sol Tax, "General Characteristics of Present Day Mesoamerican Indian Society," in *Heritage of Conquest*, Glencoe: The Free Press, 1952.
[11] Alfonso Caso, "Los fines de la acción indigenista en México," *Revista Internacional del Trabajo*, December, 1955, and G. Aguirre Beltrán, *El proceso de*

economic structures and of social relations. We no longer speak of acculturation alone, but of the Indian's integration to the nation, which is precisely the stated purpose of Indianist policy. The ecological relations between the metropolis and its satellites are only a part of the complex system of social relationships characteristic of this region. These relations can be divided into those of "class" and those of "stratification."

THE LAND AND CLASS RELATIONS

Class relationships in any society become clear only through the analysis of the whole socio-economic structure. In the Indian region of Chiapas and Guatemala these relationships do not appear through the study of cultural differences between the two ethnic groups, nor do they show in all of the social situations in which there are inter-group relations. Class relationships emerge clearly through an analysis of the distribution of land as a means of production, and the labor, trade and property relations which link one part of the population to another.[12] Thus, we first concentrate on relationships between classes of men based on production or property criteria. Later, relationships of status or prestige will be considered under the rubric of "social stratification."

Production Relations

Subsistence Agriculture. The basis of regional production is agriculture, and the basis of agriculture is maize (corn), principally for domestic consumption. Even when other crops are cultivated, maize is the primary agricultural product without which the rural family, the productive unit, would not survive. The soil is poor, agricultural techniques are primitive, and yields are therefore small. Rainfall allows two harvests a year in some regions. The farmer devotes a great part of his time to subsistence farming with the participation of family labor. Produce is consumed by the family. Sometimes, when the farmer needs money, he sells part of the harvest, but later, when his reserves are exhausted, he must buy his corn back again. In his position as a maize producer, the farmer remains isolated and does not enter into relations with other sectors of society.

---

aculturación, México, UNAM, 1957, which still constitutes the most complete theoretical exposition on Mexican Indianist theory. See also his recent *Regiones de Refugio*, México, I.I.I., 1967.

[12] I use here the terms "class," "class relations," and "class situation" as analytical concepts and I completely distinguish them, as shall be seen later, from the concept of social stratification generally associated with them. For theoretical justification of this methodological procedure see my article on "Estratificación y Estructura de Clases," in *Ciencias Políticas y Sociales* (Mexico), No. 27, 1962, and my paper on "Las relaciones entre la estratificación social y la dinámica de clases," presented at the Seminar on Social Stratification and Mobility, Rio de Janeiro, 1962.

There are exceptions to this situation. Some communities in the area have become specialized in maize production to the exclusion of any other important agricultural activity. Santiago Chimaltenango, in Guatemala, regularly produces a surplus of maize which is sold at the local markets.[13] In this case, the subsistence farmer becomes, in part, a peasant producing for the market. I say in part because due to the fact that the bulk of his production is consumed at home, he remains within a subsistence economy. It is important to stress the fact that maize is grown almost exclusively by the Indians. Even though the majority of the communities have also a Ladino population, these rarely grow maize. When they devote themselves to agriculture, it is usually to produce cash crops.

We find here a first element for differentiation of the population into social classes: one part of the population predominantly devotes itself to subsistence maize farming — even while it sells some surplus — and another sector does not participate in subsistence agriculture.

Commercial Agriculture. Almost all of the rural communities also participate in agricultural activities whose purpose is not domestic use but commerce. The subsistence farmer is also a producer for the market. Even while he may not devote the greater part of his time to this activity, it allows him to obtain the money he needs. At altitudes lower than 5,000 feet, the maize economy is complemented with that of coffee, a cash crop *par excellence*. There are also cacao, onion, and vegetables of all kinds; at higher altitudes there are fruits. All of these food products are destined for sale, and the different communities specialize in production of one or the other. Maize and coffee (within their geographic limits) are found everywhere. Coffee is destined to national and international markets, while the majority of the other products appear only in local markets. The coffee-growing communities are usually richer than those which, located on higher and poorer lands, do not grow it. But the subsistence farmer who grows some coffee or other products for the market does not neglect growing his maize, partly because he cannot buy it elsewhere.

Besides corn, in Panajachel, Guatemala, the Indians are able to grow both vegetables and coffee.[14] They grow mainly vegetables, notwithstanding the fact that these pay less than coffee. Coffee is a perennial plant, and the establishment of plantations requires time and capital. Since the Indians lack the means, they prefer to grow vegetables, with which they are able to obtain quicker, if smaller, benefits. Sol Tax describes the Panajachel Indians' economy as being a "penny capitalism," because they produce cash crops for the market, because they are oriented toward a profit economy, and because they like to make "a good deal." Nonetheless, Tax himself shows that their economy is dominated in the

[13] Charles Wagley, *Santiago Chimaltenango*, Guatemala, 1957.
[14] Sol Tax, *Penny Capitalism, op. cit.*

first place by the needs of maize farming, and that they prefer to grow vegetables rather than coffee, although coffee pays more. The reason for this apparent contradiction lies in the fact that the Indians lack capital and credit institutions. As Wolf has pointed out,[15] it is precisely these two factors — non-existent in Panajachel — which define a capitalist system. The Panajachel Indian *is* integrated to the capitalist system, through the sale of his coffee and acquisition of industrial products, but not in the sense suggested by Tax. The subsistence farmer, the Indian, is not the "capitalist" in this case. On the contrary, he is placed at the opposite pole. His agricultural labor is not essentially a commodity, and the money he earns through the sale of his vegetables is not reinvested but spent in current consumption. There is no accumulation of capital.

In contrast to the Indians, Ladinos do not grow maize but only cash crops. They settled in the region in the course of the past century, following the expansion of coffee. In the rural communities the Ladino farmers are few in number, and farming is never their only occupation. In Panajachel, they grow the greater part of the coffee, and their farming is exclusively commercial. The coffee producer always employs salaried labor; he therefore has the necessary capital available. He is, in fact, a capitalist farmer, and he is able to afford it because, in contrast to the Indian, he does not devote his time to subsistence farming. The growing of coffee, as well as those who grow it, were introduced from outside. The Indians have accepted this new kind of farming only as a complementary economic activity.

Here we have a second element for the differentiation of social classes. We distinguish on the one hand, the farmer devoted to commercial agriculture as a complementary activity, and who obtains from it only minimal profits which are wholly destined for consumption; and on the other, the farmer (especially the coffee-grower) who accumulates capital, employs labor, and who usually also performs other non-agricultural activities. Again, the former are Indians and the latter Ladinos.

The Agricultural Workers. Until now we have spoken only about independent farmers, but a large part of the farming population is composed of day-laborers. In Jilotepeque (Guatemala), day-laborers constitute 90% of the active population, of which only 9% are Ladinos. All of the wage laborers work for Ladinos; there is not one Indian in this community who employs wage labor.[16] In the highlands of Chiapas, the peasants regularly work as wage laborers in the big coffee plantations, where they spend many months a year. Until recently, this was forced or semi-forced labor, and the contract and employment conditions were notoriously bad. At present there exist labor unions of Indian workers, and the Mexican government has taken measures for the protection of

---

[15] Eric Wolf, "The Indian in Mexican Society," *loc. cit.*
[16] Melvin Tumin, *Caste in a Peasant Society*, Princeton, 1952.

migrant workers. Nonetheless, recruitment of laborers is still done by pressures and coercion which sometimes exceed the legal limits of what is called a free contract. From an Indian population totalling 125,000 persons in this area of Chiapas, 15,000 laborers are employed on a seasonal basis.[17] In Guatemala's coffee plantations compulsory labor for Indians existed until recently, up to a maximum of 150 days per year, depending upon the amount of land which they possessed. The pretext for this recruitment was the fight against idleness; yet no Ladino, even those possessing no lands, was forced to perform this kind of work.

These laborers are not separated from the social structure to which they belong; they remain subsistence farmers. They go in search of wage work only when their corn crop is secure. Writing about the Chamulas, Pozas says that they do not want to work in coffee plantations, and that they do so only when compelled by economic needs.[18] In Guatemala, temporary migrations in search of work annually affect 200,000 Indians,[19] and more than one half of the big plantations' laborers are migratory. "This recruitment," one author says, "is the means by which the plantations have extended their influence over virtually every Indian community in Guatemala."[20]

Insofar as the monetary needs of these rural communities are concerned, wage labor has in some of them the same economic function that commercial agriculture has in others. From the point of view of the global economic structure, the self-subsisting community functions as a reservoir of labor.[21] The degree of economic exploitation inflicted upon this labor force is shown by the following item: in Jilotepeque, a Ladino laborer earns 50% more than an Indian laborer, yet the cost of supporting a mule is even higher than a Ladino's wage![22]

It can thus be seen that wage work and commerce notwithstanding, the structure of self-subsisting communities has not been wholly broken. In Cantel, a Guatemalan community, only when the farmer does not possess enough land to feed his family does he seek work in the local

[17] A. D. Marroquín, "Consideraciones sobre el problema económico de la región tzeltal-tzotzil," *América Indígena*, Vol. XVI, No. 3, 1956.

[18] R. Pozas, *Chamula, un pueblo indio de los Altos de Chiapas*, México, 1959.

[19] M. Monteforte Toledo, *Guatemala, monografía sociológica*, México, 1959.

[20] A. Y. Dessaint, "Effects of the Hacienda and Plantation Systems on Guatemala's Indians," *América Indígena*, Vol. XXII, No. 4, 1962, p. 338.

[21] Dessaint, *loc. cit.*, writes: "obtaining an adequate labor supply to work cash-crop fields has been of prime importance ever since the Spanish Conquest" (p. 326). And Oliver La Farge has said: "Two methods have been used to tap the great source of labor of the highlands: violence and the destruction of the economic base which allowed the Indians to refuse voluntary work in the lowlands." (Cf. "Etnología maya: secuencia de culturas," in *Cultura Indígena de Guatemala*, Guatemala, 1959.)

[22] Melvin Tumin, *op. cit.*

textile factory. The industrial worker remains integrated in the structure and values of his community. The new class relationships produced by local industrialization have only partially modified traditional structure. Here industrial work has the same function as migratory work and commercial agriculture in other communities.[23]

Wage work represents a third element in terms of class differentiation in the area. The monetary income obtained by farmers in the manner described above represents the complement to a subsistence economy. We find here new production relations, in which the Indian is always the employee and the Ladino usually the employer. When there are Ladinos employed by other Ladinos, they occupy higher positions and receive higher salaries than the Indians.

We are now ready to attempt a first generalization. At the level of agricultural production, the relationships between Ladinos and Indians are class relationships. The former produce exclusively for the market, while the latter produce primarily for their own consumption; Ladinos accumulate capital, Indians sell their farm products only in order to buy goods for consumption; Ladinos are employers and Indians are laborers. These relationships will be seen with greater clarity when we consider land tenure.

Land Tenure

Traditional Communal Property. The system of land ownership in colonial times worked against Indian lands. Through various kinds of grants to the Spanish settlers, the Crown deprived the Indian communities of their lands. The tutelary legislation of *Indias*, which in theory protected communal property, was difficult to apply in practice. During the national period following independence from Spain the collective lands of the Indians survived only in the more isolated regions such as the one we are now discussing. Around the middle of the 19th Century a number of "liberal" reforms were further directed against communal property. A small part of the population, nonetheless, still possesses traditional communal lands to the present day.

The still existing collective property is generally composed of poor soils, hardly useful for farming, and of minimal productive and commercial value. These lands are usually used for pasture, and for gathering wood and wild fruit. All members of the community have a right to use these lands.

A community still possessing communal lands is also a traditional community, relatively well-integrated from a social point of view and more or less homogeneous from an ethnic point of view. For if land cannot be

[23] Cf. Manning Nash, *Machine Age Maya: The Industrialization of a Guatemalan Community*, Glencoe, 1958.

sold, it is unlikely that Ladinos will be allowed to use it. It is also a poor community, with a subsistence economy, since fertile soils and the possibilities of commercial agriculture attract the Ladinos and tend to transform collective property into private property. In other words, traditional collective lands are infrequent and do not perform an important role in the economy and social organization of the Indian communities of this region.

The Ejido.[24] Agrarian reform in Mexico reached the Indian region of Chiapas during the regime of President Cárdenas (1934-40). In some communities traditional collective lands were transformed into *ejidos;* in others, some of the latifundia were expropriated in behalf of the peasants. In general, the distribution of *ejidos* respected ethnic differences, so that each *ejido* includes in effect members of a homogeneous and socially integrated ethnic group, which accentuates its character of being communal property.

In Guatemala the existence of communal lands may be considered as a tenacious defense of traditional Indian communities against the economic system represented by private property and by the Ladino group. In Mexico, on the contrary, the new communal lands, the *ejidos,* are the result of an active struggle for the land by the Indians against the large landowners, a struggle which has often taken the shape of an inter-ethnic conflict.

Though they are collective property, *ejidal* lands are tilled individually, or rather by the family group. In Chamula, where all of the land is *ejidal,* the families control their plots as though they were private property, yet by law are not allowed to sell them. These plots can be inherited by sons and daughters alike, and this has produced a progressive atomization of family "property," the result of which has been the emigration of a large number of Chamulas in search of lands in the neighboring municipalities. In other communities, the farmer is entitled to the use of *ejido* lands only as long as he regularly works them. This condition is characteristic of traditional communal organization and follows the Mexican national agrarian reform legislation.

Private Ownership of Land. This is the more usual form of land tenure. It was introduced by the Spaniards and spread greatly after the nineteenth century's liberal reforms. Under that legislation Indian communities were forced to transform their communal lands into individual property, which often led to the loss of their lands to outsiders.

Private property means that land has an economic value and that it

---

[24] In Mexico the *ejido* is a grant of land to the community by the government under the agrarian reform legislation. It is sometimes worked collectively, but more often divided into small parcels for each family. The land cannot be sold or mortgaged to outsiders.

has been transformed into a commodity. It also means the emergence of social and economic inequalities on the basis of different farm sizes, and new social relationships, the basis of which is private property of land: sharecropping, tenant farming, wage labor, sale, mortgage, etc. In Panajachel — writes Tax — the land is fully integrated in the commercial cycles which characterize "penny capitalism." But the process is not yet finished. Tax states that in this community land is not considered to be a capital investment but only a consumption good. In Chamula, as we have seen, the land is collectively owned (*ejido*), yet the concept of private property (even without its juridical manifestations) is developing. The land can be inherited and divided, but not sold. It does not produce rent, but it can be mortgaged under certain special conditions.

In the Indian area, private landownership has stimulated Ladino penetration. First attracted by the new coffee crop, during the past century, Ladinos later took to other kinds of commercial agriculture. Freeing the land in fact accelerated the expansion of the national commercial-capitalist system. In Jilotepeque, Eastern Guatemala, the Indians have progressively lost their lands to such a degree that now only 5% of the Indians possess enough land to satisfy their needs, while 95% of them must rent land from the Ladinos. Seventy per cent of the land belongs to the Ladinos, who represent only 30% of the population; this land is primarily tilled by Indian sharecroppers or hired laborers. The Ladinos own an average of 57.3 acres of land, and the Indians 13.2 acres.[25] In Panajachel, the Ladinos represent one third of the population, but they own 80% of the land. The average Ladino owns more than eight times as much land as the average Indian. Besides, the Ladino often also owns lands in other municipalities.[26] How did it come about that the Ladinos have been able to take possession of such a large amount of land? Charles Wagley tells us: "The inevitable result of the series of laws extolling private property in compliance with modern conceptions was that many Indians who were unable to seize the meaning of the new private documents failed to register their lands, and these were often sold to the big plantations as non-validated lands."[27] These examples show that private landownership benefits the Ladinos and harms the Indians.[28]

There is a basic difference in the way that Indians and Ladinos conceive of land. The Indian is integrated in his traditional community,

[25] Melvin Tumin, *Caste in a Peasant Society, op. cit.*; John Gillin, *San Luis Jilotepeque*, Guatemala, 1958.

[26] Sol Tax, *Penny Capitalism, op. cit.*

[27] Charles Wagley, *op. cit.*, p. 67.

[28] Cf. Calixta Guiteras Holmes, *Perils of the Soul*, Glencoe, 1961, who writes: "as the years went by more than half of the lands belonging to the Pedrano Indians were acquired by wealthy and influential outsiders. . . . The man who purchased the land acquired the right to exploit those residing on it" (p. 14).

which is tied to the land. The Indian tills the soil; culturally and psychologically he ceases to be an Indian when he becomes separated from it. The tilling of the soil is intimately related to the group's social organization (lineage or tribe), and to its religious organization and belief. The Indian needs the land because without it he loses his social and ethnic identity. It does not matter whether this land is communal, *ejido*, or private. In any case, it will be property but not merchandise. It is a means of production, but it is not capital. It is a source of income, but not of rent.

For Ladinos, the private ownership of land has a different meaning from what it has for the Indians. It is associated with commercial farming (especially coffee), with a monetary economy, with wage-labor (including a type of servitude) of the Indians and, finally, with prestige and personal power. For the Ladinos land has a commercial value, independent of the group's own family and religious organization. The Ladinos' primary goal is to accumulate land and to work it through the use of wage labor. The Ladino is contemptuous of manual labor; his property serves the purpose of obtaining an income which allows him to devote himself to commerce and politics. We have already seen that the majority of the lands belonging at present to the Ladinos were obtained by them at the time of the coffee boom, during the past century. Ladinos use their accumulation of lands to obtain and control cheap labor.[29]

This brief analysis has shown that the private ownership of land has different economic and social functions among the Indians and the Ladinos. It is a social institution linked to the capitalist development of the region. But it primarily benefits the Ladino group, and is used by them as an instrument of exploitation of the Indians. The private ownership of land, introduced by the liberal regimes who, ironically, wanted the greatest good for the greatest number, has only served to dispossess the Indians of their lands, thus forcing them to go in search of wage work. The private ownership of land, therefore, constitutes one more element for the differentiation of the social classes of the region.

There are also important differences within the owners' group, but we do not have the data which would enable us to study them in relation to ethnic differences. The Ladino owners generally possess more lands than the Indian owners. Yet within each of these ethnic groups, the size of properties varies a great deal. Minifundists (owners of tiny plots) are many in number, and latifundia (large landholdings, or plantations), though small in number, concentrate the greatest part of private lands. The great latifundists are always Ladinos, of course, and the Indians cluster along the base of the pyramid. But there are some Ladinos who

[29] "La situación agraria de las comunidades indígenas," *Acción Indigenista*, No. 105, March, 1962.

own only very small parcels of land, while, on the other hand, there are a few Indians who possess, as in Chimaltenango, fifty times more land than others. The greater part of Indian owners do not possess enough land to meet their basic needs, and there are those who sell their minute properties and become day laborers in order to earn a little more.[30]

Commercial Relationships

The Indian economic world is by no means closed. Indian communities are only isolated in appearance. They participate in regional systems and the national economy. Markets and commercial relationships represent the primary link between the Indian community and the Ladino world, between the subsistence economy and the national economy. It is true that the major part of the Indians' agricultural produce is consumed by them. It is also true that the income generated by the Indians only represents a minimal part of the gross national product (even in Guatemala, where the Indian population represents more than one-half of the total). But the importance of these relationships is not to be measured by the amount of commercialized products or by their monetary value; but rather in terms of the quality of commercial relationships. These are the relationships which have transformed the Indians into a "minority"[31] and which have placed them in the condition of dependence in which they now find themselves.

Markets and commerce in the region have their background in the pre-Hispanic and colonial period. Their importance in some places is such that Redfield even speaks of a "primitive merchant society."[32] Tax calls the system "capitalist" because it rests on a "monetary economy organized around single households which are units of production and consumption, with a strongly developed market which tends to be perfectly competitive."[33] Such does not seem to be the case in other areas of the

[30] When generalizations are made about the Mayan area in Chiapas and Guatemala, certain local aspects and particular situations of great interest are necessarily neglected, the inclusion of which would perhaps modify the general scheme. It is a risk of which the author is wholly conscious, yet which he had to assume, considering the limits imposed by an article. Such is the case, for instance, of the Agrarian Reform in Guatemala, initiated with the revolution of 1944, but checked and diverted by the governments subsequent to the 1954 counterrevolution. Thus, the redistribution of the lands, the law of compulsory renting and the constitution of rural workers' labor unions during the decade of 1944-54 surely affected, in diverse ways, the class relations here analyzed. Yet as these processes are no longer in force, I have chosen to ignore them, at the risk of neglecting some facts which might be important to this analysis.

[31] In the sense given to this sociological term by Charles Wagley and Marvin Harris in their *Minorities in the New World*, New York, 1958.

[32] Robert Redfield, "Primitive Merchants of Guatemala," *The Quarterly Journal of Inter-American Relations*, Vol. I, No. 4, 1939.

[33] Sol Tax, *Penny Capitalism, op. cit.*, p. 13.

region, where the Indian market shows strongly marked monopolistic elements.[34]

Indian markets and the "constellation of regional markets" have been described in many contexts (especially in Mexico). The role of the Ladino city as the center of a region, and its position of economic, political, social, and religious dominance with respect to satellite Indian communities, is very well known. Between the city and the communities there develops a network of close and complex commercial relationships. In the city there is a weekly market of regional importance, and regular and permanent commerce in the stores and in the daily market place. At the weekly market place there is an influx of thousands of Indians from the surrounding region who come to sell their handicraft and farm products, and to buy manufactured and handicraft goods at the commercial establishments of the city. Some Indians are full-time traders who participate in the cycle of regional markets; Redfield has called them "primitive merchants." But the majority of Indian producers carry their products to the market themselves, usually accompanied by their families. Commerce is so organized that the Indian always leaves behind his small monetary income. He sells cheaply and must buy dearly, thus the Ladino trader gets a double profit.

Despite Tax's findings in Panajachel, there seems to be a general tendency towards a monopolistic structure in the Indian markets, in which the Indian producer-seller is in no way able to influence the price level. Trading of food products (the basis of Indian production) is controlled by a few Ladino monopolists from the city. As Marroquín has pointed out, the well-known bargaining of Indian markets is an instrument used by Ladinos in order to depress price levels of Indian products. In San Cristóbal de las Casas, Chiapas, for instance, the same effect is achieved through the performance of the *Atajadoras*, the Ladino women who place themselves at the city's entrance on market days and almost violently force the submissive, incoming Indians to sell them their wares at prices that they impose and which are lower than those which prevail at the market. These varied forms of exploitation which victimize the Indian trader, both as seller and buyer, are due to economic and political dominance of the urban Ladinos. This power is reinforced by their cultural superiority as expressed by their knowledge of price-building mechanisms, of the laws of the country, and above all, of the Spanish language. It is obvious that under these conditions the Indian has no access to national legal institutions to protect his individual rights.

Not only in the city but also in the "satellite communities" commerce is usually in Ladino hands. The latter are also moneylenders, which is an important function in societies where there is no accumulation of capital

[34] A. Marroquín, "Introducción al mercado indígena mexicano," *Ciencias Políticas y Sociales,* No. 8, 1957.

and where political and religious life demands considerable expenses. In order to pay their debts, Indians often mortgage their harvest (but seldom their property) and go to work on the coffee plantations.

Among the different kinds of relationships which take place between Indians and Ladinos, commercial relationships are the most important. The Indian participates in these relationships as producer and consumer; the Ladino is always the trader, the middleman, the creditor. The majority of the Indians enter into economic and social relationships with Ladinos at the level of commercial activity, and not at the level of wage labor. It is precisely the commercial relationships which link the Indian world to the socio-economic region in which it is integrated, and to national society as well as to the world economy.

Often commercial relationships go together with other kinds of social relationships such as interfamily relations. Pozas writes that "interdependence between Indian and Ladino individuals and families constitutes the real basis of relationships between the Ladino urban complex and the Indian rural villages."[35] These relationships between families can take the form of *compadrazgo* (ritual coparenthood). Although at first sight *compadrazgo* may appear to be an institution in which Indians and Ladinos face each other on a level of equality, in fact it contributes to accentuate the Indians' condition of inferiority and dependence. *Compadrazgo* is one among many institutions in a complex system which keeps the Indian subordinated to the Ladino in all aspects of social and economic life.

The conjunction of all these commercial relationships allows us to carry our analysis further. It is obvious that Indian communities are not economically self-contained. On the contrary, they are linked to regional structures by means of which they participate in the national and world economy. They are the weakest link of the national economy. On the other hand, these commercial relationships are only a part of the Indian community's economic system, but they are the part which places the Indians in a specific and special situation with respect to the Ladino population: a class situation. Commercial relationships between Indians and Ladinos are not relations between equals. The Indian, as a small producer, small seller, small buyer, and finally as a small consumer, can influence neither prices nor market tendencies. The Ladino, on the contrary, holds a privileged situation in the region. The Ladinos, small in number, are the traders and middlemen. The city, populated by Ladinos, is monopolistic. Regional production and distribution are concentrated there. True, these activities are a function of regional cities throughout the world. But here the economic inequalities between the city and the region are accentuated by the low level of agricultural production, the high cost of goods brought from other regions, and by all the other means

[35] Ricardo Pozas, *Chamula, op. cit.*, p. 111.

of political, religious, and social power which the city exerts over the neighboring rural environment.

There may be those who see in this situation only an ecologic relation, an "urban-rural" conflict. Others who will see only a situation of contact between two cultures, between two ethnic groups with different economic resources, which would explain or even justify the pre-eminence of one ethnic group over the other. Yet this would be a mistaken view. The city's privileged position has its origin in the colonial period. It was founded by the conqueror to fulfil the very same function it still fulfils; to incorporate the Indian into the economy which the conqueror had brought and his descendants developed. The regional city was an instrument of conquest and is still an instrument of domination. It is not only a matter of "contact" between two populations: *the Indian and the Ladino are both integrated within a single economic system, in a single society.* It is for this reason that inter-ethnic relations, insofar as commercial activities are concerned, bear the characteristics of class relations. The ecologic aspect of interaction between city and countryside, or between urban metropolis and community, in fact conceals specific social relationships between certain kinds of persons who hold differential positions with respect to the means of production and the distribution of wealth.

SOCIAL STRATIFICATION

There are essentially two ways in which to consider the social relationships between Indians and Ladinos: that which only considers two ethnic groups, two cultures brought to a more or less close contact, which might be called the culturalistic perspective; and that which takes as its point of departure the existence of the total society, of a single socioeconomic structure in which these two ethnic groups perform differentiated roles, and which might be called the structuralist perspective. The analysis made thus far is from the latter perspective. Yet this does not mean to deny the value of the culturalist approach. On the contrary, the perspective of cultural anthropology is valid when the analysis of social classes is set aside in order to consider other aspects of the relationships between the two ethnic groups.

In every society there may exist various systems of social stratification (that is, hierarchies of prestige and authority defined by cultural values). Here it is possible to distinguish three systems of social stratification, that is, three social universes with respect to which stratification may be studied: the Indian group, the Ladino group, and the total society in which Indians and Ladinos participate (that is, the inter-ethnic system). We may speak of two kinds of stratification: intra-ethnic and inter-ethnic.

Intra-Ethnic Stratification

Indians and Ladinos represent two different cultural communities. Each has its own value system. To the extent to which the value systems of these two communities are different, so too their systems of stratification will be different.

The Indians' Social Hierarchy. The Indian community is not stratified. All of its effective members equally participate in the same value system, and they are all equal with respect to each other. To participate in an effective manner in the Indian community means that Indians fulfil their duties in the community's political and religious structure.

The corporate Indian community controls its members through control of its resources and through the periodic redistribution of wealth. This is brought about by the cycle of religious festivities and the structure of local government. Community government has traditionally been in the hands of *principales*, family and lineage chiefs who enjoy special prestige due to services rendered to the community, and sometimes due to special supernatural powers which are attributed to them by other members of the group.[36] The council of *principales* is a group of elders who enjoy an individual preeminence; it is not a social stratum. This form of government is linked to the original kinship organization, which is now disappearing. Its real power is decaying, and effective government is in the hands of the so-called *Regional Council.* This is the pinnacle of the double political-religious hierarchy (also called *centripetal* organization),[37] in which individuals climb to higher status by alternately holding civil and religious positions in the course of their lives.

The individual named by his peers to hold a public position within this system is forced to accept it under the threat of strong social ostracism. Public functions imply a series of very heavy duties and monetary expenses. The selected individual (who always tries to escape from his functions before having been elected, but must rigorously submit to his duties once he has forcibly been sworn in) not only must abandon his farming, leaving it to the care of his family or even hired laborers, but must also spend large sums for festivities and ceremonies. Passing through the hierarchy means years of indebtedness for many. When the public position is well performed it is a source of prestige and moral authority, but it does not bring material rewards. Personal power is strictly limited by the collectivity; authority is exercised for the benefit of the whole community and not for any restricted particular group.

[36] G. Aguirre Beltrán, *Formas de gobierno indígena*, Mexico, 1954.
[37] F. Cámara Barbachano, "Religious and Political Organization," in S. Tax (ed.), *Heritage of Conquest*, Glencoe, 1952.

It has been said that the expenses involved in festivities and ceremonies represent a prestige economy, that distribution of wealth (similar to Canadian *potlatch* and African *bilaba*) is the source of prestige.[38]
Another author offers an opposite interpretation, which seems closer to
reality: it is not wealth as such, but services rendered to the community
which create prestige, yet a certain amount of wealth is necessary to carry
out these services adequately. Thus, there is not, strictly speaking,
a prestige economy, since economic pre-eminence is not automatically
translated into prestige. On the contrary, if a poor man performs his
public functions well, he may achieve a status of great prestige in the
community; that is if he finds the means to finance the festivities and
ceremonies which are his charge, even when this may mean running into
debt.[39]

Apparently economic pre-eminence of individuals is not favored by
the community. We have seen that the means available to the Indian
for accumulating capital are strictly limited. Also limited are the possibilities of investment. Basically, it is the corporate community itself
which limits the economic possibilities of its members. In Chamula,
members of the Council sometimes purposefully choose for the presidency
individuals whose relative wealth is well known. This is obviously justified
by the fact that wealthy persons can more easily perform their duties.
But the social consequence of this act is the redistribution of wealth and
maintenance of the "principle of equality" in the group's social organization.

Under these conditions it is impossible for a social stratum that stands
out among the rest of the population to emerge in the traditional corporate community.[40] Individual economic pre-eminence is not transformed
into prestige. It arises, individually, through positions held in the political-
religious structure. The political organization of the community is a way
to redistribute wealth and channel people's energy into service to the
community.

It is important to qualify the phrase "redistribution of wealth." In
effect, a fictitious redistribution occurs. It is nothing but elimination
of likely economic pre-eminence of those individuals who for some reason

[38] G. Aguirre Beltrán, *Formas de gobierno indígena, op. cit.*

[39] Ricardo Pozas, *Chamula, un pueblo indio de los Altos de Chiapas, op. cit.*
In an interesting essay F. Cancian shows that in Zinacantan (Mexico), the
prestige of a position depends on various factors which are difficult to measure,
among them the cost of the position, the authority it conveys, and "idiosyncratic"
factors. Cf. F. Cancian, "Informant Error and Native Prestige Ranking in
Zinacantan," *American Anthropologist*, Vol. 65, No. 5, 1963. See also his *Economics and Prestige in a Maya Community*, Stanford University Press, 1965,
for a detailed analysis of the system.

[40] Cancian (*loc. cit.*) suggests that in Zinacantan there does exist a rudimentary "economic stratification."

have been able to accumulate a greater amount of goods than their peers. This wealth is not reabsorbed by the community. It is consumed in liquor, ceremonial clothing, fireworks, and in hundreds of articles employed in what an observer has named "institutionalized waste."[41] These expenses required by the ceremonial pattern associated with the functioning of the political and religious organization are transformed into income for those who provide these articles for the community. These purveyors are urbanized Ladinos, many of whom are craftsmen specialized in the kinds of articles consumed by Indians. Aguirre Beltrán even states that trading of these ceremonial articles is, in Chiapas, "the real source of life" of a city of 18,000 inhabitants.[42] We may thus conclude that the structure which maintains equality within the Indian community, preventing the emergence of social classes, also contributes to the whole Indian community's dependence on the city, that is, to the differentiation of social classes between Indians and Ladinos.

There exists in the region yet another form of government: the Constitutional Council, which is a part of the national political regime and the only "legal" government, from the point of view of the national constitution. This is the link which unites the community to other political institutions such as political parties, regional and national legislatures and national executive power. It is the means employed by national governments to extend their administrative and political control over Indian populations.

The Constitutional Council is generally controlled by Ladinos, even though the municipal president may be an Indian. Local Indian government will surely disappear in time, to be substituted by the Constitutional Council. To the extent to which the Indians participate more and more in national politics and in official governmental organisms, the Constitutional Council is likely to become a means of social differentiation within the Indian community, perhaps creating a higher stratum of "court clerks" and functionaries.[43]

Social Strata among Ladinos. Ladino society, as every "Western" society, is stratified. This stratification is influenced by such factors as land ownership, income, occupation, education, and family lineage. The Ladino city is highly differentiated in terms of these diverse criteria,

---

[41] G. Aguirre Beltrán, *Formas de gobierno indígena*, p. 103.

[42] *Ibid.*

[43] In Chiapas, Mexico, the *Instituto Nacional Indigenista* (a government department) is training young Indians as municipal secretaries for the positions held by the Ladinos. In Guatemala, the penetration of the national political parties into the Indian communities during the democratic regimes of the 1944-54 decade modified the traditional structure. These problems have been treated in a collective work which the author was unfortunately unable to consult while working on this essay: *Political Changes in Guatemalan Indian Communities*, New Orleans, 1957.

even having its own local "aristocracy" descending (in fact or in fiction) from important colonial families. The status indices are correlated with one another. The family line, large land ownership, big business, and participation in local politics go together. But on the other hand, a high level of education (especially university) is more typical of the "new rich," the professionals (physicians, lawyers, engineers), who are new to the region but are developing some traditional interests, and thus frequently associate with the older families through marriage.

The number of strata used in describing Ladino society is an arbitrary matter. For Guatemala, Adams uses five "primary economic types" and four general strata or "classes."[44] On the other hand, in describing the Ladinos of Jilotepeque, Tumin uses a statistical index of standard of living to delimit three "classes," but then adds that the populace itself recognizes but two levels: the elite, called "society," composed of 20 families (less than 20% of the Ladino population), and the "people." At the lowest level of the Ladino ethnic group, it is difficult to distinguish clearly a Ladino from an Indian.[45] In Panajachel, Tax also speaks of two Ladino classes: the "upper urban bourgeoisie" and the "lower rural."[46]

Ladinos place high value on wealth and property, which are one of their *raisons d'être*. These values constitute the foundation of all of their economic activity, and there is no competing system of politico-religious offices to equalize property and prestige. Ladino society is mobile, and opportunities for upward mobility exist, in principle, for everyone. In contrast to the Indian, the Ladino perceives his own society as a stratified system. Certain activities, especially manual occupations, belong to an inferior order and must be avoided; there are others, especially commerce, to which they aspire. Finally, the condition of landowner is the most envied. "Good family" background plays an important part in these provincial societies, and the fact of being related, through kinship, marriage or *compadrazgo*, to important families is obviously a way of acquiring a high social status. Ladino culture, as opposed to Indian, is highly competitive and authoritarian.[47]

Inter-Ethnic Stratification and Mobility

Stratification means that certain characteristics or variables are unequally distributed among individuals. The combination of some of these characteristics and the value attributed to them by members of society account for the existence of a scale or continuum in which individuals occupy higher or lower positions with respect to one another. If a set of individ-

[44] Richard N. Adams, *Encuesta sobre la cultura de los ladinos en Guatemala*, Guatemala, EMEP, 1956.

[45] Melvin Tumin, *Caste in a Peasant Society, op. cit.*

[46] Sol Tax, *Penny Capitalism, op. cit.*

[47] B. Colby and P. Van den Berghe, "Ethnic relations in Southeastern Mexico," *American Anthropologist*, Vol. LIII, No. 4, 1961.

uals have in common a set of these characteristics, which distinguish them from other groupings, *and if this is recognized as such by society*, we may then speak of a stratum.

Ladinos and Indians hold different positions in the stratification scale, according to such well-known variables as income, property, degree of education, standard of living, etc. Given the fact that Ladinos concentrate along the scale's upper ranks and Indians along the lower ones, the two ethnic groups may be considered as separate strata within one stratified system. They are in effect the only strata in this system, because in the value systems of both groups ethnic characteristics (cultural and sometimes even biological) play a more important part in stratification than do other criteria. Ladinos hold a higher position not only in the objective scale of socio-economic characteristics, but they also consider themselves, *qua* Ladinos, as being superior to Indians. They are contemptuous of the Indian as such. The latter, on the other hand, are conscious of their social and economic inferiority. They know that those traits which identify them as Indians place them in a position of inferiority with respect to Ladinos.

Even while stratification is objectively presented as a scale or continuum, it in fact functions socially as a system with only two strata which are characterized in cultural and biological terms. Ladinos make use of physical stereotypes to affirm their "whiteness" in contrast to the darker Indians. As Tumin has pointed out, it is a matter of ideal types, since the Ladino population is in effect a mestizo one. This fact notwithstanding, one of the most valued criteria among the higher Ladino strata is that of their supposed "Spanish blood." Other observers have noted that, in San Cristóbal de las Casas, there appears to be a coincidence between the socio-economic scale and the biological continuum.[48] Racial criteria, nonetheless, do not perform a crucial role, precisely because it is impossible to classify the population in either ethnic group on an exclusively physical basis.

Cultural indices are essential to stratification: most important are language and dress, followed by self-identification and personal classification by others. Thus, mastery of Spanish and changes in dress do not *ipso facto* turn the Indian into a Ladino. Essentially the Indian condition lies in his being integrated to his Indian (corporate) community, and participating in the traditional social structure (kinship groups, civic-religious hierarchy). It is the "cultural" and not the "biological" Indian who constitutes the lowest stratum. The Indian is conscious of this situation. Learning Spanish not only represents for him a means of upward mobility, but also an instrument of defense in his daily relationships with Ladinos. The adoption of Ladino dress styles also reduces the stigma of his inferior condition in his relationship with Ladinos.

[48] B. Colby and P. Van den Berghe, *loc. cit.*

The definition of the two ethnic groups depends upon strictly cultural factors which, due to their historical importance in the region, subsume and impose themselves upon all other factors of stratification. While it dichotomizes social relationships, ethnic stratification diminishes the importance of the socio-economic scale or continuum based on quantitative indices, so that many Indians and Ladinos share the same socio-economic level without the disappearance of ethnic stratification. Robert Redfield noted that in a Guatemalan village, "the greater the Ladinos' upward mobility, the more they tended to be contemptuous of the Indians and to identify lower-class Ladinos with Indians."[49] And, naturally, those "lower-class" Ladinos considered themselves superior to Indians.

These cultural values are reflected in inter-ethnic relations. Ladinos always behave in an authoritarian or paternalistic manner towards Indians. The latter are treated with familiarity, yet it is expected that they show signs of respect and submission. Unskilled manual labor is considered an attribute of the Indian. Notwithstanding legal equality proclaimed in the Constitution, Indians are subject to discrimination, particularly in the cities, where they are exposed to all kinds of arbitrary and humiliating behavior by the Ladino population.

Effective social contacts between Indians and Ladinos are, with the exception of the already-mentioned economic relations, very limited. There exists no real social interaction between the two ethnic groups. Traditional religious and political activities are performed separately; common participation at parties and sports is almost nonexistent. The only non-economic relationship in which Indians and Ladinos formally participate is *compadrazgo*, yet as has already been pointed out, here too the Indian's inferiority is obvious, and here too there are economic implications.

There is some upward mobility from the Indian stratum to the Ladino; but its nature and characteristics are by no means simple and they vary from region to region. A public opinion poll carried out by Tumin in Jilotepeque showed that there are relatively more Indians than Ladinos who believe that movement from one group to the other is possible. Indians tend to believe they can achieve this through the accumulation of wealth, while Ladinos believe that the modification of cultural characteristics is needed. Given the Ladinos' superiority, they have an interest in checking the Indians' mobility. Adams has pointed out that in a community where cultural differences between Indians and Ladinos are small, the latter resort to a whole series of ruses in order to maintain their superiority — even the invocation of "racial" factors where no biological differences exist.

[49] Robert Redfield, "The Relations Between Indians and Ladinos in Agua Escondida, Guatemala," *América Indígena*, Vol. XVI, No. 4, 1956.

Upward mobility among Indians represents a process of acculturation.[50] But learning Spanish and adopting Ladino dress styles are insufficient. The Indian must also become socially (generally meaning physically) separated from his community. In order to become a Ladino, the mobile Indian must cut his ties with the social structure of his corporate community. He must not only modify his cultural characteristics, but also his "social" condition as an Indian. It is very unlikely, if not impossible, for an Indian to become a Ladino in the midst of his own community, for the "ladinoized" Indian is a marginal man.

The Indian's upward mobility means both a process of acculturation and an elevation in the socio-economic scale. It is neither the poorer Indians nor the subsistence farmers who become Ladinos. To become a Ladino in a cultural sense also means being a trader or regularly producing for the market and, in general, acquiring a higher standard of living. This does not mean that all of those who become traders or sell their produce in the market or who achieve a better standard of living necessarily become Ladinos. Nor does it mean that Ladinos who descend the socio-economic scale become Indians. In effect, a Ladino will always be a Ladino, low as he may fall in the socio-economic scale. But an Indian, provided that he ascends the socio-economic scale, may become a Ladino; what is more, he will never be a Ladino unless he does ascend the socio-economic scale.

THE DYNAMICS OF INTER-ETHNIC RELATIONS: CLASSES, COLONIALISM, AND ACCULTURATION

Let us pull together the different threads in this essay and attempt a general formulation of the system of relationships between Indians and Ladinos. Our historical point of departure will be the Spanish Conquest, although we do not deny the importance of pre-Hispanic social processes in the subsequent character of the Mayan region. The Spanish Conquest was a military enterprise, part of the political and economic expansion in post-feudal and mercantilistic Europe. The Conquest was fundamentally influenced by commercial factors — the lust for gold and spice. As a military enterprise the Spanish Conquest was a violent confrontation of two societies, two different cultures. The weaker one — the Indian — succumbed.

Historical Trends

At first, the Indians received from the conqueror the treatment accorded since ancient times to the vanquished: looting, dispossession, slavery, even extermination. Yet the Conquest of the New World was not like

[50] A detailed analysis of acculturation in this area has been made by G. Aguirre Beltrán in *El Proceso de Aculturación*, Mexico, 1957.

preceding ones. In Spain, deep transformations were taking place due
to the expulsion of the Moors. The American continent was to perform
an essential role in Europe's new economic development, and the native
populations were necessary to that role; thus, the destruction and en-
slavement of the Indians had to stop. The military conquest was transformed into a colonial system. Just as other colonial systems which the
world has known since then, this one was managed over three centuries
on behalf of the interests of certain powerful social classes of the mother
country, and their representatives in New Spain. The Crown's policy
reflected these changing and often conflicting interests.

At first the Indian chiefs and aristocracy were kept in their positions,
which suited the colonial administration's *realpolitik*. But towards the
end of the 19th century the Indian communities had become socially
and economically homogeneous. Their internal social differentiation was
no longer in the interests of the colonizer. Residential segregation of
Indians (through settlements of converted Indians and other mechanisms) and the *encomiendas* (lands which the Crown granted as trustee-
ship to the *conquistadores*) were the first instruments used by the
conquerors to levy taxes and services. Part of the Indian society's wealth
was simply transferred to the conquering society. Then Indian communities were transformed into labor reserves of the colonial economy.
Systems of serfdom and forced labor in plantations, mines, and workshops
constituted the basis of the economic system.

Colonial society was the product of mercantilist expansion: of the
dawning of the bourgeois revolution in Europe. Its structure still retained much from the feudal era, especially in the character of human
relationships. Some researchers even affirm that feudalism grew stronger
in America after it had begun to decline in Spain, and that America
"feudalized" Spain once again.[51] Exploitation of the Indian population
constituted one of the main goals of colonial economic policy. In order
to maintain this labor reserve, it was controlled by a complex of laws,
norms, restrictions, and prohibitions which kept accumulating during
three centuries of colonialism, and which resulted in the corporate "folk"
communities. A rigid social hierarchy based upon centralization of political and economic power and validated in the law kept the natives in their
position of inferiority with respect to all of the other social strata.

The colonial system worked on two levels. The restrictions and economic prohibitions which Spain imposed upon her colonies (and which
later had the effect of fomenting the independence movements) were
repeated, often aggravated, in the relations between the colonial society
and the Indian communities. The same commercial monopolies, the

[51] Angel Palerm, "Notas sobre la clase media en México," *Ciencias Sociales*
(Washington), No. 14-15 and 16-17, 1952. (Reproduced in *Las clases sociales
en México*, México, 1960.)

same restrictions on production, the same political controls which Spain exerted upon the Colony, the colonists imposed upon the Indian communities. As Spain was to the Colony, so the Colony was to Indian communities: a colonial metropolis. Thus mercantilism penetrated even to the most isolated villages of Spanish America.

Colonial relationships and class relationships underlay ethnic relationships, but in different ways. In terms of *colonial relationships*, the Indian society as a whole confronted colonial society. Contact was defined by ethnic discrimination, political dependence, social inferiority, residential segregation, economic subjection, and juridical incapacity. But *class relationships* were defined in terms of labor and property relations. These relations were not defined in ethnic, social, or residential terms. Only juridical coercion (supported by military power) as well as other economic and extra-economic pressures intervened in the establishment of labor relations. Labor relations were not between two societies, but only between two specific sectors within one society.

Colonial and class relationships appear intermixed throughout this period. While the former primarily answered to mercantilist interests, the latter met the emerging capitalist ones, and conflicts developed between them. Indian communities were constantly losing members to the emerging national society. Despite tutelary legislation, biological and cultural mixing was a constant process which kept producing new problems for colonial society. Those Indians who for various reasons were absorbed by the larger society, therefore, quit the colonial relationships to become integrated into the class structure. In consequence, they were no longer Indians, but simply peasants or workers.

These two kinds of socio-economic relationships in which the Indian ethnic groups were involved received moral sanction through the rigid social stratification in which the Indian (biologically, culturally, and juridically defined) was always at the bottom (with the exception of the slave). From these conditions there emerged the corporate community and the formation of Indo-colonial cultural characteristics, which we today call Indian culture. Ethnic relationships of the period thus presented three main aspects: two kinds of relationships of dependence and one kind of relationship of order.[52]

The dynamics of these systems of relationships were varied. The colonial relationships between Indian communities and the larger society tended to strengthen the Indian communities and foment their ethnic identity. The subordinate group usually reacts to a dominant-subordinate relationship of the colonial kind with a struggle for liberation, and in fact the colonial period was not devoid of native rebellions. But con-

[52] On the concepts of relation of dependence and relation of order and their application to the study of class structures, see S. Ossowski, *Class Structure in the Social Consciousness*, London, 1963.

versely, class relations contributed to the disintegration of the Indian community and its integration with the larger society. Both kinds of relations complemented each other in terms of the Indian's oppression. But the opposed tendencies which they engendered explain why certain Indian communities survived, while others were transformed into enclaves of peasants in the *haciendas* which displaced the *encomiendas* of the 16th and 17th centuries. Colonial relationships usually dominated class relationships, and social stratification (which has sometimes, because of its rigidity, been called a caste system) reflected more the colonial character than the class character of the Indian's subjugation. The stratification system, in turn, exerted its own influence upon the development of class relationships.

Political independence from Spain in the early 19th century did not basically change the relationships between Indians and the national society. Despite the legal equality of all citizens (including Indians), various factors joined to maintain the "colonial" character of these relations. There were internal struggles which lasted many decades, and there was economic depression during the first half of the 19th century. Both helped to keep Indian communities marginal, isolated from the outside world, and turned them inward. Another reason should also be taken into account. At the beginning of the colonial period tutelary laws were established because it was considered that Indians were inferior beings. But by the end of three centuries of colonialism, these laws had served to maintain and fix that inferiority. In consequence, when legal equality was declared, the Indian was effectively in a condition of inferiority to the rest of the population, in every area of economic and social life, and thus unable to act like a free and equal citizen.

The first effective changes occurred during the second half of the 19th century: first with the Reform Laws stressing individual property in land, and later with the introduction of new cash crops (principally coffee) into the Indian region. Both phenomena, of course, are closely related to one another. Legal equality of men and the break-up of communal land had two immediate consequences: the Indian could now freely dispose of himself in the labor market, and the land he held could become private property. In fact, this did not take place in the abstract, but in the specific situations that have already been mentioned: extension of commercial farming; penetration by Ladinos into communities inhabited by Indian ethnic groups; appropriation of land by Ladinos; formation of great plantations and the Indians' wage labor on these properties. Coffee plantations became working centers for a considerable mass of Indians, legally or illegally recruited from their communities. At the same time the first products of industrialization penetrated into the more distant villages of the Indian region in the form of goods carried by Ladino traders. In this way new economic relationships were established between the Indians and the rest of the population.

Expansion of the capitalist economy during the second half of the 19th century, together with the ideology of economic liberalism, once again transformed the quality of ethnic relationships between Indians and Ladinos. We consider this stage as a second form of colonialism, which we might call *internal colonialism*. Indians of traditional communities found themselves once again in the role of a colonized people: they lost their lands, were forced to work for the "strangers," were integrated against their will to a new monetary economy, and fell under new forms of political domination. This time, colonial society was national society itself, which progressively extended its control over its own territory.[53] Now there were not only isolated Indians who, abandoning their communities, joined the national society; but Indian communities themselves, as groups, were progressively incorporated to expanding regional economic systems. *To the extent to which the national society extended its control, and the capitalist economy dominated the area, relations between colonizer and colonized, between Ladino and Indian, were transformed into class relationships.*

Contemporary Processes

The corporate community has been characteristic of traditional colonial society in Indian America. Corporative social structure has an ecologic and economic basis. When colonial society is transformed into "underdeveloped" society, when the economic structure of the corporate community is modified (loss of lands, wage labor, commercialization of agricultural produce, etc.), then it is rather unlikely that the corporate quality of the community's internal social relationships can survive for long. As we have seen, some of the Indian's cultural characteristics are bound to the highly structured corporate community. If this structure should progressively disappear, these cultural characteristics would become weaker.

Ethnic stratification in the region is the result of this historical evolution. It reflects the colonial situation which has been maintained to present times. Behind inter-ethnic relationships, which show themselves as a stratification system, there is a social class structure. When an Indian works for a Ladino, the main point is not the inter-ethnic relationship but the labor relation. During the decade of the thirties, the Indians of Chiapas organized to defend their working conditions in the coffee plan-

---

[53] Pablo González-Casanova, in a different and independent analysis, also brings forth the existence of internal colonialism in Mexico. The present essay presents a particular case, which may be considered within González-Casanova's general approach. See his study, "Internal Colonialism and National Development," *Studies in Comparative International Development*, Vol. I, No. 4, 1965.

tations; not as Indians, but as workers. During the years 1944-1954 there were also labor unions of Indian agricultural workers in Guatemala. They have also become organized in their struggle for land, under the agrarian reform programs, not as Indians but as landless peasants. These relationships sometimes assume cultural forms. The struggle for land, for instance, is carried on in the name of restitution of communal and clan lands. At times there have also emerged messianic movements against Ladinos. Yet it was always a matter of structural changes within the traditional community.

Inter-ethnic stratification no longer completely corresponds to the new class relationships which have developed along with a monetary economy. "Colonized" Indians are not as such a social class. We are not saying that Indians and Ladinos are simply two social classes. This would be oversimplifying a deeply complex historical situation. During the course of economic development (or more precisely, of the development of economic underdevelopment, as a result of a colonial economy), various new social classes emerge. They are not yet totally formed, because "colonial" relationships still determine the social structure at different levels. The Indian participates in various kinds of socio-economic relationships. He holds various occupational roles at the same time. He may be a small farmer in the communal lands, an ambulant trader, a salaried worker during different periods of the year, or during the course of his life. These different kinds of class relationships contribute to separate the individual from his corporate community. The community's corporate structure is breaking up. Should it disappear, inter-ethnic stratification will have lost its objective basis.

Nonetheless, the inter-ethnic stratification system which, like every stratification system, is deeply rooted in the values held by the members of the society, is an essentially conservative force within the social structure. While it reflects a situation of the past (the clear dichotomy between Indians and Ladinos in every area of social, economic, and political life, characteristic of the colonial situation), it curbs the development of new class relationships. We should not forget that the landless peasant and the salaried worker are *also* Indians. Even though relations of production will be determinant of future transformations in the region, ethnic consciousness may weigh heavier than class consciousness. Thus, exploited or poor as a Ladino may be, he feels privileged as compared to the Indians, even those who may have a standard of living higher than his own. Indians, on the other hand, tend to attribute all of their misfortunes to the Ladinos as such (a position which, incidentally, is shared by certain romantic *Indigenista* intellectuals), an attitude which contributes to the concealment of objective relationships between classes. This range of problems has been little studied in the region and it represents, in my opinion, an interesting field of research.

To the extent to which class relationships become more clearly defined, there emerges a new stratification, based on socio-economic indices. This stratification already exists among Ladinos, and is progressively expanding to the Indians. The status symbols of the Ladinos are beginning to be valued by the Indians too. It is no longer sufficient — or even desirable — that the Indian should become "ladinoized." The situation will have radically changed when social stratification includes Ladinos and Indians independent of their ethnic characteristics. Ideally this would mean the maintenance of Indian cultural identity independent of stratification. To what degree this situation is workable depends on many special factors. It has been noted that in Quetzaltenango (Guatemala) something of the sort is taking place, and this also seems to be the case in Mexico among the Maya of Yucatán, the Zapotec of Oaxaca, and the Tarascans of Michoacán.

But such a situation would also depend on the attitudes and reactions of Ladinos, whose position is not stable within the class society. Ladinos have always accepted (at least from one generation to the other) the admission of acculturated Indians into their group. It is difficult to foresee reactions of the Ladino community faced with two hypothetical alternatives of the inter-ethnic stratification system's evolution: on the one hand, the complete assimilation of Indians (which is rather unlikely); and on the other, a general economic rise of the Indian ethnic group as such (which would be a challenge to Ladino superiority). Development of a class society leads toward either of these hypothetic situations. The final result will depend on how class conflicts are solved.

Contemporary inter-ethnic relations partly result from past colonial policy. They also represent the disintegration of that policy and are a function of present economic and class structures. As has been shown by various economists, underdeveloped economies tend to polarize into areas of growth and structurally related areas of stagnation. The Maya region of Chiapas and Guatemala constitutes such an area of stagnation, as do other Indian areas of Mexico. The "marginal" populations inhabiting these areas are growing in absolute numbers, despite national economic development.[54] The regional ruling class, represented by Ladinos, is not necessarily the dominant one in the national society. In Guatemala, since the defeat of the nationalist bourgeoisie in 1954, these two groups have in fact become one. There is no contradiction between landowners, commercial bourgeoisie (particularly coffeegrowers) and foreign capital.[55]

[54] Cf. Pablo González-Casanova, "Sociedad plural y desarrollo: el caso de México," *América Latina,* Vol. V, No. 4, 1962, and his article reprinted elsewhere in the present volume.

[55] Jaime Díaz Rozzotto, *El carácter de la revolución guatemalteca,* México, 1958. Also see Richard N. Adams, "Social Change in Guatemala and U.S. Policy," in *Social Change in Latin America Today,* New York, 1960.

But in Mexico the situation is different. National power is held by a bureaucratic, "developmentist" bourgeoisie, a product of the 1910 Revolution. This bourgeoisie has displaced latifundists on a national level, but in more backward regions, such as Chiapas, it tolerates them while seeking the support of a new rural bourgeoisie composed of traders, neo-latifundists and public employees.[56] In both Mexico and Guatemala the regional ruling class is composed of "power seekers" — to use Wolf's term — of mestizo origin who have come to fill the power vacuum left by the old feudal landowning aristocracy.

For purposes of analysis, four elements may be isolated in the current inter-ethnic situation: colonial relationships, class relationships, social stratification, and the acculturation process. These four elements constitute interdependent variables and with them we may attempt to build a hypothetic model of inter-ethnic relations at the present time.

Colonial Relationships. These relationships are a function of the structural development-underdevelopment dichotomy and they tend to be in force for as long as the dichotomy persists. As long as there are areas performing as internal colonies in underdeveloped countries, the relationships characterizing their inhabitants tend to take the form of colonial relationships. These are strengthened where there exist, as in the Maya region, marked cultural differences between two sectors of the population, leading to a rigid stratification defined in cultural and biological terms (which is sometimes called caste). Colonial relations tend to limit and prevent acculturation, cultural ladinoization, and to maintain a rigid stratification. There exists an obvious interest on the part of the dominant ethnic group (Ladinos) in maintaining colonial relations, especially when their predominance depends on the existence of cheap and abundant labor.

In contrast to Ladinos, the Indians — the subordinate ethnic group — derive no benefit from the colonial situation and may try various forms of reaction to it. The first is withdrawal into the corporate community, both physically and socially. As Wolf pointed out, this has happened on various occasions in the history of the region, and it represents on the part of the Indian ethnic group a latent tendency which becomes manifest when the economic and political situation allows it.[57] Next to withdrawal, the Indians also react to the colonial situation in terms of "nationalism." This form of reaction may have as its objective the strengthening of the Indian government (regional council), and possibly the struggle for the Indians' national political representation. It also shows in measures adopted to encourage education in the Indian language and development of Indian culture. It sometimes comes through an

---

[56] Cf. Rodolfo Stavenhagen, "Social Aspects of Agrarian Structure in Mexico," *Social Research*, 33 (3), Autumn 1966.

[57] Eric Wolf, *Sons of the Shaking Earth*, Chicago, 1959.

extreme anti-ladinoism and resistance to ladinoization. Other counter-acculturative factors such as messianism and, on certain occasions, armed uprisings and other forms of violence also play a role here. Finally, there is a third form of reaction to the colonial situation, and this is assimilation. It is an individual process which, as has been seen, represents a separation from the corporate structure of the community. From a cultural point of view it represents ladinoization. From a structural point of view it means that the individual becomes integrated to the class structure, no longer as an Indian (that is, a colonized person), but simply due to his relationship to the means of production. Ladinoization, as we have seen, may be the result of upward mobility in the socio-economic scale. But generally it only means the proletarianization of the Indian.

Class Relationships. We cannot over-emphasize that the class character and colonial character of inter-ethnic relations are two intimately-related aspects of the same phenomenon. They are separated here only for the purpose of our analysis. Class relationships have developed parallel to and simultaneous with colonial relations and tend to displace them more and more. But the colonial character of inter-ethnic relations impresses particular characteristics upon class relations, and tends to retard their development. In this context, class relations mean mutual interactions between persons holding opposed economic positions, independent of ethnic considerations. These relations develop together with the region's economic development. As agricultural production increases, as the market for industrial products expands, as the monetary economy develops, and as the labor market expands, colonial relations lose their importance and give way to the predominance of class relations. The latter's development also depends, to a great degree, upon structural factors of the national economy and is not the result of decision-making at the regional or local levels. At any rate, the development of class relations between Indians and Ladinos is associated with the development of capitalism while the "feudal" or "semi-feudal" aspects, so frequently indicated in the literature, tend to disappear.

Consequently, measures for local or community development such as improvement of agricultural techniques, establishment of production cooperatives, etc., may change colonial relations into class relations, but not necessarily so. This transformation can only take place if such developments are accompanied by the parallel development of the regional economy as a whole, and particularly of its Ladino metropolis. If such is not the case, the likelihood is that the fruits of local development will enter the traditional socio-economic circuits without modifying the regional structure.

It has already been seen that on certain occasions Ladinos are interested in maintaining colonial relations. There also exist circumstances in which they are interested in strengthening class relationships over and against colonial relationships. This happens particularly with the development of the productive forces: when Ladinos are presented with new opportunities for investment, when they need seasonal labor which can only be obtained through monetary incentives, or when they require non-agricultural labor (for certain manufactures or construction work in the cities or on the roads); finally, when they need to develop new regional markets and strengthen the Indians' demand for industrial goods. The Ladinos' interest in the development of class relations also arises when the agarian reform manages to really break the land monopoly and when the possession of his own land can turn the Indian back to subsistence farming. In this case, class relations develop particularly through the marketing of crops and the agricultural credit structure.

Social Stratification. Insofar as the regional system of social stratification has only two strata based essentially on ethnic characteristics it tends to maintain the appearance of a colonial situation. At the same time, as class relations develop, it tends to change into a clearly defined socio-economic stratification. The already existing stratification among the Ladino ethnic group expands to include both ethnic groups. Perhaps the day will come when both ethnic groups — independent of their cultural characteristics — will be included in a single stratification system, based exclusively on socio-economic criteria. The old stratification system, based on ethnic characteristics tends to conflict with the development of class relations and the socio-economic stratification based on them. Thus, for instance, an Indian trader or landowner receives discriminatory treatment from Ladinos who are in a socio-economic situation inferior to his own, while Indian day-laborers tend to receive smaller wages than the Ladinos who are in the same position. Among the Ladinos there exists an obvious concern over maintaining the bases of ethnic stratification; especially among the lower strata of the Ladino population, who in this way avoid competing with socially mobile Indians. This is the same phenomenon as that of the poor whites in the south of the United States.

The Indians' upward vertical mobility in the socio-economic scale is accompanied by a certain degree of ladinoization, but, as has already been pointed out, not all of the aspects of Indian culture change at the same rate. Development of class relations tends to facilitate the Indian's upward mobility, since an ascent in the socio-economic scale renders the conservation of a low status based upon exclusively ethnic criteria more precarious. Upward mobility, as much in the socio-economic scale as in the shift from the Indian to the Ladino ethnic group, is a function of the transformation of the colonial situation into a class situation.

Acculturation. The process of acculturation of the Indian is hard to place in a structural analysis, since it is used in the literature to refer to processes which are highly varied in content. In a general sense it means the adoption of Ladino cultural elements by individuals or groups (communities) of the Indian ethnic group. Thus, the change in dress, the substitution of folk medicine by scientific medicine, and the change of occupation, to take only three examples, are all part of the process of ladinoization. Yet the structural significance of these three examples, taking each by itself, is very different. Without considering for the moment the motivational determinants leading to a change in dress, this by itself has no consequences for the social structure; except if, carried out collectively by the Indians, it should lead to certain changes in the value systems of both ethnic groups, which in turn might influence the systems of mutual action and interaction, thus affecting social structures. But this kind of chain argument does not lead to a better understanding of the phenomena under study. Of the preceding examples, the second — the shift from traditional medicine to modern medicine — does not by itself represent a structural change either. But it may lead to demographic consequences which will have important structural results. Change of occupation, on the contrary, can only be understood within the frame of a structural analysis.

The above shows that the concept of ladinoization may mean anything from a simple change in the daily use of an object (using a spoon instead of a *tortilla* to eat soup), up to a complete change of the Indians' life and world view. Within the limits of this essay, concern over the process of ladinoization is only meaningful insofar as it has immediate structural implications.

In conclusion, it must be repeated that the contemporary scene involves a complex combination of elements. Using the analytic concepts of "colonial relationships," "class relationships," "social stratification" and "acculturation" helps us understand the dynamic processes at work, and relate them to historical antecedents as well as contemporary events.

Dynamics of the Class Structure

THE PROBLEM

It is commonly said that neither Marx's generalizations on the social classes of early capitalism, nor the generalizations of more recent authors, are fully adequate for the experiences of the contemporary "developing" countries. In fact, what should be looked for is the specification of hypotheses on the structure and dynamics of social classes in different types of social systems. Thus the aim of this work is to analyze Mexican society and the unique experiences it has undergone, in order to study the principle factors determining the dynamics of its social classes. They have evolved somewhat differently from what would be expected from the Marxist model of class consciousness and political action in Europe.

It is well known that the Marxist terminology presents two different concepts of social class: one concerns the phenomenon of class "in itself," based on the objective structure of the exploitation of certain groups of people by others; the other, of class "for itself," based on the realities of consciousness of that structural situation, and on the political organization which follows from it. To the first concept corresponds the definition of social class offered by Marx: "When millions of families live in economic conditions which separate their way of life, their interests and their education from those of other classes which are opposed to them, they constitute a class." Lenin further specifies this definition of social class: "Classes are groups of people, one of which appropriates to itself the work of the others, according to the position they respectively occupy in a defined economic system." The other Marxist concept of social class

From *Cahiers Internationaux de Sociologie*, XXXIX; juillet-décembre de 1965), pp. 113-136. Translated by Nina Weightman and Joseph A. Kahl, and corrected by the author. Used by permission of the author and Presses Universitaires de France (Paris).

Pablo González-Casanova, educated in history in Mexico and in sociology and political science in Paris, was for several years Director of the School of Political and Social Science of the National University of Mexico, and is currently Director of the University's Institute of Social Research.

corresponds to the transformation of these "objective interests" into class consciousness and political action. Marx is more exacting in this sphere. He draws attention to conditions to be fulfilled before a social group can constitute a class: "When there is only local contact (among the groups at a similar social level) — when the identity of their interests does not produce a community, a national association, a political organization, these groups *do not constitute a class*, because they are incapable of defending their class interests."

Thus, Marxist writing itself specifies a series of limitations on the political phenomena of social class. Lenin shows that in colonial and semi-colonial underdeveloped countries, there exists "the national duty to cope with imperialism" which prevents the establishment of "class unity." Numerous Marxist authors draw equal attention to this limitation on the integration of a class system in underdeveloped and colonial countries.

The hypothesis that we will try to outline is this: in a society such as is found in Mexico there does not exist a working class which has class consciousness "transforming its objective interests (of class) into an interest of which it is aware." Therefore, it is not led into organized action founded on conflict such as was characteristic of the classes in the type of industrialized society that Marx knew, and which led to the formation of large unions and workers' political parties. We will try to pinpoint, in the functioning of a society like the one in Mexico, the specific obstacles in its social structure which prevent the working classes from perceiving an identity of interest against the *bourgeoisie*. But before turning to consciousness and class action, we must first study the objective structure of the Mexican population, using the latest available figures from the national census.

CULTURAL AND ECONOMIC INEQUALITY

The social structure of Mexico presents great inequalities, and it is advisable, in order to analyze it, to establish first a simple and elementary dichotomous division which will allow us to distinguish those who do not participate in the development of the country from those who do.

According to the 1960 census, 38% of the population aged 6 years and more were illiterate (i.e., 10,600,000 illiterates). The proportion of children 6 to 14 years of age *not* attending school was 37% (3,100,000 children). The number of persons who did *not* wear shoes was 12,700,-000, or 38% of the population aged 1 year and over. The proportion of the population 1 year of age and over that ate *neither* meat, fish, milk nor eggs was 24% (8,100,000). Thus, about one-third of the population live outside of the modern economy.[1]

[1] The total number of inhabitants in 1960 was 34,923,000.

Mexico is a multiple society, culturally as well as economically hetero-geneous, in which there exist groups of indigenous people who have little part in the national life. In a general way they can be spotted with the help of different indices. In 1960, the indigenous population not speaking Spanish comprised 4% of the inhabitants aged 5 or more; the native population speaking both an Indian language and Spanish com-prised 6% of this age-group. On adding the two figures, we come to the total of 3 million persons or 10% of the population. These three millions constitute the core of what the anthropologists call the indigenous prob-lem. But language is not a sufficient index for evaluating the dimensions of the phenomenon. Taking other indices — work-techniques, customs, consciousness of belonging to a community distinct from the rest of the nation — certain anthropologists think that the indigenous problem ex-tends to a population of 7,000,000 inhabitants. At the outside, the num-ber of those who do not participate in the national culture rises to 10,600,000 inhabitants aged one or more years (31% of the total) cor-responding to those who do not eat wheat bread, but only tortillas of maize.

These data show the existence of one Mexico which participates in the economic development and modern national culture of the society, and of another Mexico which remains marginal to participation.

Beyond this dichotomous division of marginals and participants, there exists the possibility of dividing the population into classes of low, middle and high economic status, using the 1960 census. This possibility shows us, through all the available indices, that the middle and upper classes constitute a very small proportion of the total. If the population is classified according to the number of rooms per home, we come to the following results:

Homes with	Percentage
1 room	51.2%
2 rooms	25.2
3 rooms	10.2
4 rooms	5.2
5 rooms	2.5
6 rooms	1.5
7 rooms or more	4.2
	100.0%

On re-classifying the population in larger groups, we get: 51.2% in homes with 1 room, 35.4% in homes with 2 to 3 rooms, and only 13.4% in homes with 4 rooms or more.

Dwelling-place characteristics allow a division of the population in the following manner.

(a)	Homes without drainage	71.5%
	With drainage	28.5
		100.0
(b)	Homes without water supply, either in the home or in the building	68.4
	Water supply outside the home but in the building	8.5
	Water supply in the home	23.1
		100.0
(c)	Homes without bathrooms	79.5
	With bathroom and running water	20.5
		100.0
(d)	Homes without radio or T.V.	64.6
	With radio only	28.7
	With radio and T.V.	6.7
		100.0

These indices correspond to different types of standards of living. In some cases they correspond to basic necessities, like drainage; in some cases to standards of living in keeping with the urbanization and industrialization of the country, such as a bathroom; in other cases, they reveal relatively high standards of living within urban and industrial society, like possessing *both* a radio and a television. Whichever the case, the percentage of the population that has a standard of living and consumer-habits proper to an urban and industrial society is very low, and even lower still is the percentage of those who have consumer habits proper to the middle and upper classes.

In accordance with these above indices, the middle- and upper-class population could be established as follows:

UPPER AND MIDDLE CLASS POPULATION

Loose Definition		*Tight Definition*	
With water supply in building	31.6%	Water supply in the home	23.1%
With drainage	28.5	With bathroom and running water	20.5
Use of kerosene, gas or electricity	33.2	Use of gas or electricity	15.5
With radio or T.V. or both	35.4	With radio and T.V.	6.7
3 rooms or more	23.6	4 or more rooms	13.4

Using criteria that were mainly cultural, such as Indian language or illiteracy or the complete absence of the simplest modern consumer goods, we stated above that about one-third of the population is marginal by a loose definition, and at least ten per cent by a very rigid definition. At the opposite end of the hierarchy, and using criteria that involve access to urban styles of life, such as adequate housing, bathrooms, and television sets, we can say that about fifteen per cent of the people have a high standard of living, and perhaps another fifteen per cent have an intermediate standard of living.[2]

EDUCATIONAL INEQUALITY

Another index of social stratification encountered in the 1960 census is that which shows the levels of education of the population; using it, one can conventionally identify the lower, middle and upper classes with primary, secondary and advanced education, respectively.

If we classify the population aged 6 or more according to the level of education reached, we get the following groupings:

Years of Schooling	Percentage
0	43.7%
1 to 3	31.1
4 to 6	19.6
7 to 9	3.5
10 to 12	1.3
13 to 15	0.4
16 and above	0.4
	100.0%

Adjusting our base from the point of view of age by choosing the population aged 30 or more, thus dealing with those who have completed their schooling, and combining into larger categories, we get:

No education	46.0%
Primary education	48.3
Secondary education	3.7
Advanced education	2.0
	100.0%

Since women get less education than men, it is useful to adjust our base even further by limiting ourselves to the male population aged 30 or more:

No education	40.6%
Primary education	52.8
Secondary education	4.5
Advanced education	2.1
	100.0%

[2] Another consumption index can be used to identify those with high standards of living: only 7.1% of the families in the population owned an automobile, and only 2.2% had a private telephone.

Whichever educational measure is used, the middle and upper classes together do not amount to more than 6.6% of the population.

LABOR FORCE PARTICIPATION

If we classify the economically active population, the following groups emerge:

Children 8-11 years of age, working for pay	0.7%
Non-paid family workers	1.0
Manual laborers	50.5
Self-employed	33.9
Non-manual employees	13.1
Employers	0.8
	100.0%

Among those categories used in the census there is one which is particularly ambiguous, in that it engulfs otherwise normally distinct groups, namely, the category of those who are "self-employed." In it are merged under-employed marginal peddlars, petty farmers, small property-owners, artisans and shopkeepers. Part of the category thus corresponds to the proletariat and even to the "lumpen-proletariat," and another part to the middle class. In the same confusing way, the census proclaims high officials as well as routine clerks to be included among the "non-manual employees." In any case, the percentage of non-manual employees and employers is very low, for both groups together constitute no more than 14% of the economically active population. The census permits some further useful specification of type of employment in various sectors of the economy:

	Primary Activity (agriculture)	Secondary Activity (industry)	Tertiary Activity (commerce)
Employees, non-manual	0.43%	11.55%	39.85%
Employers	0.32	1.30	1.22
Others	99.25	87.15	58.83
	100.00%	100.00%	99.90%

From the foregoing figures, we can note that the proportion of white-collar or non-manual employees increases enormously as we move from agriculture to industry, and from industry to commerce. It is this creation of new types of jobs through industrialization that expands the middle classes in society. Yet the proportion of owners, or upper-class persons, expands at a much slower rate.

INCOME DISTRIBUTION

From the point of view of income, the Ministry of Industry and Commerce has published the results of an investigation undertaken in 1961-2.

This information, which comes from a sample survey, allows one to stratify the population in the following ways:

(a) Monthly family income (1961-62)	Percentage
Up to 300 pesos	22.5%
From 301-500 pesos	23.4
From 501-1,000 pesos	27.8
From 1,001-3,000 pesos	22.7
More than 3,000 pesos	3.6
	100.0%

(b) Monthly income per economically active person (1961-62)	Percentage
Up to 300 pesos	41.5%
From 301-500 pesos	26.1
From 501-750 pesos	12.5
From 751-1,000 pesos	9.5
From 1,001-2,000 pesos	7.5
Above 2,000 pesos	2.9
	100.0%

Note: A dollar is equivalent to 12.50 Mexican pesos.

If the monthly family income shows a more equitable distribution than the monthly income per active person, this is explained by the fact that there are often several employed persons in each family, and one finds this more frequently in low-income families.

The Gross National Product was 145 billion pesos in 1962, the number of economically active persons was 10,750,000, and the number of families was 6,740,000. Thus the mean annual income per family was 21,513 pesos (or 1,721 dollars), and the mean monthly income per family 1,793 pesos (or 143 dollars). The distribution of income in the above tables is so unequal that only a little more than 10% of the total of economically active persons have incomes above the mean, and only 15% of the families have incomes higher than the mean.

The upper classes are particularly difficult to detect from income data. Normally, one leaves the top category an "open" one — such as 2,000 pesos or more — which prevents separation of the very rich from the others. Likewise, the concealment of high incomes from the interviewer makes the description of this group particularly difficult. Nevertheless, if one considers other researches and the fact that the distribution inside the upper range is highly unequal, the groups with family income of 10,000 pesos and more (which would correspond to the upper-middle class) and of 20,000 pesos and more (which would correspond to the upper class) very definitely constitute less than 1.3% of the total of the population, i.e., about 100,000 families.

RURAL AND URBAN DIFFERENCES

All the foregoing differences are accentuated when we classify the population according to its rural or urban character. In the Mexican census the population living in localities of 2,500 inhabitants and more is considered as urban, and the population living in localities of less than 2,500 inhabitants is considered as rural. Although this limit appears arbitrary, the truth is that high correlations are encountered between the population considered thereby as rural and the marginal population, and between the urban population and the participating population, as defined above.

Accepting the limit of 2,500 inhabitants per locality, 49% of the population is rural and 51% urban. Indeed, 23% of the population lives in localities of less than 500 inhabitants, and 35% in localities of less than 1,000 inhabitants. Taking other standards for the definition of an urban locality, 30% of the population lives in cities of over 20,000 inhabitants, and 19% in cities of over 100,000 inhabitants.

In underdeveloped countries, the gap between the urban and rural zones is very wide. For example, in Mexico the mean annual income *per capita* (not per family) for the rural sector in 1960 was 1,500 pesos, compared with 6,300 pesos for the urban sector. Taking the limit of 2,500 inhabitants per locality to distinguish the urban from the rural population, we get the following distributions:

	Percentage	
(a) *Monthly family income* (1961-62)	*Rural*	*Urban*
Up to 300 pesos	39.9%	6.6%
From 301 to 500 pesos	28.4	19.0
From 501 to 1,000 pesos	21.2	33.8
From 1,001 to 3,000 pesos	10.0	34.3
More than 3,000 pesos	0.5	6.3
	100.0%	100.0%
(b) *Monthly income per economically active person* (1961-62)		
Up to 300 pesos	65.3%	20.6%
From 301 to 500 pesos	21.7	30.0
From 501 to 750 pesos	6.3	17.9
From 751 to 1,000 pesos	3.9	14.4
From 1,001 to 2,000 pesos	2.5	12.0
More than 2,000 pesos	0.3	5.1
	100.0%	100.0%

It is obvious that the rural population is greatly disadvantaged. In the rural population, only 10.5% of the families have more than 1,000 pesos (80 dollars) monthly income, whereas this level of income is received by

40.6% of the urban families. Of course, the cost of living is somewhat less in rural zones, but nevertheless the population is much worse off.

Furthermore, even within a given income group, those in rural zones get less education; for example, among the poorest persons (individuals earning less than 300 pesos), only 11% of those in the rural areas went beyond third grade, but 53% of the urbanites did. Secondary education is almost exclusively confined to the urban zones.

These educational differences between the urban and rural populations are shown (independently of income) in the following distributions:

Years of Schooling	Rural	Urban
0 to 3	81.2%	29.4%
4 to 6	16.3	45.5
7 to 9	1.9	14.8
10 or 11	0.2	2.9
12 and more	0.4	7.4
	100.0%	100.0%

We come across a similar contrast with regard to housing characteristics. We find that for each income group, there are more rural people living in homes without drainage, water supply, or electricity. For a group of the rural population to have running water installed in more than half of the homes, an income level of more than 1,000 pesos must be reached; whilst in the urban population, we find the same service in the group earning more than 301 pesos.

In the case of electricity, these differences are emphasized even more; whilst the poorest urban groups have electric lighting in a large proportion of the homes, only the richest rural families enjoy its benefits.

	Homes with Electricity	
Monthly Income	Rural	Urban
Up to 300 pesos	20.3%	75.7%
From 301 to 500 pesos	21.7	81.7
From 501 to 1,000 pesos	36.8	90.6
From 1,001 to 3,000 pesos	53.2	95.6
More than 3,000 pesos	89.2	98.5
All incomes	26.7	89.4

One can easily conclude from the foregoing information that the income level in Mexico is very low, and that the middle and upper classes form a very small proportion of the society. Furthermore, the rural zones are especially disadvantaged: their income is lower on the average, and fewer services are available at any given income level. Indeed, the rural gap is so great that some of the indices we use to identify the upper and middle classes in the urban population do not serve for the same purpose regarding the rural population: for instance, secondary and higher education are so scarce in the countryside as to be useless as indicators. By contrast, the existence of electricity in the home can serve as an indicator of middle-class status in the countryside but not in the city. Thus, we must recognize again that there are really two Mexicos: one is rural, poor, uneducated, and partly marginal to the national life; the other is urban, developing, and mainly participant. The differences between the two Mexicos are so great as to require different indicators for dividing the population into social classes.

Furthermore, Mexico's regional development is extremely unequal, a fact which is also characteristic of underdeveloped countries. To the differences observed in the social domain within a region, we must add differences between regions and states. In 1960, areas with a third of the country's population controlled more than three-quarters of the industry. These differences in industrialization are associated with differences in standard of living. While in the Federal District and in the northern states the population attains a higher standard of living than the national average (from 35% to 100% above the norm), the southern states have standards of living two-thirds below the national average. Concerning mortality and illiteracy, the differences between the regions and states are more than doubled; the differences are almost quadrupled concerning the teacher/pupil ratio, and also for running water supply; and almost five-fold for the legal minimum salary.

THE RELATIVE ABSENCE OF CLASS CONSCIOUSNESS AND CLASS POLITICS

The social structure of Mexico — highly unequal and differentiated — makes one think that the European Marxist model would surely apply. One expects class consciousness and class-oriented political action. However, the reverse is in fact the case. Most of the Mexican proletariat are grouped in official government parties and unions; they support the existing order. Opposition parties and unions are very weak in power, and they can only be considered as political organizations based on class (or with class consciousness) with great difficulty.

Let us begin with the problem of political structure. It is very difficult to ascertain the exact power of the official government party in contrast to the other parties, taking as a starting-point the number of those with party affiliations. The government party[3] possesses a collective-type affiliation (that is, various unions and peasant groups are constituent members) and the parties in opposition either do not keep a register of their members, or keep their statistical information secret. In these conditions, the only way left of analyzing the party situation is through election results. Since 1929, the year in which the government party was founded, the latter has not lost a single presidential, gubernatorial or senatorial election. During this period, the party has raised to power 6 Presidents,

[3] The Institutional Revolutionary Party, or simply PRI, its initials in the Spanish language.

nearly 200 governors, and 282 senators. As for the deputies in the lower house of the Congress, from 1929-40 all belonged to the government party. Since 1940, the parties in opposition have managed to obtain up to 4% of the seats.

In no presidential election since the revolution in 1910 has the opposition managed to obtain more than 25% support, and that only once (in 1952). Normally, the opposition candidate or candidates together do not manage to register more than 10% of the total of votes. And although there are electoral frauds of various kinds, the true vote clearly favors the government party. It is a fact that in Mexico a predominant one-party system has existed since 1929. Parties do not alternate in the exercise of power, and there is no special party for the laboring masses. The labor force, politically organized, is in the vast majority controlled by government organizations, and in one form or another, complies with the government system. Although the opposition parties and their leaders claim that the working masses are maneuvered from above as much in politics as in unionism, a more penetrating and objective study of the problem reveals the workers' agreement with government organizations, their conformism, and their scepticism toward the creation of independent organizations following a distinct line of policy. Two-thirds of the unionized workers belong to The Mexican Workers' Confederation, which is closely linked to the official party through its working-class sector, and is linked to the government through the official jobs of its leaders. Other unions, not linked to this central one, maintain equally close relations with the official party and the government. For example, during the 1952-55 legislature, there were 35 workers' delegates, 19 of whom came from the large central government union.

During the constitutional period of the Mexican Revolution (1918-1962), at least 52 seats held by senators from the working-class sector can be counted (33 from 1940-1961), and more than 250 occupied by deputies from the same sector (150 since 1940). But a study of their participation in Congress could hardly reveal the weight and the characteristic attitudes of the representatives of the workers' movement.

An index of the dependence of the Mexican unions upon the government, and in particular upon its presidential-type policy, is that of strikes. If one observes the strikes which break out on a large scale in varying presidential regimes, one can establish the fact that it is when the Presidents are known for their populist and pro-worker policies that the greatest number of strikes occur, as if the union leaders and the workers felt themselves protected or even encouraged by the presidential power. Precisely the opposite effect is produced when the Presidents follow a less radical policy, or a more open alliance with the property-owning national and foreign sectors. Thus we can see that during President Obregón's stay in power (1920-24), who counted among his followers the "Red Battalions" and the working-class leaders, the national average of strikes rose to 197; during the conservative period of Calles and the so-called "Maximato" (1925-34), the average went down to 41; it rose again to 478 with Lázaro Cárdenas' pro-agrarian and working-class government (1934-40). Later the average was 387 in Avila Camacho's moderate government; 108 with Alemán (under the regime in which the trend in income distribution was unfavorable to the working-class sector), and 248 with Ruiz Cortínes, whose policy was above all reformist. The annual average of strikers was 64,000 (Obregón); 4,000 (Calles and followers); 61,000 (Cárdenas); 56,000 (Avila Camacho); 19,000 (Alemán); 25,000 (Cortínes).

The workers' movement follows the policy of the Chief Executive, and is protected by his power: the number of strikes and strikers increases when the President's policy is reformist or radical, and decreases in the contrary case. There were, in sum, three exceptions to this tendency. The strikes of 1933 revealed the discontent of the workers' movement in the face of a conservative and anti-worker policy; the strikes of 1943-44 in Avila Camacho's time, in which the workers' movement wanted to demonstrate its power, ignored by the new government; and the strikes of 1958, in the course of which a dissident sector of the workers' movement (telegraphers, railwaymen, electricians, etc.) were struggling to recapture their independence and improve the representational character of their unions.

The effects of these manifestations were clear. The 1933 strikes, together with other factors, fostered the popular and agrarian policies of the Cárdenas government which entered office the next year. Indeed, workers' organizations gave important support to Cárdenas' policy of expropriating national and foreign firms, including the oil companies. The 1944 strikes gave rise to considerable repression but the workers adapted themselves to the new situation. The 1958 strikes allowed the dissident workers' movement to attain partial political and economic success, especially in those cases in which the tactics of the new leaders coincided with the conciliatory and negotiational spirit characteristic of modern trade union movements. In the opposite instance, the repression of resistant leaders was simultaneous with a government policy of increases in salary and benefits to rebellious workers — a policy of benefits which, moreover, sometimes went beyond the protests of the fallen leaders. Because of this policy, the majority of the masses accepted the economic and political conditions that were determined for them. The discontent was not channelled into revolutionary workers' organizations, nor into characteristic mass movements. There was a government policy of concessions in the economic domain and resistance in the political domain. The discontent was reduced to a purely verbal radicalism, and at times emotional manifestations.

The proletariat has been generally reformist and conformist; it has followed and even relied on governmental policy without any symptoms of mass working-class organizations of a revolutionary character, and even less of the birth of party ideologies and radical organizations for the workers, similar to the standard Marxist model.

AN ESSAY IN INTERPRETATION

The first explanation of this anomalous Mexican situation is that it is manifested in a structure internally different from "classical" capitalism. Although there are some parallels to earlier European capitalism, there are basic differences as well. Contemporary capitalism has discovered a series of ideological and structural responses to the development of a society based on class, in the political sense of the term. Thus, let us take it that the most plausible explanation of the phenomenon must be looked for in structural factors rather than in psychological factors of alienation, or in purely political factors concerning the management of power.

It is true that sustained growth is not enough, by itself, to efface class consciousness and class policy: during the classical development of capitalism economic growth certainly took place, but the population movement to which it gave rise (from country to town, from agriculture to industry) did not coincide with the type of advancement in the social sphere which occurs today. Under present conditions, these population movements signify a considerable advancement in the standard of living of the mobile people.

Let us begin by studying to what degree the movement of the masses into participant status in the modern sector can coincide with conformism and moderation. Our analysis of Mexico's development must include what one might call the "hope factor," that is, the idea that the individual can personally escape misery, that he can resolve his personal and family problems while following the ways which the development of the country afford him, without substantial modifications or radical attitudes — with, at the most, a reformist attitude.

The development of Mexico began with a gigantic redistribution of wealth, and in particular of agricultural property. The revolutionary governments redistributed 43 million hectares among 2,200,000 heads of families. These peasants own or control their land, and although their standard of living is normally very low, in general they have the mentality of proprietors, and the corresponding stabilizing behavior. In the nation, 54% of the heads of family are owners of the houses they live in; in the countryside, 70% own their homes, and in the towns 38% own theirs (1960 census). In the countryside, the number of owners increases in proportion as the family income decreases, according to the 1961-62 inquiry, and among the urban population, one comes across a considerable proportion of proprietors among families of lower incomes (46% of groups earning less than 300 pesos per month are proprietors). In this instance, the fact of owning one's home and land, even in very poor living conditions, has a stabilizing function which did not exist before the Revolution.

The development of the country brings about a constant migration of the rural population towards urban centers. The proportion of the population which is rural progressively decreases — from 80% in 1910 to 49% in 1960 — while the urban population increases correlatively. Large groups of peasants hope to escape poverty by migrating toward the towns, for the differences in income and standard of living between the country and the town constitute an attractive passage from an inferior to a superior status. Others see how their rural milieu itself is becoming urbanized. In both cases, the urban society effaces many class differences; many benefits and services which, in rural life, are exclusive to high-income groups, are available in urban areas to most groups of the population: *e.g.*, electric light, water, drainage, a radio, and education.

The general "mobilization" of the population into the modern sector is perhaps an even more important fact, for it constitutes, in one generation, a passing from marginal life which offers nothing, to the life of someone who has possessions — perhaps a low standard of living, but one which is participating in development. The annual rate of growth of the literate population aged 11 and more was 8.3% for the period from 1930-1960; the annual rate of growth of the population eating wheat bread was 6.3% (1940-50); it was 9.5% (1950-60) for the population wearing shoes.

The development of the country also brings about large movements across social class lines. These movements depend on, (a) the process of redistribution of the wealth in land; (b) the process of expropriation of foreign concessions; (c) the establishment of a public sector in the economy coming to almost 50% of annual investments; (d) the process of industrialization; (e) the process of urbanization; (f) the process of social policy in the domain of public works, salaries, fiscal affairs, and education; (g) changes in consumer habits; (h) the process of social policy concerning population mobility, allowances and differential salaries for the working classes.

According to Cline's calculations (partially based on Itturriaga's previous calculations), between 1895 and 1960 the middle class increased from 7.8% to 33.5% of the population, while the lower class shrank from 90.7% to 60.0%. In another, perhaps less optimistic grouping, but closer to reality, González-Cosío calculates that between 1900 and 1960 the upper class has remained practically unchanged (about 0.5%), the middle class doubled (8.3% to 17.1%), and the lower class decreased from 91.1% to 82.4%. In another kind of grouping, based on income, Ifigenia Navarrete calculates that from 1950-1957 the lower class diminished from 70% to 65%; the lower-middle class grew from 18%

to 19%, the upper-middle class grew from 7% to 11%, and the monied class remained stable at 5%.[4]

This information, although uncertain in detail, suggests a characteristic trend of all economic development, which is even more accentuated by the social revolution that occurred in Mexico: the vertical mobility of the lower classes towards higher classes. This circulation is added to the rise in the average standard of living brought about by development, and above all the tremendous increase of the percentage of the population participating in this development. This process of social mobility and mobilization stimulates the individual's hope of bettering himself. It creates pride in being allowed to participate in the national development, and a spirit of reform within the limits of the path that the nation has outlined.

Moreover, Mexican development has been strongly influenced by political measures of redistribution and expropriation of wealth which go beyond the redistribution that has been brought about automatically, thanks to urbanization and industrialization. The political and social vision of development is oriented in a way which does not exist in the political model of "classical" capitalism, and tends toward the integration of all the inhabitants into "full citizenship," as T. H. Marshall would say. This policy accentuates the differences among the workers themselves, and thus diminishes class consciousness based on homogeneity.

The differences among the manual workers are certainly greater than those existing between non-manual employees and manual workers. Frequently "blue-collar" workers earn several times as much as "white-collar" workers. Above all, great differences exist between marginal workers and participating ones. But even in the participating sector, notable differences in salary and allowances and benefits occur. Individual workers are constantly improving their relative position. Every year more than 167,000 new workers enter the Social Security system, which includes medical care. And the average wage of workers inside this system is double the national minimum.

All these differences come into play in two ways: firstly, the fact of being a manual worker is not of basic import, nor does it correspond to a general social category; the group divisions within the working class are more important than the divisions between the working class and the other classes. In any case, when the skilled workers talk of "class struggle" and handle the union contest adroitly, they obtain better wages and

[4] Sources: Howard F. Cline, Mexico: Revolution to Evolution (London: Oxford, 1962); Arturo González-Cosío, "Clases y estratos sociales," in México: cincuenta años de revolución, Tomo II (México: F.C.E., 1961); Ifigenia M. Navarrete, La distribución del ingreso y el desarrollo económico de México (México, D.F.: Instituto de Investigaciones Económicas, U.N.A.M., 1960).

then forget the general concept of class. Secondly, the development of the country has allowed, as we have seen, a movement of people from regions, sectors, and branches of industry where work is poorly-paid, towards regions and branches where it is well-paid, and the rapid rate of industrialization has given rise to a large vertical mobility. If a policy of allowances, salaries and differential treatment is added to this, according to the workers' standards of cultural and political participation, one would see an integration of a general explanation of factors which have worked against the existence of a "class consciousness" and "class political action" in the working-class sector.

These structural trends are reflected in political propaganda. Among the proclamations, manifestos, talks and reviews issued by the participating groups of the working classes, one notices the constant references to "national unity." There is an identification of class problems with those of the Nation and the State — an identification of "class consciousness" with "Revolutionary ideals." There are panegyrics on nationalization and the independent attitude of the Mexican government against the great powers of world politics. There are idealizations of the government's social measures in favor of the working class: social security benefits, public housing, school-books free of charge for working-class children, etc. When Marxist terminology and rhetoric are used — a cultural heritage of the radical steps of the last Revolution — it is said that the class struggle should be based on the principles of the Mexican Revolution; one praises simultaneously the "class struggle" and the Mexican national Revolution; capitalism as opposed to feudalism is praised; imperialism is criticized and unionism, as an anti-imperialist factor, is praised; the pro-imperialist bourgeoisie is attacked, but not the "good" nationalist bourgeoisie; there is the demand that the State not be a class state; the President is praised for his Revolutionary actions and attitudes, for the help he offers to the workers in salary increases; the government is praised, and accusations are made against "capitalists" only insofar as they are the enemies of the government and the working class; it is asserted that the "exploited class" is solidary with the government, that the best instrument for the working class struggle is the P.R.I. (the government political party), and that the final aim of the working class is to "have done with" the pro-imperialist bourgeoisie.

CONCLUSIONS

In Mexico, the organized working class does not appear to be conscious of the problem of the marginal population; rhetorically, one speaks of the "exploited," of the "workers" and of unity with the peasants, but the limited concrete pressures exerted on the government only operate in favor of the participating sector, leaving the marginal sector isolated. The problem of the marginal population rests in the political and moral conscience of the ruling class; it has no organizational expression from below.

From the political point of view, the ruling class is more or less aware of the fact that it is necessary to continue absorbing the marginal population in order to maintain the political stability of the country. Since the time when the rebellious peasants under Zapata were approaching the capital, the ruling class has realized that the political union of the participating and marginal masses would be a toublesome and explosive element. From the moral point of view, it is the intellectuals and civil servants of the ruling class who are preoccupied with inquiries into the solution of these problems. As for the radical groups, steeped in Marxist ideology as they are, with attitudes of intellectual dependence and automatic imitation of Marxist models, when they do not recognize the priority of the national struggle as opposed to class struggle, they try to force reality until they can find an imagined "class struggle" corresponding to the standard Marxist model; and then they explain the lack of class consciousness by resorting to saying that the working class finds itself alienated, without considering the structural differences between the marginal sector and the participating sector as the most characteristic and dynamic fact of Mexican society.

To the above considerations, we may further aod another fact which merits emphasis, and which goes against the emergence of a class system of the European type in Mexico. The fatalism and paternalism which characterize traditional societies appear to have an even greater vitality in societies undergoing industrialization and urbanization, when, as in Mexico's case, a social policy is outlined partially favoring the working classes. They are moving very rapidly from one form of civilization to another, and they turn to the government and its leaders for emotional as well as material support. When they are fully adjusted to the new society, emotional dependence will disappear, but in a country in transition, such as Mexico, paternalism and fatalism combine with nationalism to weaken class consciousness.

So long as the country maintains a high rate of development, and so long as a policy of balanced mobilization continues, the economic and political security of the system as it now exists has all the chances of lasting. The social structure of Mexico will probably approach more and more that of a neo-capitalist society, without ever going through the "classical" period of capitalism. One can perceive in Mexican society a pattern that reflects its own special history, its own blend of underdevelopment, capitalism and socialism, and it cannot be understood by automatic use of models from other societies.[5]

[5] For further elaboration of the themes of this article, see the same author's *La democrácia en México* (México, D.F.: 2a edición, Era, 1967) — editor's note.

*Selective
Bibliography*

Brandenburg, Frank, *The Making of Modern Mexico* (Englewood Cliffs, N.J.: Prentice Hall, 1965).
A synthesis of economic, sociological and political materials in a detailed portrait of the new society, particularly concerned with the workings of politics and the control exercised by the inner circle at the top.

Cline, Howard F., *The United States and Mexico* (New York: Atheneum, revised edition, 1963).
A good historical treatment of the Revolution and its aftermath to the present time, with special emphasis on United States policy toward Mexico during the revolutionary period.

Erasmus, Charles J., *Man Takes Control* (Minneapolis: University of Minnesota Press, 1961).
A study of a region in Northwestern Mexico which describes the changes in social structure in rural regions that follow economic growth based on new irrigation works and roads.

Fuentes, Carlos, *Where the Air is Clear* (New York: Obolensky, 1960).
Translation of a great modern novel portraying the interplay between the social classes.

Lewis, Oscar, *Five Families* (New York: Basic Books, 1959).
Tape-recorded conversations of four families in Mexico City and one in Tepoztlán which portray in vivid terms the daily lives of some Mexicans, mostly very poor.

Redfield, Robert, *The Folk Culture of Yucatan* (Chicago: University of Chicago Press, 1941).
A classic in anthropology, although a bit dated in theoretical outlook, which contrasts four communities ranging from a city to an isolated Indian tribe, and shows the blending of indigenous, Spanish and contemporary cultures.

Scott, Robert E., *Mexican Government in Transition* (Urbana: University of Illinois Press, 1959).
Detailed analysis of the workings of the official political party, the PRI, and the rest of the apparatus of government.

Tannenbaum, Frank, *Mexico, the Struggle for Peace and Bread* (New York: Knopf, 1950).
An excellent account of the Revolutionary ideology and its translation into practice, particularly during the Cárdenas period.

Vernon, Raymond, *The Dilemma of Mexico's Development* (Cambridge: Harvard University Press, 1963).
Analysis of the Mexican economy since the Revolution, with sharp insight into its political and institutional framework.

Whiteford, Andrew H., *Two Cities of Latin America* (Garden City, New York: Anchor Books, 1964).

A comparison of the social strata in two provincial cities, Querétaro in Mexico, and Popoyán in Colombia, which shows the greater dynamism of the Mexican social structure.

II

Great Britain
Continuity Amidst Change

We have been dealing to this point with Mexico, one of the newest countries to embark upon industrialization. Thus, our study of Mexican stratification inevitably led us to emphasize the impact of the modern economic forces upon older social structures, to highlight the growth of the new strata and the decline of the old ones.

But Great Britain, to which we now turn, is the oldest industrial country in the world, so we must expect different problems to concern her analysts of stratification. The vast movement of people from farm to city is a thing of the distant past; the proportion of the labor force engaged in manufacturing has hit a peak and begun to decline, as automation advances; the spread of literacy is long since complete. The problems of British society are those of mature industrialization, such as maintaining a competitive position in world markets with other advanced economies; the expansion of secondary and higher education, and its adaptation to the ever-increasing demands of complex technology and scientific practices of administration; the provision of equal access to the educational system, which has become decisive to career life chances; the development of adequate welfare services so that no stratum of society remains "marginal" to its current standards of health and minimum comfort.

The meaning of the word "tradition" is quite different in the two

83

countries. In Mexico it refers to patterns of thought and action that stem from the rural society of pre-Revolutionary days: *hacendados*, illiterate peasants, *tortillas* made of maize, paternalistic forms of social relations. But in England tradition refers to the culture of high capitalism and imperialism, now under attack from the energies of a new mass society of producers and consumers that is supposed to include all citizens on an equal basis.

There is a marked tension in British society between its elitist traditions and its equalitarian goals. The former reflect a sense of "status consciousness" that is shown through respect for: the Queen, men of leading families, established patterns of higher education based upon the humanities and set by Oxford and Cambridge, the versatile all-rounder rather than the technical specialist, precedent and continuity instead of innovation and change. Sir Winston Churchill was the epitome of British elitism, and more recently the Tory cabinet of Sir Alec Douglas-Home in 1964 showed that the tradition lingers. It comprised twenty-three men; ten were graduates of Eton, ten came from other elite "public" (i.e., fee-paying private) schools, and only three from state-maintained grammar schools.

But modern Britain also has a strong equalitarian thrust. At the end of World War II, at the peak of his glory, Churchill was defeated by the socialists. Later, the Home government fell as Harold Wilson led another socialist victory. These Labour regimes have attempted major reforms in British society. They built a free national health service that provided care from "cradle to grave." They (in cooperation with the Tories) established secondary education for all children until the fifteenth birthday, and developed the "11-plus" examinations, which were aimed at a method of selecting children for entry into university-preparatory education by "objective" tests at the age of eleven rather than by family background and ability to pay. The post-war educational reforms not only made free secondary schools and universities more widely available, but added subsistence grants for most university students. The socialists raised income taxes above ninety per cent for the very rich, and they tried to tax away large inheritances. They gave government subsidies to vast housing estates for the poor. In addition to these deliberate measures, the economic circumstances and policies of Britain during most of the post-war period have permitted full-employment, even for teen-agers of the working class. One result has been an upsurge of youthful "pop-culture," from the Beatles to the mini-skirt, which represents a reversal of elitist traditions. Many observers are saying that creativity in contemporary Britain comes from the young and from the working class, rather than from the old and established groups.

Sociological research always reflects the political currents of its environment. Thus, it is not surprising to find that much of the recent investigation in Britain has been concerned with the tension between continuity and change, between elitism and equalitarianism, between traditional culture and deliberate attempts by government for reform of the stratification system. Perhaps three themes have dominated: the effect of housing policies on community and family life, the consequences of full-employment on the class system, and the results of new educational policies on mobility chances.[1]

There has been a long series of penetrating studies of local communities, and the impact on them of the enormous amount of publicly-supported housing construction since the war. Many of these studies have been synthesized in Josephine Klein's *Samples From English Cultures*.[2] They are mainly descriptive and qualitative, and difficult to compress, thus, they are not represented in the present volume.

The second series of researches, those concentrating on the "affluent worker" who has emerged as a result of full employment and technical advance, are represented here by two examples from the continuing investigations of the Cambridge group led by David Lockwood and John H. Goldthorpe. Lockwood begins by creating a theoretical synthesis of many past studies of the working class. He notes that three types of workers are described in the literature: (1) the traditional proletarian, best illustrated by men in homogeneous communities of miners or dockers, and probably most vividly alive in Richard Hoggart's reminiscence of his youth in Northern England, *The Uses of Literacy*. They seem a declining group; the mines are substituting machines for men, the docks too are becoming mechanized, and the closed communities of militant men who divided the world sharply into "us" and "them" are losing shape. (2) The traditional deferential, the worker in the small community dominated by the gentry. He is the chap who is expected to tip his cap, and to vote Tory because he trusts his betters to run things. He has not been studied in depth, except as one of many types of men in small towns. (3) The new privatized worker, the man on the modern assembly line. He has achieved an income that takes him into the middle class, but does not move fully into a middle-class style of life. He buys more things than the traditional worker, but does not enter into the interactional system of the middle classes. He sees the system in individualistic terms that reflect his own geographic mobility and his own concentration on his private family life.

The data on this new type of worker are more fully presented in the

[1] Although there are signs of change, until now research by academic sociologists as part of normal university work has not been strongly supported; thus much of the actual investigation has been carried out by marginal institutions depending upon government agencies for funds. Housing and education (along with health) have been of central concern to these agencies, who have needed research to guide administrative policy.

[2] See Selective Bibliography, below.

essay by Goldthorpe, Lockwood and their colleagues. Here they give the preliminary results of a careful quantitative study, choosing machinists and automobile assemblers, and contrasting them with white-collar workers (or, to use an old English term, black-coated workers) in the same town. The picture that emerges is of men who have moved out of traditional working-class communities, who are developing a new way of life based on higher incomes and more movement from one part of the country to another, but who remain workers: they vote Labour, they remain aloof from middle-class cliques and formal organizations, and they do not expect to advance very high in the occupational hierarchy. They appear to represent a new variety of manual worker in England.

Regarding mobility chances, the first major post-war research was that of D. V. Glass and his co-workers. They demonstrated that there was a lot more movement in the system than popular stereotypes recognized. For example, although about one-third of adult male Britons had jobs at the same level as their fathers', thirty per cent had risen and a slightly larger percentage had fallen. Some of this movement was independent of education — a man could become a business manager, for example, without a university degree (much more easily in Britain than in the United States). Yet, through time, selection via education was increasing, and deliberate reforms in the school system were hastening that process. Thus, the bias by social class within the school system became a crucial subject of study.

Jean Floud's paper integrates many studies of the effects of the post-war educational reforms. She emphasizes that at first the need for change was felt in terms of making education more easily accessible to the poorer classes of society. There were "barriers to opportunity" that had to be removed. So new "grammar schools" (university-preparatory and thus highly selective) were opened with state funds, and the universities themselves were multiplied and expanded. The results were these: entry into grammar school was increased up to about 23 per cent of the age cohort.[3] Furthermore, the chance for a boy from a working-class home of getting into a grammar school went up from 10 to 15 per cent (comparing the pre-war and the post-war rates). The chance for a boy from a middle-class home went up from 40 to 50 per cent. But during the years of grammar school the working-class boys are squeezed out at a much higher rate than the middle-class boys, thus their chance of graduating is much less than their chance of entering. And regarding university admission, the chance for a working-class boy seems to have declined slightly since the reforms (dropping from 1.7 to 1.6 per cent of the age cohort), whereas the chance for a middle-class boy has greatly increased (rising

---

[3] In the United States, about 80 per cent graduate from high school, about 40 per cent enter college, and about 20 per cent graduate. However, the content of the curricula at each level differs substantially from the English counterparts.

from 9 to 19 per cent). Thus, one effect of the reforms has been to make free education much more readily available to the middle classes! As these facts have become evident, the focus of research has changed. As Floud expresses it, new attention is being paid to the "educability" and motivation of children from different social classes rather than to barriers that keep children out who are begging to be admitted. For a few at the bottom of the hierarchy, deep poverty is condemning. If parents cannot afford enough space for a child to study, or adequate clothing, or to forego his income after he reaches the legal age of work, then of course the child has little chance of staying in school. But there are influences far more subtle than material poverty. The researches of Basil Bernstein, just beginning to be published, show that in England as in a Negro slum in America, deficiencies in language and in powers of conceptualization related to language skills are endemic in certain sections of the lower class. These weaknesses keep the child from doing well in school.

Furthermore, lower-class parents are less interested in school, and do not push their children to study as much as middle-class parents do. Perhaps the revealing longitudinal research of J. W. B. Douglas provides the best illustration. He followed a large sample of children from England and Wales from birth until entry into secondary school. He showed that parents from the working class had poorer standards of infant care; they rarely visited elementary schools to inquire about their children's progress (5 per cent made visits, compared to 42 per cent in the middle class); they expressed a wish that their children stay in school beyond the legal minimum in only 13 per cent of the cases (compared to 78 per cent in the middle class). As a result of the cumulative effect of these parental attitudes, working-class children's behavior showed performance in school below the level mental ability would predict; indeed, entry into grammar school was about 50 per cent less than I.Q. alone would dictate, using averages from the middle class as norms.

The value orientations of the classes are different, and these differences are expressed in a variety of concrete attitudes and behaviors. Values are "intervening variables" — that is, they are predicted by class indices, but are more the direct causes of children's behavior than are the socio-economic traits that compose these indices. Thus they explain in part the specific influences of class position upon children, and they also explain why some children are mobile. The latter are likely to be from families where the values of the parents are atypical of their class.

Perhaps the theme of continuity amidst change is best shown in the essay by Richard Titmuss which opens this selection of studies of contemporary Britain. He balances the gains of the new Welfare State against its many hidden biases. For example, the income tax deductions for children given to a man with a high income are many times greater than the direct family benefits given to a poor man. The medical benefits, just as the educational benefits, that have flowed from the post-war reforms, have not seeped down to the poorest who need them most. The increasing pressure to bureaucratize industry, to increase technical competence, means that the upper sections of the educational system will become more selective and even harder for children from the bottom to penetrate. He puts it in a sentence: "Equal opportunity of access by right of citizenship to education, medical care and social insurance is not the same as equality of outcome."

In some ways, Britain is the world's most advanced industrial country. She invented the machines that made the Industrial Revolution; she has long been the most urban of nations; she has been a leader in many forms of social welfare that spring from the problems, as well as the affluence, of advanced industrial society. Yet in other ways she is backward by comparison. Her percentage of students in secondary school and university is lower than that of France, or Japan, or the United States. Her university system is more traditional, more elitist, not only in number and types of students admitted, but also in curriculum and style. Her occupational structure is moving toward a bulge among middle-class jobs — more clerks and technicians, fewer manual workers (especially unskilled) — yet more slowly than in the United States.

The comparative theorist is tempted to say that these discrepancies show that there are varieties of form possible for industrial society, rather than a single ecumenical type. Yet these variations may be but small differences in degree, rather than basic differences in kind. And the very slowness of change in the educational system in Britain is bringing enormous pressures for reform from within the society. The "lags" are felt to be not variations of approach to industrial society, but deficiencies to be remedied. Since we have no clear criteria to separate minor differences from basic variations of type, the theoretical question continues to be debated, and may be unsolvable.

For men of affairs in Britain, the lesson is less theoretical. They realize that the traditions of social inequality die hard. Those traditions have been built into class cultures over the centuries, and the value orientations of lower-class families, combined with their continuing relative as well as absolute material deprivation, make it hard for them to take full advantage of the new opportunities opened up by the Welfare State. If deliberate government action is to reduce even further the social inequalities that most Britons deplore, it will have to seek new tools, and these in turn will increasingly depend upon the skills of social research that are illustrated by the essays which follow. It is worth noting that these new forms of government action will probably include deliberate attempts to change the motivations of lower-class people, thus raising an ethical question: How far should society go in imposing its values on "deviants"? The spector of "1984" cannot be ignored; many sociologists are reluctant to become the technicians of "Big Brother," and yet the increasing practical power of their research leads in that direction in Britain as in the United States.

4 RICHARD M. TITMUSS

Goals of Today's Welfare State

One point of view which is strongly held in the West (particularly the far West) is that welfare inhibits economic growth; it discourages thrift and savings; it encourages high absenteeism from work and low productivity; it diminishes family responsibility.[1] An opposing point of view — equally strongly held — believes that welfare has more to do with humanitarian values than economic efficiency; with the social and ethical texture of society; with the exercise of compassion and reason in social relations.

Both these points of view have one thing in common. They are largely assertions and do not rest on any firm basis of fact. The concept of welfare has indeed suffered much in the past from stereotypes of deserving or undeserving recipients of charity; from images of well-meaning but muddle-headed social workers cheerfully ignoring the harsh realities of economic life. We all drag about with us the chains of history — includ-

From *Towards Socialism*, edited by Perry Anderson and Robin Blackburn. © New Left Review 1965. Used by permission of the author, Cornell University Press, and Fontana Books.

Richard M. Titmuss' career began in the business world, transferred to the Civil Service, and led to the London School of Economics and Political Science, where he is Professor of Social Administration. He is the outstanding analyst of contemporary British welfare institutions, as demonstrated in his *Essays on the Welfare State* (2nd edition, 1963), and *Income Distribution and Social Change* (1963).

[1] With some additions and revision this essay embodies the main part of a lecture given at the Hebrew University, Jerusalem, in August, 1964 in opening a Seminar on "Objectives for Social Services in Israel."

ing an outdated one about the social worker — but it is time we recognized the evidence for a third point of view. Briefly, this is to see economic growth and social growth as interdependent in the sense that lagging behind in one has, necessarily, negative consequences on the other. Unbalanced economic growth may, for instance, generate a need for greater public expenditures than would otherwise be the case. The social costs of technological change, if allowed to lie where they fall, may result in larger costs in the future in the shape of physical and psychological handicap, destitution, deprived children, ill-educated workers unable or unwilling to acquire new skills, and a general slackening in the sense of social involvement and participation in the life of community.

The case for social growth, in making a positive contribution to productivity as well as reinforcing the social ethic of human equality, depends to a large extent on which forms of welfare are developed, how they are administered, and the education and skills of those who staff these services. We know now from experience in Britain that we did not abolish the spirit of the old and hated poor law by enacting new legislation in 1948. The same people — the same administrators and workers — still had to run the hospitals, public assistance offices and welfare services. They poured into the new social service bottles the old wine of discrimination and prejudice. What was needed was a major effort of training, retraining and separation of functions of administrators, social workers and local officials. This, I believe, is one of the less dramatic but important goals of welfare: a more humane and informed administration of social service. This is a prerequisite to "reaching the unreachables" in our society. We have to realize that in this matter there is an enormous gap between the best we are capable of and what goes on; that reducing this gap is not simply an affair of spending more money; and that it is in great part the responsibility of public authorities to challenge whatever attitudes and conventions stand in the way of improvement, and to initiate themselves the move to higher standards of service everywhere.

This is one of the major goals in the development of welfare as an aid to economic growth. It means efficient and more effective welfare. Before, however, turning to my next point I must say something about the definition of the term. How do we define welfare? What are the main areas of collective action which may be designated as social policy?

I do not wish at this stage to embark on a long essay on definition. It will be sufficient to indicate the main areas of public (or publicly subsidized) social and welfare services, namely:

1. Education from the primary school to the university.
2. Medical care, preventive and curative.
3. Housing and rent policies.

4. Income maintenance (including children's allowances, old age pensions, public assistance, and schemes for unemployment, sickness and industrial injuries benefits).

5. Special services in kind for dependent groups, the old, deprived children, unsupported mothers and various handicapped classes.

All these services are redistributive in their effects. They cannot be neutral, whether they are provided only for certain groups in the population or on the principle of universality. They change patterns of getting, spending and storing. In terms of total government expenditures they may absorb anything from 10 per cent to 30 per cent of the annual budget.

In looking to the future and asking questions about the major objectives of these services we must first inquire how they are functioning at present in the modern state. Are they in reality achieving what they were intended to achieve? To what extent and in what sectors are they redistributing resources on criteria of need or on criteria of productivity — on Myrdal's principle of Cumulative Causation? In attempting to answer such questions we must also take account of the operations of the income tax system with all its complex indirect subsidies and transfers towards meeting the cost of different types of services and needs; for example, allowances for children, deductions for education, medical care, old age pensions, life assurance, owner-occupied houses and so forth. For those who pay income tax, these are welfare contributions and their general tendency in Britain and other countries is to reduce the progressiveness of the taxation system. They are, in short, redistributive in effect just as the formal welfare services are.

I cannot, of course, try to answer these important questions so far as other countries are concerned. However, from social policy studies in the last few years in Britain and the United States it has become increasingly clear that certain tendencies are at work which conflict with the general model of a "Welfare State" redistributing resources in favour of the poor and those with the greatest need.

In Britain, for example, we have begun to ask statistical and sociological questions about the utilization of the high-cost sectors of social welfare and the low-cost sectors of social welfare. We have been led to do so by the recognition that the Beveridge principle of universality in welfare — comprehensive systems of education, medical care and pensions of all citizens — does not, by itself alone, solve the problems of the underclass in our societies; the fifth or quarter or more of the population who are badly educated, badly housed, badly fed and who often have greater need for medical care and services of many kinds than the general population.

Universality in welfare is needed — and was needed in Britain — to reduce and remove barriers of social and economic discrimination. Separate services for second-class citizens invariably become second-class services — whether they are organized for 10 per cent or 50 per cent of the population. Moreover, those who staff these services may come to believe that they themselves are second-class workers. Hence, when exercising discretionary powers in giving or withholding benefits and services they may adopt a more punishing attitude to those whom they may disapprove of.

The principle of universality applied in 1948 to the main social welfare services in Britain was needed as a major objective favouring social integration; as a method of breaking down distinctions and discriminative tests between first-class and second-class citizens. But equal opportunity of access by right of citizenship to education, medical care and social insurance is not the same thing as equality of outcome. It is only a prerequisite — though a necessary one — to the objective of equalizing the outcome. Other and more precise instruments of social policy are required in addition to achieve equality of outcome irrespective of race, religion or class.

I will now give a few examples of what we have been learning in the past ten years about the actual functioning of universally provided services in Britain.

1. Under the National Health Service we have learnt that the higher income groups make better use of the Service; they tend to receive more specialist attention; occupy more of the beds in better equipped hospitals; receive more elective surgery; have better maternity care; and are more likely to get psychiatric help and psychotherapy than members of the so-called working classes — particularly the unskilled.

2. In the field of financial provision for old age (which dominates the budget for national insurance) we have learnt that the State now makes a larger contribution on average to the pensions of the rich than it does to the pensions of the poor. This has come about as a consequence of the combined action of the principle of universality, of tax allowances, subsidized pension schemes sponsored by employers, deductible life assurance and other factors.

3. Under the universal system of family allowances and children's allowances a man earning £20,000 a year with 2 children will receive from the State (pay less tax) £5 a week for the children. At the other end of of the scale a man with 2 children and earning £500 a year will receive from the State 8/- a week. The rich father thus gets thirteen times more from the State than the poor man in recognition of the dependent needs of children.

4. In the field of housing the subsidy paid by the State to owner-occupiers of many categories of houses is on average greater than the subsidy received by most tenants of public housing (local government) schemes. This has come about as a consequence of the differential

effects of local rate payments, housing subsidies, interest rates, tax deductibles for mortgage interest, and other factors. To arrive at this conclusion for housing (as for pensions and benefits for children) calls for a complex and intensive analysis of many diverse systems of Government intervention.

5. For my last example, I take education. Next to the ownership of land and property, this (and the lack of it) is today the most revolutionary and explosive force in developed and developing economies. Earning power, life chances, achievement, position and class, and even the level of pension in old age depend on education and training, and on society's investment of scarce resources in those who are educated. In highly-developed countries today the total value of the capital sunk in the education of the population is immense. It has been estimated for the United States that in 1957 the capital sunk in the education of the population represented 40 per cent of the total of physical tangible capital plus intangible educational capital.[2]

This, of course, is not to say that education can be viewed simply as another form of productive capital investment. It confers other benefits: social and spiritual. It enables the educated person to enjoy more freedom and a fuller life. But education does have value as a straightforward commercial investment. The return on higher education as a purely commercial investment for the individual is probably larger today in most Western countries than any other form of investment. If heavily financed by the State, and if proportionately more children from better-off homes benefit, then the system will be redistributive in favour of the rich.[3]

In the past, the spread of the first stages of education to all children — the principle of universality — was a major equalizing and integrating force in our societies. It functioned in this way partly because the problem of earnings and labour forgone was less of a problem. But we are now entering in the West a new era in which secondary and higher education may become one of the major disequalizing and socially disruptive forces. There are three reasons for this.

One is that scarce resources only allow a small proportion of young people access to good secondary and higher education. (The principle of universality cannot be applied to higher education in any country of the world in this century.)

The second is a greatly intensified problem of earnings and labour forgone (associated, of course, with the problem of educational motivation) which leads to the exclusion of working-class children. Immense

[2] T. W. Schultz, *The Economic Value of Education*, 1963, p. 51.
[3] This process has been well illustrated in a recent study by Dr. Ben-David of the Hebrew University, "Professions in the Class System of Present-Day Societies," *Current Sociology*, vol. xii, No. 3, 1963-4.

sacrifices are called for from parents and children living in poor conditions and bad housing if earnings are given up in favour of study.

And the third is that as industrial, scientific and technological developments demand more people with higher education there will be, as in Britain, pressures to invest more scarce resources in such education at the expense of education for the masses, and also to concentrate secondary education on those who will go on to higher education. These pressures, we must recognize, are growing stronger in our societies.

These five examples I have given of trends and tendencies in the functioning of social welfare services provide us with some glimpses of the magnitude of the task that lies ahead in redefining the goals of welfare. The major beneficiaries of the high-cost sectors of social welfare are the middle and upper income classes. The poor make more use of certain services (for instance, public assistance) but these tend on a *per capita* basis to be the low-cost sectors.

In addition to these trends, Britain and other Western countries have experienced in the last fifteen years a rapid growth in what we may call "non-wage income." This has taken the form of services, fringe benefits, privileges and perquisites which are not generally or wholly subject to tax. The major beneficiaries have been the middle and upper income groups.

In short, we can now say that the advent of "The Welfare State" in Britain after the Second World War has not led to any significant redistribution of income and wealth in favour of the poorer classes. According to the most recent estimates,[4] 5 per cent of the population of the United Kingdom owned 87 per cent of all personal wealth in 1911-13, 79 per cent in 1936-8 and 75 per cent in 1960. The decline in the concentration of wealth, although insignificant over the period of fifty years, is less marked since 1938 than during the years of mass unemployment and economic depression between 1913 and 1938. The trend towards a somewhat less unequal concentration in the ownership of wealth appears to have slowed down in the past twenty-five years. This is all the more remarkable when we consider the effects since 1938 of substantially higher rates of taxation and estate duty, the equalizing forces of the Second World War, full employment and a far greater employment of married women, and the supposedly redistributive effects of "The Welfare State." Full employment for nearly twenty years, considered alone, might have been expected to have brought about a markedly less unequal concentration; a much greater proportion of workers have had opportunities of accumulating some savings.

Moreover, it has to be remembered that all these figures are expressed

[4] By J. R. S. Revell of Cambridge University published in J. E. Meade, *Efficiency, Equality and the Ownership of Property*, Allen and Unwin, 1964, p. 27.

in terms of *individual* holdings. We do know from various studies that
since the 1930s there has been an increasing tendency for large owners
of property to distribute their wealth among their families.[5] The British
fiscal system is almost unique in the Western world in its generous
treatment of wealth-holders in allowing them to use family settlements,
discretionary trusts, gifts, family covenants and other legal devices for
redistributing and rearranging income and wealth. This trend is reflected
in the startling fact that in the mid-1950s and within age groups, it was
in the young adult age group that the tendency for wealth to be concentrated in a few hands was most marked. If it were possible to measure
the distribution of wealth in terms of family holdings it might thus be
found that inequality had increased since 1938. There is certainly evidence from the United States, which has experienced a marked increase
in individual wealth inequality since 1949, that measurement in terms of
family holdings does make a significant difference.[6]

Yet since the end of the 1930s it has been the broad intention of welfare measures to facilitate a more equal distribution of economic resources. Why then, it may be asked, have these unintended consequences
of social policy come about? There are, of course, many reasons and I
can only mention a few. For one thing, our conceptual frame of reference
was too narrow and too romantic. We have associated "Welfare" with
the "Poor"; it has given us a nice feeling. Secondly, we too readily assumed that social legislation solves social problems. As every social worker
knows (or should know) it does not. Thirdly, we failed to develop in
the 1950s techniques of social analysis as we have developed techniques
of economic analysis. Fourthly, we have tended to "compartmentalize"
welfare; to put it in a separate conceptual box; to see it as a hindrance to
economic growth in the long-run — as it may be in the short-run. Accordingly, therefore, we failed to relate the functioning of services and
the measurement of social need with the dynamics of change — economic,
technological, social and psychological.

Lastly, we lacked vision and we lacked social inventiveness. We did not
see that the task of reaching the poor and minority groups, of redistributing resources in their favour, of getting them to use and benefit from
health, education and social services was a far more formidable one
than most reformers imagined. We gravely under-estimated the growing
strength of the forces working in the other direction — forces stemming
from economic and technological change, specialization and the class
division of society. And we failed to grasp the importance of the connections between, for instance, bad housing and inability to profit from

[5] Richard M. Titmuss, *Income Distribution and Social Change*, 1963,
chapter 5.
[6] R. J. Lampman, *Review of Economic Statistics*, 41, November 1959, pp.
379-92.

education; between an inadequate command over language and the
need for more social workers to help to interpret and manipulate the
resources of a complex society; and between social policies and the in-
adequacy of the administrative machine (particularly at local levels) to
translate policies into effective action.

In short, because we were complacent, because we looked inwards and
backwards to the 1930s, our social diagnosis was inadequate. Only now
are we coming to see that we need much sharper tools of social study and
measurement; more precise social analyses of conditions, needs and the
actual functioning of services; more attempts at social planning in
alliance with economic planning. How many hospital beds shall we need
in 1975? How many more social workers, welfare workers, and other
staff will be required? What problems of crime, delinquency and deprivation will confront our societies in ten years' time?

These and similar questions are admittedly difficult ones to answer. But
if we wish to redefine the goals of welfare then we cannot escape the
responsibility of being more intelligent about what is happening and
what is likely to happen in our societies.

We shall not make progress in identifying and measuring the future
tasks of welfare unless we relate need and response to the ongoing forces
of change. If we accept that two of the major positive goals of welfare
are to increase and spread the impact of equalizing factors and to speed
up the impact of factors favouring integration then we must base the
many practical details of policy and action on a more informed diagnosis
of change. From recent advances in the social sciences we can be reasonably sure about the continuation of certain trends, for example.

To achieve economic growth and innovation, modern societies need to
apply the lessons of advances in technology and science. This means
more division of labour and specialization; more education and specialized
training; more specificity in manpower recruitment and deployment;
longer hierarchies in occupational positions in the labour force; larger incentives for training and mobility; more and probably larger differentials
in rewards. These processes, necessary as they are, tend on balance to
generate disequalizing forces and, by demanding higher standards of
education, training and acquired skills, they can make more difficult the
task of integrating people with different cultural backgrounds and levels
of motivation. While we may rise expectations in people's minds about
what the future may hold, technology simultaneously raises the barriers
to entry. This process, now becoming known in the U.S.A. as "credential-
ism," is believed to be partly responsible for the solidifying of a permanent underclass of deprived citizens, uneducated, unattached and
alternating between apathetic resignation and frustrated violence.

A second process, built-in among modern societies and related to
technological change, which we also need to understand, is represented

by growth of professionalism. In Britain and other countries, the professions are largely recruited from the middle classes; professional workers come from homes and educational institutions where they have little contact with manual workers and people from different cultures. Thus, they bring to their work middle-class values in the processes of giving or withholding medical care, education, legal aid and welfare benefits. Their model of the ideal pupil, student, patient and client is one with middle-class values and a middle-class tongue.[7] This process, subtle and often unconscious, partly explains why in Britain, under universally available welfare services, the middle classes tend to receive better services and more opportunities for advancement. This is understandable; we all prefer the co-operative patient or client; motivated to achievement, anxious to learn, anxious to work. Of all professions in contact with the poor, only social workers in their training learn to understand the significance of this factor in their relationships. They recognize the importance of guarding professionalism against functioning as a disequalizing force.

While I have not attempted any precise description of today's welfare goals, I believe that some of them are implicit in the lessons of experience. These I have set within the context of certain general principles of economic management. In doing so I have stated a case for a balance of economic and social growth. We want higher productivity for a higher standard of living and we want a more equal society. We want individual advancement and we want an integrated community of self-respecting human beings. In achieving these goals systems of welfare have a major contribution to make. They will, of course, present us time and time again with conflicting ideologies and conflicting policies.

In the choices that we have to make I would like, in conclusion, as a student of welfare, to offer two personal prescriptions.

The world desperately needs standard-bearers of social inventiveness and personal integrity; examples to look up to; precepts to learn from. In a world made smaller by modern communications what we do in the field of welfare and how we do it has an influence far outside national boundaries. Men are still moved by the ideas of compassion. So we need pioneers in the art of giving. Secondly, I believe that when conflict in policies presents itself we should take risks in welfare choices. We should trust rather than distrust people and put our faith in the ultimate reasonableness of man.

To me, the "Welfare State" has no meaning unless it is positively and constructively concerned with redistributive justice and social participation. These goals may collide in the short-run with the need to increase economic productivity and to raise the general standard of living. Although we cannot be sure that this collision is inevitable it is, nevertheless, tempting to argue — tempting to take the safe side — that when we

[7] See B. Bernstein, *Brit. Journal of Sociology*, vol. 15, No. 1, 1964.

are richer we can afford to be more generous to the less fortunate. But, equally, can we be sure that in the processes of getting richer and of concentrating only on getting richer we shall not, as a society, lose the impetus to create a more equal and socially just community?

5   DAVID LOCKWOOD

Sources of Variation in
Working-Class Images of Society

For the most part men visualise the class structure of their society from the vantage points of their own particular *milieux*, and their perceptions of the larger society will vary according to their experiences of social inequality in the smaller societies in which they live out their daily lives. This assumption that the individual's social consciousness is to a large extent influenced by his immediate social context has already proved its usefulness in the study of "images of society" and it has been stated most clearly by Bott, who writes: "People do have direct experience of distinctions of power and prestige in their places of work, among their colleagues, in schools, and in their relationships with friends, neighbours, and relatives. In other words, the ingredients, the raw materials, of class ideology are located in the individual's various primary social experiences, rather than in his position in a socio-economic category. The hypothesis advanced here is that when an individual talks about class he is trying to say something, in a symbolic form, about his experiences of power and prestige in his actual membership groups and social relationships both past and present."[1] Working from very similar premises, several

Reprinted by permission of the author and publisher from *Sociological Review*, Volume 14, November 1966. (Originally given as a lecture at the University of Göttingen, February, 1966.)

David Lockwood, educated in sociology at the London School of Economics and Political Science, became well known with his work on *The Black-coated Worker: A Study in Class Consciousness* (1958). He is now at Cambridge University, and has recently been Visiting Professor at Columbia University in New York.

[1] Elizabeth Bott: *Family and Social Network*, London, 1957, p. 163.

quite independent investigations have suggested that there seem to be two broad ways in which individuals conceptualise class structure: "power" or "conflict" or "dichotomous" models on the one hand; and "prestige" or "status" or "hierarchical" models on the other. Further it has been proposed that the social ideology of the working class tends to take the form of a power model whereas that of the middle class approximates the hierarchical model. Although some of these studies have noted variations in social imagery within the working class, they have concentrated chiefly on explaining the variations between the classes. Thus the power or dichotomous ideology of the working class and the hierarchical ideology of the middle class have been accounted for primarily in terms of differences in the industrial life chances and life experiences of manual and non-manual employees.[2]

While the similarity of the findings of these various investigations is very striking, it is also quite clear from other studies that the industrial and community *milieux* of manual workers exhibit a very considerable diversity and it would be strange if there were no correspondingly marked variations in the images of society held by different sections of the British working class. Indeed, on the basis of existing research, it is possible to delineate at least three different types of workers and to infer that the work and community relationships by which they are differentiated from one another may also generate very different forms of social consciousness. The three types are as follows: first, the traditional worker of the "proletarian" variety whose image of society will take the form of a power model; secondly, the other variety of traditional worker, the "deferential," whose perception of social inequality will be one of status hierarchy; and, thirdly, the "privatised" worker, whose social consciousness will most nearly approximate what may be called a "pecuniary" model of society.[3]

[2] See E. Bott, *op. cit.*; O. A. Oeser and S. B. Hammond: *Social Structure and Personality in a City*, London, 1954; H. Popitz, H. P. Bahrdt, E. A. Jueres, and H. Kesting: *Das Gesellschaftsbild des Arbeiters*, Tuebingen, 1961; A. Willener: *Images de la société et classes sociales*, Berne, 1957; R. Hoggart: *The Uses of Literacy*, London, 1957; A. Kornhauser, H. J. Sheppard and A. J. Mayer: *When Labor Votes*, New York, 1956; A. Andrieux and J. Lignon: *L'ouvrier d'aujourd'hui*, Paris, 1960. Ralf Dahrendorf was the first to draw attention to the similarity of the conclusions of Popitz, Willener, and Hoggart, in his book, *Class and Class Conflict in Industrial Society*, Stanford, 1959, pp. 280-289.

[3] On the traditional and privatised working class see David Lockwood: "The 'New' Working Class," *European Journal of Sociology*, Vol. 1, No. 2, 1960; and John H. Goldthorpe and David Lockwood: "Affluence and the British Class Structure," *Sociological Review*, Vol. 11, No. 2, 1963. The present paper may be regarded as an extension of these earlier statements and in particular as an elaboration of one major element in the normative dimension of "class." John Goldthorpe and I have worked together so closely on the wider problem of which this paper is a part that I find it difficult to say where my thoughts end and his begin. Although he may not fully agree with my interpretation, the

The "traditional worker" is, of course, a sociological rather than an historical concept; a concept relating to workers who are located in particular kinds of work situations and community structures rather than one purporting to give a description of the working class as a whole at some particular point of time. Moreover, the concept encompasses not only the most radical and class conscious segment of the working class (the proletarian worker) but also its most socially acquiescent and conservative elements (the deferential worker). Yet, distinct as the two traditionalists are from one another in social and political outlook, they do share several characteristics which make them traditionalists and thus distinguish them from the privatised worker. It would seem best, then, to begin with an account of the work and community structures underlying proletarian and deferential traditionalism.[4]

The most highly developed forms of proletarian traditionalism seem to be associated with industries such as mining, docking, and ship-building; industries which tend to concentrate workers together in solidary communities and to isolate them from the influences of the wider society.[5] Workers in such industries usually have a high degree of job involvement and strong attachments to primary work groups that possess a considerable autonomy from technical and supervisory constraints.[6] Pride in doing "men's work" and a strong sense of shared occupational experiences make for feelings of fraternity and comradeship which are expressed through a distinctive occupational culture. These primary

present essay draws much from a paper of his entitled "Attitudes and Behaviour of Car Assembly Workers," which will be published shortly in the *British Journal of Sociology*.

[4] Work and community relations do not, of course, exhaust the range of variables which may affect the formation of models of society. In particular, the experience of social mobility (in the present context, downward mobility) is most likely to have the effect of predisposing a worker towards a hierarchical, rather than a class, model. This is so for two reasons: first, because the experience of social mobility makes a person more sensitive to the fact of hierarchical social distance; and secondly because the downwardly mobile worker is likely to have been socialised into a set of values ordered around a concept of status hierarchy. However, the number of socially mobile persons in any particular section of the working class will be determined to a large extent by the self-same factors that shape their work and community relationships, i.e., by the industrial and occupational structure of a particular locale.

[5] The first to draw attention to this phenomenon in a systematic way were C. Kerr and A. Siegel: "The Inter-industry Propensity to Strike: An International Comparison," in A. Kornhauser, R. Dubin, and A. M. Ross: *Industrial Conflict*, London, 1954. See also, for example, *The Dock Worker*, University of Liverpool Department of Social Science, Liverpool, 1954; and N. Dennis, F. Henriques, and C. Slaughter: *Coal Is Our Life*, London, 1956.

[6] R. Blauner: "Work Satisfaction and Industrial Trends in Modern Society," in W. Galenson and S. M. Lipset: *Labor and Trade Unionism*, New York, 1960, p. 343, *et seq.*

groups of workmates not only provide the elementary units of more extensive class loyalties but work associations also carry over into leisure activities, so that workers in these industries usually participate in what are called "occupational communities."[7] Workmates are normally leisure-time companions, often neighbours, and not infrequently kinsmen. The existence of such closely-knit cliques of friends, workmates, neighbours and relatives is the hallmark of the traditional working class community. The values expressed through these social networks emphasize mutual aid in everyday life and the obligation to join in the gregarious pattern of leisure, which itself demands the expenditure of time, money and energy in a public and present-oriented conviviality and eschews individual striving "to be different." As a form of social life, this communal sociability has a ritualistic quality, creating a high moral density and reinforcing sentiments of belongingness to a work-dominated collectivity. The isolated and endogamous nature of the community, its predominantly one-class population, and low rates of geographical and social mobility all tend to make it an inward-looking society and to accentuate the sense of cohesion that springs from shared work experiences.[8]

Shaped by occupational solidarities and communal sociability the proletarian social consciousness is centred on an awareness of "us" in contradistinction to "them" who are not a part of "us." "Them" are bosses, managers, white collar workers and, ultimately, the public authorities of the larger society. Yet even though these outsiders are remote from the community, their power to influence it is well understood; and those within the community are more conscious of this power because it comes from the outside. Hence the dominant model of society held by the proletarian traditionalist is most likely to be a dichotomous or two-valued power model. Thinking in terms of two classes standing in a relationship of opposition is a natural consequence of being a member of a closely integrated industrial community with well-defined boundaries and a distinctive style of life. It may well be, as Popitz has argued, that the propensity to hold a dichotomous social imagery is a general one among industrial workers in large establishments: certainly

[7] The defining characteristics of an occupational community are: (1) Workers in their off-hours socialize more with persons in their own line of work than with a cross-section of occupational types; (2) Workers "talk shop" in their off-hours; (3) The occupation is the reference group; its standards of behaviour, its system of status and rank, guide conduct. *Ibid*, p. 351.

[8] The one-industry town with its dominant occupational community would seem to produce the most distinctive form of proletarian traditionalism. But, given a relatively isolated community with a stable and preponderantly working class population, a quite high degree of proletarian traditionalism is perfectly compatible with industrial diversification. Indeed, industrial diversification may promote the stability of the population by allowing a man to change his work without leaving the locality.

the social divisions of the workplace, the feeling of being subject to a distant and incomprehensible authority, and the inconsiderable chances of escaping from manual wage earning employment are all conducive to the formation of such an ideology.[9] But it is probable that this image of society is fully developed only among those workers whose sense of the industrial hiatus is strengthened by their awareness of forming a quite separate community. Moreover, to anticipate the subsequent discussion, it would seem that the tendency to adopt a power model of society is most evident among workers who have a high degree of job involvement and strong ties with their fellow workers. In other kinds of work situations, where these factors are absent, or nearly so, the whole significance of the workplace as a determinant of a dichotomous class ideology is correspondingly reduced.

Our knowledge of the second variety of traditional worker is rather skimpy and results mainly from the efforts that have been made to track down that elusive political animal, the "deferential voter."[10] It may be assumed, however, that the model of society held by the deferential worker is a prestige or hierarchical, rather than a power or dichotomous model. In fact, given that people who think of social divisions in terms of status or prestige usually distinguish higher and lower strata as well as status equals, his model is likely to be at least a trichotomous one.[11] Further, the deferential worker does not identify himself with his superiors or strive to reach their status; he defers to them socially as well as politically. His recognition of authentic leadership is based on his belief in the intrinsic qualities of an ascriptive elite who exercise leadership paternalistically in the pursuit of "national" as opposed to "sectional" or "class" interests. But how refined his image of the status hierarchy really is, or how exactly he perceives his own position in it, is not known. It is merely suggested that he has a conception of a higher and unapproachable status group of leaders, his "betters," the people who "know how to run things," those whose performance is guaranteed by "breeding"; and that he himself claims to be nothing grander than "working class."

[9] Popitz, et al., op. cit., pp. 237 et seq.

[10] For an exposition of the political philosophy to which he is held to respond, see S. M. Beer: Modern British Politics, London, 1965, pp. 91-102. For a preliminary report on the investigation by R. T. McKenzie and A. Silver, see: "Conservatism, Industrialism, and the Working Class Tory in England," Transactions of the Fifth World Congress of Sociology, Louvain, 1964, Vol. III, pp. 191-202. See also R. Samuel: "The Deference Voter," New Left Review, January-February 1960; Mark Abrams: "Class and Politics," Encounter, October 1961; W. G. Runciman: Relative Deprivation and Social Justice, London, 1966, Chapter IX. Probably the best description of the deferential traditionalist and his social context is by Margaret Stacey: Tradition and Change, Oxford, 1960. See also the highly instructive paper by D. E. G. Plowman, et al.: "Local Social Status in England and Wales," Sociological Review, Vol. 10, No. 2, 1962.

[11] E. Bott, op. cit., p. 176.

However, given these elements, it is possible to go a little further and to draw the not unreasonable, but wholly speculative, conclusion that the deferential worker thinks in terms of at least a four-fold division of society. Since he thinks in terms of "genuine" or "natural" leaders in both a local and a national context, it is likely that he thinks also of "spurious" leaders and, by implication, of "misguided" followers. Spurious leaders are those who aspire to leadership, and indeed from time to time acquire it, without possessing the requisite qualities. They may have achieved wealth, power and position, but they lack the heredi-tary or quasi-hereditary credentials which the deferential worker recognises as the true marks of legitimacy.[12] Misguided followers are those, broadly in the same layer of society as himself, who refuse to acknowledge the objects of his deference, and who aid and abet the spurious leaders in usurping authority.[13] If the deferential worker has an image of society as a status hierarchy, then the existence of "undeferential" workers is almost a necessary condition for the protection of his own sense of self-esteem. There are few instances of lower status groups who both accept the legitimacy of the status hierarchy and fail to discover groups with an even lower status than their own.

Whatever niceties of status differentiation enter into the ideology of the deferential traditionalist, it would seem that he does hold a hier-archical model of some kind, and it would seem worthwhile exploring the hypothesis that such a model of society will be the product of very special work and community relationships. Here, studies of the deferential voter do not take us very far. The findings that these voters are more likely than non-deferentials to be elderly, to be women, to have low in-comes and to come from rural areas are demographic facts relating to the properties of individuals rather than facts relating to the properties of the social systems in which these individuals are located.[14] Nor is it to be assumed that all deferential voters will be deferential traditionalists. The latter, like proletarian traditionalists, must be thought of as an extreme type, characterised by a combination of social roles which, taken together, are most likely to lead to a hierarchical social imagery.

The typical work rôle of the deferential traditionalist will be one that brings him into direct association with his employer or other middle class influentials and hinders him from forming strong attachments to workers

[12] See M. Stacey, op. cit., pp. 159-160, on the tensions between the traditional and non-traditional segments of Banbury.

[13] "They support the parties of their 'social betters' while insisting on their own position at the bottom of the social ladder. Compared with their neigh-bours, they are not interested in a party which stands for the ordinary working class and which aims to raise the standard of living of ordinary people." M. Abrams, op. cit., p. 42.

[14] M. Abrams, op. cit., p. 42; R. Samuel, op. cit., p. 11; R. T. McKenzie and A. Silver, op. cit., p. 199.

in a similar market situation to his own. These work conditions are most clearly present in the sorts of occupations that are to be found in small towns and rural areas, although they are by no means entirely absent in larger urban centres. Workers in various kinds of service occupations, in non- (or rather pre-) industrial craft jobs, those working in small scale "family enterprises," and in agricultural employment, are workers who are most exposed to paternalistic forms of industrial authority.[15] The essence of this work situation is that relationship between employer and worker is personal and particularistic. The worker has an unique position in a functional job hierarchy and he is tied to his employer by a "special relationship" between them and not only by considerations of economic gain.

In the making of the deferential traditionalist certain features of community life will also play an important part in fixing and sharpening the sense of hierarchy that he acquires in his rôle as worker. Small, relatively isolated and economically autonomous communities, particularly those with well-differentiated occupational structures and stable populations, provide the most favourable settings for the existence of "local status systems." The key characteristic of such systems is that the allocation of status takes place through "interactional" rather than through "attributional" mechanisms.[16] The boundaries of the several status groups making up the local system are maintained by various means of social acceptance and rejection in both formal and informal association. People do not judge one another from a distance and attribute status on the basis of a few, readily observable criteria, such as the amount of an individual's material possessions. Status groups (or rather the cliques of which they are constituted) are membership as well as reference groups. Through close acquaintance, people have a detailed knowledge of each other's personal qualities and can apply relatively complex criteria in deciding who is

[15] See the account of "traditional" firms in M. Stacey, op. cit., pp. 27-28; and the discussion of paternalism in D. Lockwood, The Black-coated Worker, London, 1958, pp. 78-81 and 141-149. A more fully developed system — "patriarchalism" — is portrayed by Solomon B. Levine: Industrial Relations in Postwar Japan, Urbana, 1958, pp. 36-38.

[16] On the concepts of "local status systems" and "interactional" status systems, see D. E. G. Plowman, et al., op. cit., especially pp. 186-195. The distinction between interactional and attributional status systems is also made by M. Young and P. Willmott when they contrast the "face-to-face" relationships of Bethnal Green with the "window-to-window" relationships of Greenleigh. See M. Young and P. Willmott: Family and Kinship in East London, London, 1957, especially pp. 134-135. The perception of status groups as interactional groups is basic to the fully developed status or hierarchical model of society as E. Bott makes clear when she writes that: "status was not conceived in relative terms as a continuum. Each class was given a specific subculture" and "each category differed from others in sub-culture and prestige" so that "individuals in one class, if they happened to meet, might associate with one another as equals in informal interaction." E. Bott, op. cit., pp. 176-177.

worthy of membership of a particular status group. There is also wide-spread consensus about the rank order of status groups in the community, so that lower strata regard their lowly position less as an injustice than as a necessary, acceptable, and even desirable part in a natural system of inequality. Local status systems, therefore, operate to give the individual a very definite sense of position in a hierarchy of prestige, in which each "knows his place" and recognises the status prerogatives of those above and below him. For the deferential traditionalist, such a system of status has the function of placing his work orientations in a wider social context. The persons who exercise authority over him at his place of work may not be the same persons who stand at the apex of the local status system, but the structural principles of the two social orders are homological; and from neither set of relationships does he learn to question the ap-propriateness of his exchange of deference for paternalism.

Although in terms of social imagery and political outlook the proletarian and deferential traditionalists are far removed from one another, they nevertheless do have some characteristics in common. They are first of all traditionalists in the sense that both types are to be found in industries and communities which, to an ever increasing extent, are backwaters of national industrial and urban development. The sorts of industries which employ deferential and proletarian workers are declining relatively to more modern industries in which large batch or mass production tech-niques are more and more the major modes of production. Again, the small isolated country town, or the mining village, or the working class enclave, such as is represented by the dockworkers' community, are gradually becoming linked with, or absorbed into, larger urban concen-trations and with an increased amount of voluntary and involuntary residential mobility of the labour force the close link between place of work and community is being broken down.

They are also traditionalists in the sense that their horizons of ex-pectations do not extend much beyond the boundaries of the communities in which they live and of which they are, so to speak, "founding mem-bers." This again is largely a product of the social isolation and social stability of both the deferential and proletarian communities. Workers in such environments are as unlikely to change their patterns of con-sumption as they are their political loyalties, because in both cases they are encapsulated in social systems which provide them with few alterna-tive conceptions of what is possible, desirable, and legitimate.

Finally, and perhaps most significantly, the work and community rela-tionships of traditional workers involve them in mutually reinforcing systems of interpersonal influence. The effect of group membership on class ideology will, of course, vary depending on the type of traditional worker under consideration. In the case of the deferential worker, his rôle in a paternalistic authority structure at work and his position in a

local status system in the community both predispose him to think of
society in terms of hierarchy. In the case of the proletarian traditionalist,
his membership of the work gang and his participation in the system of
communal sociability lead to a conception of a "class-divided" society.
But although the effects of group membership are very different in the
two cases, both the deferential and the proletarian traditionalists are
highly integrated into their respective local societies; and this means that
their attitudes and behaviour are to a large extent influenced and controlled by means of direct face-to-face encounters. In this way, they experience a sense of belonging to actual social groups which are marked
off from other groups by boundaries that are maintained through social
interaction. This consciousness of definite social placement in turn affects
their perception of the class structure. Whether their models of society
are basically hierarchical or basically dichotomous, the fact that traditional workers have a strong sense of group membership means that they
will tend to see "strata" or "classes" as active social formations and not
merely as amorphous aggregates of individuals. In this respect, the social
consciousness of the traditional worker differs markedly from that of the
privatised worker, whose model of society is shaped by work and community relationships which do not convey, to the same extent, an awareness of group affiliation.

The social environment of the privatised worker is conducive to the
development of what may be called a "pecuniary" model of society. The
essential feature of this ideology is that class divisions are seen mainly in
terms of differences in income and material possessions. Naturally, there
will be few individuals who think of class divisions in purely pecuniary
terms. But the social consciousness of many individuals in the "new working class" may be closer to this pecuniary model of society than to either
of the two types of social imagery previously discussed.[17] Basically, the
pecuniary model of society is an ideological reflection of work attachments that are instrumental and of community relationships that are
privatised.[18] It is a model which is only possible when social relationships
that might provide prototypical experiences for the construction of ideas
of conflicting power classes, or of hierarchically interdependent status
groups, are either absent or devoid of their significance.

The work situation of the privatised worker is such that his involvement in the job and his attachments to the enterprise and to his fellow
workers are slight. Numerous studies have provided us with the generalisa-
tion that workers employed in large factories with mass-production tech-

[17] See J. H. Goldthorpe and D. Lockwood, *op. cit.*, pp. 149-154, for a discussion of these two terms.
[18] R. Dubin: "Industrial Workers' Worlds," *Social Problems*, Vol. 3, January 1956, p. 135. Also see C. Argyris: *Personality and Organization*, New York,
1957, especially Chapter IV; R. Blauner, *op. cit.*

nologies and doing jobs which are highly specialised, repetitive, and lacking in autonomy, are workers for whom, in Dubin's words, "work and the workplace are not central life interests" and for whom work is viewed "as a means to an end — a way of acquiring income for life in the community."[19] Under these conditions, work is a deprivation which is performed mainly for extrinsic rewards; and "money-mindedness," the calculative exchange of labour power for maximum pay, is the predominant motive for remaining in the job. Frequently isolated from their workmates by the constraints of technology, and seeking no close relationships in a work situation that is viewed in purely instrumental terms, such "alienated" workers do not form cohesive groups inside the factory and they are not prone to form occupational communities outside the factory. Their main attitude to work is that of its being a necessary evil; and given this orientation they have no desire to carry over into their leisure time the atmosphere and associations of work.[20] In all these respects — the low involvement in the job itself, the lack of cohesive work groups, the absence of occupational communities — privatised workers differ significantly from the traditional worker, and more especially from the proletarian traditionalist. Relative to the latter, the privatised worker finds himself in a work situation that is socially isolating and, to a large extent, socially meaningless; a situation in which the dominant relationship is the cash-nexus. But, although he is "alienated" labour, he is unlikely to possess a strongly developed class consciousness because his involvement in work is too low to allow for strong feelings of any kind, except perhaps the desire to escape from it altogether. He is neither deeply involved with his work-mates nor deeply antagonistic to his employer; on the whole his attitude to both more nearly approximates one of indifference.[21]

These tendencies of the work life are reinforced and accentuated by a certain form of community life which is increasingly representative of the new working class: namely, the social structure of the council, or the private, low-cost housing estate.[22] From the present point of view, the most salient feature of these estates is that they bring together a population of strangers, who have little in common, save that they have all ex-

[19] The general theme is quite old. See, for example, Karl Marx on "The Power of Money in Bourgeois Society," *Economic and Philosophical Manuscripts of 1844*, London, 1959. A more recent Marxist interpretation which concentrates on the work situation is that by Andre Gorz: "Work and Consumption," *Towards Socialism*, edited by Perry Anderson and Robin Blackburn, London, 1965, especially pp. 348-349.

[20] R. Blauner, *op. cit.*, p. 351.

[21] On the significance of intensity, as opposed to direction, of involvement, see A. Etzioni: *A Comparative Analysis of Complex Organizations*, New York, 1961, p. 9.

[22] Some of the abundant literature on this topic is summarised in J. Klein: *Samples from English Cultures*, London, 1965, Vol. II, Chapter 5.

perienced residential mobility and that most of them gain their livelihood
from some kind of manual labour. In such communities, social life is
very different from the communal sociability of the traditional working-
class community. Unrelated by the ascriptive ties of kinship, long-standing
neighbourliness and shared work experiences, and lacking also the facility
for readily creating middle-class patterns of sociability, workers on the
estates tend to live a socially isolated, home-centred existence. Such
conditions favour the emergence of attributional rather than interactional
status systems. Whereas in the traditional proletarian community status
is allocated (or more precisely made indeterminate) through the individual's participation in several overlapping cliques, the status order of
the housing estate is based on conspicuous consumption, by means of
which people judge their social standing relative to others without usually
associating with them in formal or informal leisure-time activities. The
low housing density of the estate, its lack of recreational amenities, the
uprootedness of its inhabitants and their limited capacities for creating
new styles of sociability produce a society in which residents are only
superficially acquainted and associated with those who live around them.
The attributional nature of the status ranking that arises from this situation in turn induces an acquisitiveness and a sensitivity to competitive
consumption that are quite alien to the communal sociability of
proletarian traditionalism.

The work and community settings just described are the breeding
grounds of the privatised worker, and his socially isolated existence not
only predisposes, but also enables, him to adopt a pecuniary model of
class structure. In the first place, he is strongly motivated to view social
relationships in pecuniary terms. Lacking close primary group ties inside
and outside the work situation, at work he is wage-oriented and in the
community consumption-oriented. Just as money wages become of salient
importance in attaching him to his work rôle, so, too, consumer durables
are of primary significance in mediating his status with his neighbours.
This pattern of motivation is neither natural nor accidental. If the
privatised worker is more of an economic man than the proletarian or the
deferential traditionalist, it is because his environment conspires to make
him so.[23] Secondly, however, the work and community relationships that
foster this pecuniary outlook are unlikely to give the individual a feeling
of definite social location through membership of either a status group or
a class fraternity. The privatised worker may be a trade unionist and he
may live in a community where status is reckoned by material possessions;

[23] It is of course possible that, in addition, a process of "self-selection" occurs,
so that those workers who are more instrumental in their work orientations
and less well integrated into their local communities than other workers are
more likely to enter and remain in the jobs and communities of the kind
described.

but from neither of these sources will he derive more than a rudimentary awareness of belonging to a cohesive group and hence of the social distance between such groups.

By contrast with the proletarian traditionalist, the privatised worker will tend to join and support his trade union for instrumental rather than class solidaristic reasons. Given his materialistic, home-centred aspirations, the trade union for him is less the symbolic expression of an affective attachment to a working class community than a utilitarian association for achieving his private goal of a rising standard of living. Lacking the class consciousness which the proletarian traditionalist acquires from his involvement in solidary work groups and communal sociability, the privatised worker expects his union to devote itself exclusively to bettering the economic position of his own job category rather than to dissipate any of its resources in pursuing the more distant political objective of changing the wider society. As far as he is concerned, the trade union is a "service organisation," not part of a social movement; and, far from his union membership providing him with a consciousness of class, his orientation to trade unionism reflects precisely his lack of such a sentiment.

By contrast with the deferential traditionalist, the privatised worker is unlikely to be made aware of a system of status groups arranged in a stable hierarchy of prestige. His neighbours on the estate are mostly manual wage-earners like himself, socially undistinguished from one another save by marginal differences in their ownership of consumer durables. This means that whatever status distinction arises from the competition to possess these goods is inherently unstable and too superficial to be the source of a sense of unbridgeable social distance. Moreover, in so far as status groups fail to coalesce, the pattern of sociability in the community will remain privatised and there will be small opportunity for the individual to experience personal acceptance by his status equals or personal rejection by his status superiors. Hence, in the typically attributional status system of the housing estate, the worker will not learn to perceive status as a phenomenon that manifests itself in group relationships.

The daily social encounters of the privatised worker do not, therefore, lead him to think of a society divided up into either a hierarchy of status groups or an opposition of class. His model of society is one in which individuals are associated with, and dissociated from one another less by any type of social exchange than by the magnitude of their incomes and possessions.

Before going on to outline the elements of this pecuniary model of society, it may be useful to summarise the argument thus far by a table which differentiates proletarian, deferential, and privatised workers in terms of work and community variables. The meanings of the terms used to describe these variables should now be evident from the foregoing discussion.

WORK SITUATION

	Involvement in Job	Interaction and Identification with Workmates	Interaction and Identification with Employers
Middle Class[24]	+	+	+
Deferential	+	−	+
Proletarian	+	+	−
Privatised	−	−	−

COMMUNITY STRUCTURE

	Interactional Status System	Occupational Community	Occupational Differentiation
Middle Class	+	+	+
Deferential	+	−	+
Proletarian	+	+	−
Privatised	−	−	−

[24] Since this paper concentrates on manual workers, only the briefest comments on the position of the middle class employee are called for. Here "middle class" refers to the administrative, managerial, technical and professional white collar group (i.e., excluding lower grade clerical employees, who in many respects are similar to the privatised worker, as well as entrepreneurs). This group is included in the paradigm partly because their presence gives it a certain pleasing symmetry; but also because the same variables that are used to differentiate the three types of manual worker would also appear to be relevant in analyzing the social situation of non-manual employees. From the paradigm, it can be seen why the white collar employee is predisposed to hold a hierarchical model of society. What cannot be seen is why his hierarchical ideology differs from that of the deferential worker. This is because a variable relating to chances and expectations of upward mobility is not included in the table, which, since it was designed to show differences within the manual group, implicitly assigns a low and constant value to this variable. It is also quite obvious from the work of Prandy that there is much more variation in the work situation of the white collar employee than is suggested by the above scheme (see K. Prandy: *Professional Employees*, London, 1965). The characterisation of the middle class employee in terms of community variables is likewise undoubtedly something of an oversimplification. However, even as it stands, the following points can be made in defence of the present scheme. First, there is ample evidence that middle class employees of the kind in question do find their work intrinsically more rewarding and are more highly involved in their jobs than most industrial workers. Secondly, because their working relationships usually bring them into close contact with higher management and administration as well as with small groups of workers of their own rank, they are likely to identify themselves with both "the firm" and their colleagues. Thirdly, because of their high job involvement, they are likely to form occupational communities; and this tendency should be more pronounced the more they are geographically mobile and thus the more they are dependent on friendships acquired through their occupational rôles. Fourthly, middle class

The social isolation of the privatised worker reflects itself in his ideology of a "de-socialised" class structure.[25] The single, overwhelmingly important, and the most spontaneously conceived criterion of class division is money, and the possessions, both material and immaterial, that money can buy. From this point of view, for example, education is not thought of as a status-conferring characteristic, but rather simply as a good that money can buy and as a possession that enables one to earn more money. In general, power and status are not regarded as significant sources of class division or social hierarchy. Power is not understood as the power of one man over another, but rather as the power of a man to acquire things: as purchasing power. Status is not seen in terms of the association of status equals sharing a similar style of life. If status is thought of at all it is in terms of a standard of living, which all who have the means can readily acquire. It may not be easy to acquire the income requisite to a certain standard of living and hence qualify for membership in a more affluent class; but given the income there are no other barriers to mobility.

Within this pecuniary universe, the privatised worker tends to see himself as a member of a vast income class which contains virtually the great mass of the population. This class may be called "the working class" or "the middle class." Whatever it is called, it is a collection of "ordinary people" who "work for a living" and those who belong to it include the majority of manual and non-manual employees. They are united with one another, not by having exactly the same incomes, but by not having so much or so little income that their standard of living places them completely beyond the upper or lower horizons. A minority of persons in the society have either so much wealth or such an impoverished existence that they lie outside the central class. They are the very rich and the very poor.

---

employees are likely to live in occupationally mixed communities. Simply because there are relatively so few men in the middle ranges of white collar employment, it is almost inevitable that their neighbours will include small-scale entrepreneurs, independent professionals, lower grade clerical and sales employees, and perhaps even highly paid manual workers. Finally, white collar employees are likely to be involved in interactional status systems. Whether social visiting, or membership of and participation in voluntary associations is taken as a measure of communal (and hence status) interaction, the middle classes rank so much higher than the privatised working class that the difference is qualitative.

25 In singling out the basic features of this model of society I have been influenced by my reading of the responses to an open-ended question on class which was part of the interview schedule used in a study of a sample of affluent workers. I should stress, however, that the responses to this particular question have not yet been systematically analyzed, and that the present paper can in no way be regarded as a description of the findings of this part of the study. For an account of the study, see John H. Goldthorpe, David Lockwood, Frank Bechhofer, and Jennifer Platt: "The Affluent Worker and the Thesis of *Embourgeoisement:* Some Preliminary Research Findings," *Sociology,* Vol. *I,* No. 1, 1967. [See following article, Ed.]

Since the main criterion of class membership is money, the lower and, especially, the upper limits of the central class are hard to define, and are consequently defined arbitrarily or regarded as indeterminate.[26] In general the "upper" or "higher" or "rich" class is not perceived as wielding power or deserving of respect. It is simply a vague category of "all those up there" who have incomes and possessions and a standard of life that are completely beyond the bounds of possibility as far as the ordinary worker is concerned.[27] The rich, however, are different from the rest only in the sense of Hemingway's rejoinder to Scott Fitzgerald: that they have much more money.[28]

Finally, the central class with which the privatised worker identifies himself is seen as a relatively new phenomenon, brought about by the incorporation of the old middle class into the new "working class," or, alternatively, by the incorporation of the old working class into the new

[26] To take two examples from our own study: First, a man who has a conception of a two-fold class system: the "rich" and the "middle class." "Q — What is the main thing that decides which class someone's in? A — Money. Q — Just money? A — If you've got an income coming in, say £5,000 a year, that brings you a rich person; if you've got an income of £1-2,000 or just under, you're middle class." (034) Secondly, a man who holds a two-class model, and calls his classes the "higher class" and the "working class." "Q — What's the one main thing that decides which class a person's in? A — Money. The more money a person has the better he can live. Q — Where does the working class end and the higher class begin? A — The more money you have, the higher you get — but there *isn't* an end to the working class. Q — Are there any other differences between classes? A — No, its just the money." (035)

[27] This tendency of persons in socially ambiguous positions to enlarge their own class and to relegate the remainder of the population indiscriminately to the periphery is well known. "Some people who placed themselves in the 'working class' made differences within it but lumped together everyone else as 'the rich.' The more remote the people of another class, the less opportunity there is for checking fantasy against fact, so that the individual can see in such people what he wants to see." E. Bott, *op. cit.*, p. 165. "The earnings of these suburbanites permit some of them to call themselves 'middle class' but the framework of hierarchy of class that is meaningful to these workers is not a conceptual framework that applies to society as a whole, but one that is limited to what is possible for them . . . there is a tendency to lump together as 'way up there' everyone whose income is greater than the upper limit of what is possible for them . . . to be 'middle class,' then, probably means to them, not what sociologists mean by middle class, but rather the *middle of the working class* . . . the 'upper' middle class, white collar worlds of engineers, junior executives, professionals and would be professionals are completely beyond their ken; this latter milieu is alien to them, beyond their limits of possibility." B. M. Berger: *Working Class Suburb*, Berkeley, 1960, pp. 85 and 89.

[28] This is, of course, an extreme position. In fact, deviations from a purely materialistic interpretation of class structure are likely to occur in both an ascriptive and moralistic direction. Thus, the "rich" class may be seen as containing persons whose wealth is inherited and/or undeserved ("The idle rich"). Similarly, the "very poor" may be seen as containing persons who are lacking in ability and/or lacking in motivation to raise themselves ("poor character").

"middle class." Whether the end result of the change is seen as a "working class" or a "middle class," its identity is basically an economic one; people are assigned to this central class because they have roughly similar levels of income and possessions. Because the convergence of the "old" working and middle classes is seen in essentially economic terms, the designation of the new central class as "middle" or "working" would seem to be largely a matter of how the change is perceived as having taken place rather than an expression of status- or class-consciousness.[29] Indeed, the logic of a purely pecuniary model of society leads to neither class consciousness nor status consciousness but to commodity consciousness. Class and status models entail a perception of social groups whose boundaries are identifiable by acts of power and deference. But the pecuniary universe is one in which inequalities are not expressed through social relationships at all. Income and possessions may be the marks of persons, but unlike power and status they do not involve persons in relationships of inequality with one another. Inequalities take on an extrinsic and quantitative, rather than an intrinsic and qualitative form. In fact, compared with power and prestige, money is not inherently a divider of persons at all; it is a common denominator, of which one may have more or less without its thereby necessarily making a difference to the kind of person one is.

In so far as the privatised worker thinks in terms of the pecuniary model, he has, of course, a somewhat distorted view of the class structure. All available evidence indicates that the amount of informal social interaction between the lower middle and upper working classes is very small and that, in this sense at least, class boundaries are still quite distinct. The privatised worker's idea of a vast central class, differentiated only by marginal differences in income and possessions, is not, therefore, an accurate sociological picture. At the same time, it must be noted that the boundary between the middle and working classes is probably maintained as much by work and residential segregation as by personal exclusion. Thus, from this point of view, the mechanisms of class dissociation operate in a way which is not entirely incompatible with an image of a "de-socialized" class structure.

There is, finally, no suggestion that the pecuniary model of society is to be thought of as a direct product of working class affluence.[30] The

---

[29] If the pecuniary model of society appears to resemble the "sociology" of class that is frequently purveyed via mass media ("We're all middle class nowadays" or "We're all workers nowadays"), the reason for this may very well be that the privatised worker is more likely to be reached by mass communication and more readily influenced by its message. Because of his relative social isolation, he may be more exposed to impersonal influence; and, given his affluence and privatisation, the view that class differences are on the wane is a plausible one for him to maintain.

[30] Renate Mayntz, in her study of social class in Euskirchen, notes the

pecuniary model is an outcome of the social rather than the economic situation of the privatised worker; and he is only able to hold such a theory of society in so far as his social environment supports such an interpretation. His relative privatisation, his lack of a sense of class cohesion and his isolation from any system of hierarchical social status are the conditions under which he can view his society simply in pecuniary terms.

A purely pecuniary ideology is, of course, just as much of a limiting case as a purely class or purely status model of society. But it may be that it is at least as relevant as the other two in understanding the social and political outlook of the increasingly large section of the working class that is emerging from traditionalism.[31]

---

contrary tendency: for income models to increase in importance, the lower the income of the respondent, and suggests that this is so because at the lower levels "diese materielle Frage ein wichtiges, oft sorgenvolles Problem des taeglichen Lebens ist." *Soziale Schichtung und Sozialer Wandel in einer Industriegemeinde*, Stuttgart, 1958, p. 99. This essentially *ad hoc* explanation is not very convincing. In the absence of privatisation there is no sociological reason why privation any more than affluence should lead to a pecuniary model of society.

[31] The related concepts of *privatisation, instrumentalism,* and *pecuniary ideology* are merely intended to serve as points of reference for the study of the new working class. As such, they help to specify the conditions affecting the direction of working class politics, and yield the conclusion that this will take the form of "instrumental collectivism." Recently, Perry Anderson has argued that instrumental collectivism could be the basis for the development of a new "ideological collectivism" (a sort of Hegelian synthesis in which the rational elements of an otherwise apolitical instrumental collectivism combine with the radical elements of an otherwise parochial solidaristic collectivism). The major activating force of this new radicalism could in turn be a sense of relative deprivation arising from new aspirations for power and status. Thus, John Westergaard has suggested that working class radicalism could have its sources in workers' aspirations for middle class status in the community; and others, including Gorz and Mallet, see the work situation as the potential locus of a new radicalism stemming from workers' demands for "control" over production. However, in so far as the work and community *milieux* of the new working class generate "privatisation" and "instrumentalism," neither of these radicalizing aspirations is likely to emerge and to lead to ideological collectivism. On the contrary, since a privatised style of life is likely to create aspirations for higher consumption rather than for higher status, and since instrumentalism devalues work save as a means to higher consumption, the most probable form of radicalism is that which centres on immediate "shop-floor" demands for maximizing earnings; a form of radicalism in its way just as parochial, if not more so, than the solidaristic collectivism of the traditional worker. See *Towards Socialism, op. cit.,* pp. 108, 265, 317, *et seq.*

6   JOHN H. GOLDTHORPE, DAVID LOCKWOOD,
       FRANK BECHHOFER, AND JENNIFER PLATT

The Affluent Worker and the Thesis of
Embourgeoisement: Some Preliminary
Research Findings

The theme of "the affluent worker" is not new: it has been a recurrent
one from the earliest years of Western industrial society. It antedates, in
fact, the Marxian themes of "proletarianisation" and the growing im-
poverishment of the industrial labour force. For example, around the
year 1790, John Millar of Glasgow, one of the great Scots forerunners
of modern sociology, made the following observations on the society of
his day:

> When a country . . . is rapidly advancing in trade, the demand for
> labourers is proportionately great; their wages are continually rising,
> instead of soliciting employment, they are courted to accept of it;
> and they enjoy a degree of affluence and importance which is fre-
> quently productive of insolence and licentiousness.
>
> That the labouring people in Britain have, for some time, been
> raised to this enviable situation is evident from a variety of cir-
> cumstances, from the high price of labour; from the absurd attempt
> of the legislature to regulate their wages, and to prevent them from
> deserting particular employments; from the zeal displayed by the
> lower orders in the vindication of their political, as well as of their
> private rights; and, above all, from the jealousy and alarm with
> which this disposition has, of late, so universally impressed their
> superiors.[1]

Reprinted by permission of John H. Goldthorpe and The Clarendon Press
(Oxford) from Sociology, Volume I, January 1967.
John H. Goldthorpe was educated first in history at University College, London, then in sociology at the London School of Economics and Political Science.
He lectured at the University of Leicester, and is now at Cambridge University.
  [1] John Millar, "The Advancement of Manufactures, Commerce, and the Arts,
since the Reign of William III; and the Tendency of this Advancement to
diffuse a Spirit of Liberty and Independence," an essay appended to An Historical
View of the English Government from the Settlement of the Saxons in Britain to
the Revolution in 1688, London: Mawman, 1803.

This passage is of interest, and is quoted, not only because of its date. It is also significant because it provides the basic pattern for most subsequent discussion on the matter of the affluent worker. This pattern is as follows: First, reference is made to aspects of economic progress – in Millar's case, the rapid growth of trade and rising demand for labour – which are directly responsible for the spread of prosperity. Secondly, certain consequences of this affluence are postulated for workers' social consciousness and conduct – for Millar, increasing awareness of their social importance, the decline of deference, independence vis-a-vis employers, and so on. Then finally, these developments are in turn related to certain significant features of the current *political* situation – in 1790, the concern of the lower orders to claim political as well as civil rights. In other words, underlying Millar's observations there is a theory – which he in fact develops more explicitly elsewhere in his work[2] – of the primarily economic determination of political behaviour and institutions, with changes in the objective and subjective aspects of social stratification being seen as a crucial mediating process.

A broadly comparable theory is, of course, central to the work of Marx and Engels. Indeed Millar may well have been an important influence in the development of Marx's sociological thinking.[3] However, on the particular question of the affluent worker, the interesting point is that this theoretical affinity co-exists with a complete reversal of perspective. Millar, as we have seen, regarded the growing affluence of the labouring population as a threat to the established hierarchy of social ranks and to the political system associated with this. For Millar, the affluent worker was a potentially dynamic factor in a relatively stable social order. For Marx and Engels, on the other hand, the more prosperous stratum of the working class was an essentially conservative element, hindering the growth of true working-class consciousness and of a revolutionary working-class movement, and thus holding back the inevitable crisis of capitalist society.

Engels, in particular, gave a good deal of attention to this problem of working-class conservatism in his writings of the 1870s and 1880s.[4] In this

[2] See John Millar, *The Origin of the Distinction of Ranks*, London: Murray, 1779; *cf.* also W. C. Lehmann, *John Millar of Glasgow*, Cambridge University Press, 1960, Ch. XI esp.

[3] Cf. R. L. Meek, "The Scottish Contribution to Marxist Sociology" in John Saville (ed.), *Democracy and the Labour Movement; essays in honour of Dona Torr*, London: Lawrence and Wishart, 1954.

[4] See, in particular, "The English Elections," 1874 and "Trades Unions," 1881; *cf.* also Engels' letters to Marx, 7 October 1858; to Marx, 18 November 1868; to Kautsky 12 September 1882; to Kelley–Wischnewetzky, 10 February 1885; and to Sorge, 7 December 1889. All the above are reprinted in Karl Marx and Frederick Engels, *On Britain*, Moscow: Foreign Languages Publishing House, 1953.

he was activated chiefly by the failure of the industrial workers of Great Britain to exploit the new franchise of 1867 and to secure working-class dominance in Parliament. Engels' explanation of this failure emphasized the British worker's craving for "respectability" and enhanced social status which thus led to a willingness, indeed eagerness, to accept bourgeois social values, life-styles, and political ideas. But Engels then went on to argue further that this process of the *embourgeoisement* of the British working class had itself to be explained by reference to Britain's exceptional economic position in the mid-nineteenth century as the world's leading industrial nation. Only because of this national economic supremacy was it possible for the theory of working class "immiseration" to be controverted and for a sizeable section of the British labour force to enjoy living standards which were such as to encourage their bourgeois aspirations. In this way, then, in spite of their radically different standpoints, Engels' analysis is very similar to Millar's in its basic form. In their discussion of the affluent worker, both are ultimately interested in a certain political situation; and this they seek to understand in terms of the dynamics of social stratification, which they in turn relate to the secular trend of economic development.

From the end of the nineteenth century, a Marxian, or more accurately, a para-Marxian perspective on the question of the affluent worker has been the dominant one; that is to say, it has been generally argued (or assumed) that affluence is conducive to *embourgeoisement* which itself leads to political conservatism, or at any rate to political apathy, within the working class. During certain periods of labour unrest and socialistic fervour, such arguments may have been somewhat subdued; but, unfailingly, they have re-emerged with conditions of greater economic and political stability. However, one basically important development from the original Marxian position should be noted. With the decline in faith in the predictive aspects of Marx's thought, *embourgeoisement* has ceased to be regarded as a purely temporary process which would sooner or later be checked and reversed as part of the logic of the auto-destruction of the capitalist system. Rather, it has come to be seen as a permanent and progressive process which is inherent in the "affluent society" of the modern West and which reflects, in fact the logic of the long-term evolution of *industrialism*. The industrial society of the future, it has been claimed, will be an essentially "middle-class" society; as the age of scarcity gives way to the age of abundance, the idea of a working class with its own distinctive way of life, values, and goals is one which becomes increasingly obsolete.[5]

So far as Great Britain is concerned, this new version of the *em-*

[5] For a critical discussion of theories of this kind, see John H. Goldthorpe, "Social Stratification in Industrial Society" in P. Halmos (ed.), *The Development of Industrial Society*, Sociological Review Monographs, No. 8, Keele, 1964.

bourgeoisement thesis came to particular prominence in course of the last decade. The circumstances which lent it force are now part of the familiar history of these years and we need refer to them here only very briefly. Economically, the 1950s were characterized by a relatively rapid rise in living standards and, most significantly, by a marked growth in the number of "middle-range" incomes. This resulted in an increasing overlap, in terms of income, between those in white-collar and manual occupations; and, concomitantly, former differences in patterns of consumption were also much reduced as manual workers considerably increased their ownership of consumer durables and, in a growing number of cases, began to buy their own homes. Politically, these same years were ones of undisputed Conservative dominance. The three successive electoral victories of the Conservative party, with rising majorities, were without historical parallel, while the Labour vote showed ominous signs of secular decline. Moreover, there were indications that in the areas of the country which were economically most progressive, this fall in the Labour vote was due to some significant extent to loss of support from among the industrial working class, either through defections or through new voters failing to follow in the traditional pattern.

In these circumstances, then, it can scarcely be regarded as surprising that the thesis of the progressive *embourgeoisement* of the British working class should prove to be an attractive one. The argument that British society was becoming increasingly middle-class provided the obvious means of linking together the outstanding economic and political developments of the period. It was, in fact, an argument accepted by spokesman of both the right and left, by numerous journalists and social commentators, and by not a few political scientists and sociologists. However, the existence of this general consensus of opinion did not alter the fact — though it may have served to obscure it — that the thesis of "the worker turning middle-class" lacked any satisfactory validation. It remained merely as an assumption, or at best an inference, which it seemed reasonable to make in interpreting the socio-political situation in Britain at the end of the 1950s. Although the circumstantial evidence might be persuasive, very little *direct* evidence could be presented to support the specific proposition that manual workers and their families were in the process of being assimilated on a relatively large scale into middle-class ways of life and middle-class society.[6]

This situation may be regarded as the point of departure of the research project on which this paper gives a preliminary report. Primarily,

[6] For an elaboration of this argument, see David Lockwood, "The 'New Working Class,'" *European Journal of Sociology*, Tome I, 1960, No. 2, 248-259, and John H. Goldthorpe and David Lockwood, "Affluence and the British Class Structure," *Sociological Review*, Vol. XI (n.s), No. 2, July, 1963, 133-163.

the aim of the project was to investigate the thesis of working-class *embourgeoisement* in an empirical way, and with it the generally accepted view of the relationship between working-class affluence and working-class politics in contemporary British society. From the outset we felt, on theoretical grounds, that this view was a highly questionable one. Thus, in planning our project we decided to seek a *locale* for the field research which would be *as favourable as possible* for the validation of the arguments about which we were doubtful. In this way, we gave ourselves the possibility of providing a test of the *embourgeoisement* thesis which might be critical in the sense that if it were to be shown that a process of *embourgeoisement* was *not* in evidence in the case we studied, then there would be strong grounds for arguing that such a process was unlikely to be occurring to any significant extent within British society at large.

This strategy involved, therefore, first, an attempt to specify theoretically what a *locale* of the kind in question would be like; and then, secondly, discovering some adequate real-life approximation. These proved to be no easy matters. Eventually, though, it was decided that the town of Luton would come nearest to meeting our requirements, and for the following major reasons: (i) it was a prosperous and rapidly growing industrial centre in an area of the country now experiencing general economic expansion; (ii) in consequence of this, the town's labour force contained a high proportion of geographically mobile workers; (iii) also in consequence of the town's rapid growth, a high proportion of its population lived in relatively new housing areas; and (iv) the town was somewhat removed from the older industrial regions of the country and was thus not dominated by their traditions of industrial relations and of industrial life generally.[7]

We thus based our research primarily upon a sample of 229 manual workers drawn from the hourly-paid employees of three progressive manufacturing firms sited in Luton.[8] All these firms had advanced personnel and welfare policies and were noted for their good industrial relations records. Our sample was limited to men who were (i) between the ages of 21 and 46; (ii) married; (iii) earning regularly *at least* £17 per week (October 1962); and (iv) resident in the town of Luton itself or adjacent housing areas. The sample was also constructed so as to enable comparisons to be made between workers at different skill levels and involved in

---

[7] The theoretical basis for our choice of Luton will be given in full in our final report on the research. However, further relevant discussion of factors favourable to *embourgeoisement* can be found in David Lockwood and John H. Goldthorpe, "The Manual Worker: Affluence, Aspiration and Assimilation," paper presented to the Annual Meeting of the British Sociological Association, 1962.

[8] Vauxhall Motors Ltd; The Skefko Ball Bearing Co. Ltd; and Laporte Chemicals Ltd.

120GOLDTHORPE, LOCKWOOD, BECHHOFER, AND PLATT

different types of production system.[9] For further comparative purposes, we also took a sample of 54 lower-level white-collar workers based on two of the firms. The manual workers were interviewed twice; once at their place of work and then again, together with their wives, in their own homes. The white-collar workers were interviewed at home only.[10]

Our manual workers proved to have a broadly comparable range of incomes to the white-collar workers and also differed little from the latter in their ownership of various high-cost consumer goods and in house ownership. Other characteristics of the manual sample which should be noted were the following: (i) a majority (55 per cent) lived outside of typically working-class localities such as those in the centre of the town or the council estates; (ii) 71 per cent were not natives of Luton or of the Luton district; and (iii) only 13 per cent had ever had the experience of being unemployed for longer than a month. We would then claim that such a sample could be regarded as one that was reasonably appropriate to our purposes.[11]

We cannot here present anything like a full account of the findings of our research; for apart from obvious limitations of space, the analysis of our material is still incomplete. What we aim to do is to set out some general results which have a direct bearing on what we believe must be regarded as major elements in the *embourgeoisement* thesis. In an earlier paper distinctions were made between the economic, normative and relational dimensions of change in class structure;[12] and it is in terms of

[9] Three different skill levels were represented: 56 men were craftsmen (tool-makers, millwrights and other maintenance men from Skefko and Laporte); 23 were setters (from Skefko); and 150 were semi-skilled production workers. This latter category comprised men in jobs which were characteristic of the main type of production system operating in each of our three firms: viz. Vauxhall assemblers (86) Skefko machinists (41) and Laporte process workers (23). In effect, then, our sample was one of a population made up of men who met the criteria referred to above and who were employed in certain selected occupations in the three firms with which we were concerned. Caution must be exercised in regard to data relating to the sample as a whole in cases where there are marked differences between the occupational groups on which the sample is based; for in these cases "overall" figures will reflect the weight given to particular groups through variations in our sampling ratios. Where references are made in the text to the sample as a whole without qualification, it may be assumed that inter-occupational differences are not, so far as we can discover, of any great significance.
[10] The response rate for the manual workers (i.e. on the basis of the 229 agreeing to both interviews) was 70 per cent and for the white-collar workers, 72 per cent.
[11] We would emphasize the preliminary nature of all the findings reported in this paper. The detailed results of our research will be presented in monographs dealing with different aspects of the study — industrial, political etc. — and these monographs will then, it is hoped, provide the basis for a final report aiming at a *vue d'ensemble*.
[12] Goldthorpe and Lockwood, "Affluence and the British Class Structure," pp. 135-6. In general, the "Note on Concepts and Terminology" appended to

these that the following discussion proceeds. First, we shall be concerned with some basic features of the work situation of the men in our sample. This is a most important aspect of their class situation viewed in economic terms — although one which has tended to be neglected because attention has been focussed on "affluence" in the sphere of consumption. However, from our standpoint, it is not enough to know that certain manual workers can earn high incomes: what must also be known is under what conditions this affluence is achieved, and their human and social implications. Secondly, in regard to both the normative and relational aspects of class, we present data on the nature and extent of our workers' participation in community life; including data on the further vital but again often neglected question of the extent to which the manual-non-manual division in work continues to coincide with a major line of status-group demarcation. Then finally, and again under the normative heading, we concentrate on the political attitudes and behaviour of our sample. As we have already observed, political orientations have been the matter of ultimate interest in most discussions of "the affluent worker" thus far; and it is for this reason that they are singled out for special attention in this paper.

Employment and the Work Situation. An obvious but basic fact about the men in our sample is that they are "affluent" primarily because of their employment in large-scale, technologically advanced manufacturing enterprises. Their role as wage workers in such enterprises is indeed fundamental to the understanding of their entire social existence. On the one hand, it is through filling this role that they are able to achieve a level of income which makes a "middle-class" standard and style of living available to them. On the other hand, however, it can be shown that, as rank-and-file industrial employees, their typical life experiences and life chances are in several ways significantly different from those of most workers in distinctively "middle-class" occupations.

To begin with, it could be said that many of the workers with whom we were concerned appear to experience their work as little more than mere *labour*; that is, as an expenditure of effort which offers no reward in itself and which is motivated primarily by the extrinsic reward of payment. It is true that the men performing the more skilled jobs — toolmakers, millwrights, setters — could derive some degree of satisfaction directly from their work. But for the large number of those in the less skilled jobs — in particular, the machinists and assemblers — it was rather the case that their work, as experienced, involved various kinds of *deprivation*; for example, lack of variety, lack of challenge, lack of autonomy and often too relatively unpleasant physical conditions.

"Affluence and the British Class Structure" has been followed throughout the present text.

This situation was indicated by the answers we received to a number of questions in our interview schedule. For instance, of the machinists and assemblers, 60 per cent reported that they found their work monotonous, 84 per cent that it did not command their full attention, and 47 per cent that it was physically tiring. Moreover, we also asked our respondents in a quite general way: "Did you like any of your other [i.e. previous] jobs more than the one you have now?" In the case of the machinists and assemblers 62 per cent said that they had, as too did 47 per cent of the more skilled men and 44 per cent of the process workers. And the reasons given revealed that overwhelmingly these men assessed previous jobs as being preferable on the grounds of the greater *intrinsic* rewards which they had offered when compared with their present work or, at any rate, because the deprivations they had entailed were less severe. The kinds of jobs most frequently referred to in this respect were either ones at a higher skill or status level than the individual's present work, or jobs in agriculture, transport, services, and other forms of employment which do not usually involve the physiological or psychological rigours of mass-production industry. Over a quarter of the more skilled workers and over three-quarters of the semi-skilled men had held jobs in one or the other of these two categories at some earlier time in their working lives.

The implication of these findings is, then, that for a sizeable proportion of the workers in our sample, their attachment to their present employment is mainly of a pecuniary kind. In other words, it would appear that these men have in some way arrived at a decision to abandon work which could offer them some greater degree of immediate satisfaction in order to take a job which enables them to gain a higher level of monetary reward. Confirmation that such an instrumental view of work was in fact the prevalent one, within all groups in the sample, was provided by the answers we received to a further question of a more direct kind. After enquiring of our respondents if they had ever seriously thought of leaving the firms for which they now worked — just under half said they had — we went on to ask: "What is it, then, that keeps you here?" From the replies which were made, it was clear that by far the most important consideration was the high level of pay which could be earned. This was mentioned by 65 per cent of the more skilled men and by 69 per cent of the semi-skilled workers. Moreover, of the latter 1 in 4 (24 per cent) stated that "the money" was the *only* reason why they remained in their present employment.[13] By contrast, less than 1 in 3 (29 per cent) of the

[13] The factor next most frequently referred to — by 47 per cent of the more skilled men and 33 per cent of the semi-skilled — was that of security; and in many cases it was made clear that the main concern here was with long-run income maximization rather than with the minimum requirement of having a job of some kind. Also worth noting is the fact that those men who said they *had* thought of leaving gave reasons for this in preponderantly *non*-economic terms; less than 1 in 12 (7 per cent) referred to any dissatisfaction with pay. On the

skilled men and only 1 in 7 (14 per cent) of the semi-skilled made any mention of staying in their present job because they liked the work they did.

When this same question was put to the men in our white-collar sample, a significantly different pattern of response was produced. Only two men out of the 54 said that they stayed in their present jobs simply because of the level of pay, and only 30 per cent made any reference to pay at all. On the other hand, liking the work they did was the reason which was most frequently mentioned, being given by 2 white-collar workers out of 5 (39 per cent).[14]

It would appear, then, that for many of the affluent workers we studied, affluence has been achieved only at the cost of having to accept work as an activity largely devoid of immediate reward – as an activity which is chiefly a means to the end of a high level of income and consumer power. In this respect, the more skilled men may be regarded as fortunate in being able to find high-paying jobs which can also offer some opportunity for fulfilling more expressive needs – even though they too, it would seem, still view their work in a largely instrumental way. For the men lacking in skills – or, more accurately, skills in high demand – the road to affluence has often been a much harder one. Most commonly, on our evidence, it has meant taking and holding down jobs which offer higher pay than do most other types of manual work *because of* their inherent strains and deprivations. In this way, therefore, a "middle-class" standard of income and consumption has been brought within reach; but only through a kind of work which is not typically part of white-collar experience.[15]

Moreover, it may also be observed that the nature of the work they perform is not the only cost of affluence to the men in our sample: the amount of work they do and when they do it are also important considerations. Even with the relatively high rates of pay which they enjoyed, the workers we studied could rarely earn wage packets of upwards of £20 for a normal week's work. For the majority, overtime formed a regular part of their employment and was an essential element in their high standard of living. During the period, in which our interviews were being carried out, we estimate that the men in our sample were averaging around 5½ hours overtime per week. This would imply an average work-

---

other hand, in the reasons given by semi-skilled men, the nature of their work and working conditions figured more prominently than any other source of discontent.

[14] Of the 35 white-collar workers who had thought of leaving, poor pay was given a reason by 9 (26 per cent) and together with the desire for wider job experience was the reason most often mentioned.

[15] For a more detailed discussion of the working lives of the assemblers in our sample, see John H. Goldthorpe, "Attitudes and Behaviour of Car Assembly Workers: a deviant case and a theoretical critique," *British Journal of Sociology*.

ing week of from 48 to 50 hours. Furthermore, three-quarters of those in our sample were also permanently on shift work, which is, of course, an increasingly common aspect of employment in modern capital-intensive plants. The majority of the men on shifts were required to do regular periods of night work, while the remainder were on some kind of double day-shift system. In this latter group, those who were favourably disposed towards shift work and those who disliked it were roughly equal in number. But among the men who had to work "nights," unfavourable attitudes were twice as frequent as favourable ones. The most common complaints of these men were to the effect that night working impaired their physical or psychological well-being, that it led to the disruption of family living, and that it interfered with their leisure and "social" pursuits.

Systematic overtime and shift working must then be seen as an integral part of the way of life of most of the affluent workers we studied. Not only are these characteristic features of their employment, but they also have consequences for workers' activities outside the factory — consequences of a constraining kind. Moreover, in the particular form in which our workers experience them, such constraints could not be said to figure prominently in the social life of those in white-collar occupations.

Finally, on the theme of employment, there is one other way in which the manual workers with whom we are concerned remain significantly differentiated from most varieties of white-collar man. This is in terms of their chances of advancement — of making a career — within the enterprise in which they work. In general, opportunities for rising from the ranks, whether of manual or non-manual employees, are known to be contracting in most kinds of business organization. But still, the prospects for office workers, technicians, sales personnel, and so on are appreciably better than are those for men on the shop floor. For the latter, even where their firms follow policies of "promotion from within" — as our Luton firms attempted to do — the chances of being promoted must inevitably be slight, if only because of the small number of openings which exist in relation to the large number of possible candidates.

Among the manual workers we studied, the fact that advancement within the enterprise was unlikely was fairly well recognized. In reply to a question on our interview schedule, only two men out of our sample of 229 were prepared to rate their chances of promotion even to foreman level as being "very good"; 37 per cent of the skilled men and 30 per cent of the semi-skilled thought their chances in this respect were "fairly good," but 37 per cent of the former group and 41 per cent of the latter felt they were "not too good" and 19 per cent and 25 per cent respectively regarded the position as being "hopeless."[16] We also put the following

---

[16] We asked: "One way a worker might improve his position is by getting promotion, say, to a foreman's job. If you decided to have a go at this how would you rate your chances of getting to be a foreman? Would you say they

question to our respondents: "If a worker of ability really put his mind to it, how far up this firm do you think he could get in the end?" The answers we received were clearly influenced by the different "myths and legends" of the three firms from which our workers came; but overall less than half (45 per cent) believed that such a man would achieve managerial level; 40 per cent thought he would reach a supervisory grade, and most of the remainder (13 per cent) said that he would get nowhere at all.

When comparable questions were put to our white-collar sample, a notably different picture emerged: 63 per cent believed that their chances of promotion to the next highest grade were "very good" or "fairly good," as against 37 per cent having more pessimistic views; and similarly, 65 per cent of the sample believed that a rank-and-file white-collar worker with ability and determination would be able to make his way into a managerial position.

These varying assessments of chances of promotion are not only significant in reflecting, as they do, differences in objective life situations: they are important also in the way in which they are associated with marked differences in the entire pattern of aspirations between the two occupational groups in question. For example, among the white-collar workers the greater optimism about promotion coexists with a general desire to achieve advancement within the firm. When asked how they would like the idea of promotion, 87 per cent of the white-collar workers responded positively. By contrast, when the manual workers were asked how they would like the idea of being made a foreman, a positive response was forthcoming from 62 per cent of the more skilled men and from only 43 per cent of the semi-skilled.[17] On the other hand, though, one alternative means of "getting ahead" had more often been hopefully thought about by the manual workers: nearly two-fifths of the latter (37 per cent) as opposed to one fifth of the white-collar sample (19 per cent) had seriously considered starting up in business on their own account; and in fact there were 28 men in the manual sample (12 per cent) who were actually trying to do this at the time or who had tried in the past.

However, undoubtedly the greatest difference of all in this respect lies in the fact that for manual wage workers — whether affluent or not — the main hope for the future cannot be in "getting ahead" in any of the more usual "middle-class" senses. Rather, it must rest in the pro-

---

were very good, fairly good, not too good or hopeless?" There were 4 "Don't knows."

[17] The white-collar workers were asked: "What about the idea of promotion? Would you like this very much, quite a lot, not very much, not at all?" The manual workers were asked: "How about the idea of becoming a foreman? Would you like this very much, quite a lot, not much, not at all?"

gressive increase of the rewards which they gain *from their present economic role*. Individually, they can certainly help to realize this by being occupationally and geographically mobile — by being prepared to "follow the money." And it was clearly in this way that many of the men in our sample had achieved their affluent condition. But even then, to a greater extent than with most white-collar employees, in industry at least, the economic future of these workers still remains dependent upon *collective* means; that is to say, upon trade-union representation and trade-union power.

In this latter connection, two basic points may be anticipated from the fuller treatment of unionism among our affluent workers which we shall present elsewhere. First, our research provides no indication that affluence diminishes the degree of workers' attachment to unionism — although it may well be important in changing the meaning of this adherence. The factories with which we were concerned were, in effect, quite valuable recruiting grounds for the unions in that they attracted a high proportion of workers who were not union members but who subsequently became enrolled; 38 per cent of the men in our sample had become unionists only after taking up their present employment. Secondly, while the large majority of the workers we studied could not be said to be men committed to their union as part of a great socio-political movement or even as a "fraternity," they nonetheless recognized well enough the practical importance of the union and of union strength in regard to the day-to-day issues of industrial relations — and at shop and factory levels in particular. In brief, one could say that for most of the men in question a union was, at least, an organization to which, as wage workers, it paid them to belong; it had definite instrumental value. The fact that the same could now also be said of an increasing number of non-manual employees, notably in commerce and administration, cannot be denied. But this, of course is not so much evidence of *embourgeoisement* as of a reverse process in which the work situation of many white-collar employees is becoming in various ways closer to that of their blue-collar counterparts.

Community Life. As we have already noted, the majority of our sample of affluent workers were not natives of Luton. They were, rather, men who had migrated to the town during the last two decades in search chiefly of higher wages and better housing. We have also observed that more than half now live in areas which could not be described as typically working-class. This is closely associated with the fact that a similar proportion (57 per cent) own or are buying their homes. These characteristics of the sample are then perhaps sufficient in themselves to indicate that many of the men we studied do not share in what is thought of as the "traditional" pattern of community life among urban industrial workers and their families; that is, a pattern based upon residential stability and social homogeneity in which kinship and various forms of communal sociability play a dominant part.[18]

On the matter of kinship, this conclusion can be supported more directly by other of our data. For example, as a result of their geographical mobility, a high proportion of the men in our sample had become physically separated from their kin to a degree which made day-to-day contact impossible — and so too had many of their wives. Thus, of those who still had parents alive, only 13 per cent of the men and 18 per cent of the wives had parents living within ten minutes' walk of themselves; and in the case of 56 per cent of the men and 48 per cent of their wives, their parents were all living entirely outside the Luton area. The degree of separation from siblings was slightly less marked, since sometimes they too had moved to Luton. But, even so, only 36 per cent of the couples we studied had a majority of their closer kin (parents, siblings, and in-laws) living in the Luton area. The remaining couples were almost equally divided between those with the majority of their kin living within a 50-mile radius of Luton and those whose kin were for the most part yet further afield.

Given, then, that many of the couples we studied were not members of largely kin-based communities of the traditional working-class kind, the question arises of whether this situation was associated with any shift towards patterns of community life which were more typically middle-class and at the same time with any substantial degree of social mixing with recognizable middle-class persons. For if *embourgeoisement* is a likely concomitant of working-class affluence, then one would expect that middle-class life styles and society would be most readily sought after among those manual workers who, as well as being affluent, have also been freed from the social controls of an established working-class community and, in particular, from the essentially conservative influence of the extended family. The findings of our research which bear on this point are, in detailed form, rather complex: nonetheless, in general terms they are clear enough and they tend to give little support to the thesis of *embourgeoisement*, at least in the crude form in which it has usually been advanced.

The first point to be made is that in spite of the limits set by physical distance, kin were still relatively prominent in the social lives of the couples we studied. As might be expected, for those couples whose closer kin were for the most part in the Luton area, social contacts with kin were far more frequent than those with persons in any other comparable

---

[18] For a useful survey of the research on the basis of which some generalized picture of the "traditional" working class way of life may be formed, see Josephine Klein, *Samples from English Cultures*, London: Routledge and Kegan Paul, 1965, Vol. I, ch. 4.

category, such as neighbours, workmates, or other friends. However, even in the case of the other couples — almost two-thirds of the sample — whose kin were mostly outside of Luton, the part which kin played in their social lives was far from negligible. For example, we asked our respondents, both husband and wife: "Who would you say are the two or three people that you most often spend your spare time with [apart from spouse and children]?" For those couples whose kin were largely in the area, kin made up 41 per cent of the persons named; but still with the remaining couples, 22 per cent of those mentioned were kin none-theless. Similarly, when we asked wives about the persons they had visited, or had been visited by, during the past week, kin accounted for 52 per cent of the total for wives in the former group but still for 20 per cent for those in the latter. In the case of those couples who were largely separated from their kin, these findings would, then, suggest one or both of two things: first, that the few kin which these couples had in the Luton area tended to be seen quite often and, second, that fairly close contact was kept with other kin regardless of their distance.[19]

However, what is perhaps of greatest significance about the couples in question is the way in which their relative isolation from kin is compensated for. Primarily, it would seem, the place of the absent kin is taken not by friends chosen from among the community at large but, rather, by *neighbours*, roughly defined as persons living within ten minutes' walk. For instance, in answer to the question on the two or three people with whom spare time was most often spent, neighbours represented 47 per cent of those mentioned but other friends only 12 per cent.[20] Again, on the question of wives' visiting and visitors, neighbours accounted for 54 per cent of those involved and other friends for only 26 per cent. In this connection, a comparison with the white-collar sample is instructive. The white-collar couples, being less mobile, were somewhat less likely to be separated from their kin than the manual sample as a whole; and kin were a clearly more important element in their pattern of sociability than in that of the manual couples who had moved away from the centres of their kinship networks. But the further interesting difference between these two groups was that the white-collar couples, *in spite of* their greater amount of contact with kin,[21] *also* had far more contact with

[19] Even in the case of the third of the sample the majority of whose kin were located more than 50 miles from Luton, the proportion of kin among the persons with whom spare time was most often spent remained at 22 per cent, and kin also accounted for 16 per cent of the wives' visiting partners.

[20] The remaining 19 per cent (after adding in the 22 per cent who were kin) were workmates or ex-workmates. The "neighbours" category includes "ex-neighbours"; i.e. persons whom the respondents first came to know when they were living within ten minutes' walk.

[21] Kin accounted for 31 per cent of the persons with whom the white-collar

friends who were not neighbours or workmates. Thus, of the persons with whom the white-collar couples spare time was mostly spent, 29 per cent were friends of this kind, and such friends also accounted for 31 per cent of the persons the white-collar wives visited or were visited by.[22]

What this suggests to us is, then, that among the affluent workers we studied, middle-class norms had, as yet at least, only a very limited influence on patterns of sociability. In cases where kinship could not provide the basis of social life, these workers and their wives appeared to turn most readily for support and companionship to those persons who, as it were, formed the next circle of immediate acquaintance — that is, persons living in the same neighbourhood. Making numbers of friends from among people with whom their relationships were not in some degree "given," in the way that relationships with kin and neighbours are, was still not a highly characteristic feature of their way of life. Compared with the white-collar couples, they were apparently lacking in motivation, and probably also in the requisite skills, for this kind of social exercise.[23]

One further finding from our interviews supports this interpretation. It is a typical feature of middle-class social life that couples entertain each other in their own homes. We therefore asked our respondents how often they had other couples round and who were the people who regularly came. Briefly, what emerged was that the couples in the manual sample did not entertain at home anything like so frequently as did the white-collar couples and, further, that they were more likely to confine such entertaining to their kin. Workmates and neighbours, as well as other friends were all less often invited than in the case of the white-collar couples.[24] In other words, it would seem that among our affluent workers

couples reported most often spending their spare time, and for 28 per cent of the wives' visiting partners.

[22] As against 15 per cent and 41 per cent respectively who were neighbours. The remaining persons mentioned by the white-collar couples as leisure time companions were workmates.

[23] In regard to the comparisons which we have made both between the white-collar couples and the manual couples who are largely separated from their kin and between the latter group and the other manual couples, it should be noted that no great differences occur in the actual *numbers* of persons mentioned either as leisure time companions or as wives' visiting partners. Thus, to think in terms of the "substitution" of neighbours (rather than of other friends) for absent kin would appear appropriate.

[24] The questions asked were: "How about having other couples round, say for a meal, or just for the evening: how often would you say you do this, on average?" and then "Who is it you have round — are they friends, relatives or who?" 15 per cent of the manual sample as against 7 per cent of the white-collar sample said that they never had couples round, and 54 per cent as against 76 per cent said they entertained in this way once a month or more. Of the couples entertained by the manual workers, 57 per cent were kin compared with 45 per cent in the case of white-collar workers.

middle-class styles of sociability remain less influential than the "traditional" working-class belief that the home is a place reserved for kin and for very "particular" friends alone.

Finally, there is the question of how far our affluent workers and their wives were actually involved in what might be regarded as middle-class society. To what extent did white-collar persons figure in their social lives? In this respect, the interpretation of our findings is not very difficult. They point fairly clearly to a considerable degree of status segregation. For example, to revert to our question on persons with whom spare time was mostly spent, 75 per cent of those named by couples in the manual sample were also manual workers and their wives, and only 17 per cent were persons of clearly higher status in occupational terms. Moreover, of the latter, 29 per cent turn out to be kin. We can in fact say that 20 per cent of the couples in our sample find their chief companions entirely among their kin and a further 47 per cent entirely among kin or persons of similar occupational status. On the other hand, only a very small minority — about 7 per cent of the sample — appear to associate predominantly with unambiguously middle-class people.

A similar picture also emerges if we turn from informal relationships to examine participation in formal organizations. Such participation was not at a high level among our affluent workers or their wives, and was significantly lower than in the white-collar sample. For the men, the average number of organizations belonged to (not counting trade unions) worked out at less than 1.5 and for the wives was as low as 0.5. However, more relevant than their number for present purposes was the character of these organizations; they were not of a kind likely to lead to association with middle-class people, or at least not in any intimate way. Predominantly, they were ones either almost entirely working-class in membership — such as working-men's clubs, angling or allotment societies — or, if more mixed in their social composition, organizations which had some fairly specific purpose — religious, charitable, sporting etc. — and a well defined internal hierarchy. What was largely lacking among couples in the sample was participation in organizations with some middle-class membership but with primarily diffuse, "social" functions — such as, say, drinking or recreational clubs — or participation in organizations of any kind in which other manual workers and their wives were not in a large majority.

In general, then, one may say that there is little indication that the affluent workers we studied are in process of being assimilated into middle-class society. Nor, in the great majority of cases, do they even appear to see in this a style to be emulated. On our evidence there is thus little need, and little basis, for the hypothesis that non-traditional norms and status aspirations accompany these workers' enjoyment of a relatively high standard of living. Furthermore, the small number of cases where some degree of *embourgeoisement* does appear to be in train suggests that many other factors are involved here apart from that of affluence itself. For the most part, those ways in which the social lives of the men and women in our sample do most obviously diverge from a more traditional working-class pattern are, in our view, largely to be explained as the consequences of job and residential mobility, and also perhaps of the constraints imposed by overtime and shift working; that is, as the consequences of certain objective conditions of their relatively prosperous existence to which these workers and their wives have been obliged to adapt. And the *direction* of these changes, we would suggest, is not towards "middle-classness," but rather towards what might be termed a more "privatized" mode of living.[25] In contrast with the communal and often kin-based sociability of the traditional working-class locality, the characteristic way of life among the couples we studied would appear to be one far more centred on the home and the immediate family; a way of life in which kin and neighbours, although still relatively important, figure in a more selective and limited way, and in which friends and acquaintances in the middle-class style do not, as yet at least, play any major part.[26]

Political Orientations. It was not the aim of our research to provide a direct test of the argument that growing affluence and the process of *embourgeoisement* were causing national, secular decline in the Labour Party's electoral support among the working class. For this purpose, a very different kind of research design would have been required. With our relatively small sample of affluent workers, we sought not simply to discover the pattern of their voting behaviour but also to set this in its socio-economic context and to form some idea of the *meaning* which party support held for our respondents. However, in presenting our findings in this section some straightforward voting figures are a necessary starting-point and are in themselves not without interest.

At the General Election of 1959, 212 out of our sample of 229 were eligible to vote. Of these 212, 71 per cent reported voting Labour as against 15 per cent Conservative and 3 per cent Liberal, with the remainder abstaining. Some variations in voting occurred between the different occupational groups within our sample, and thus this overall

[25] Cf. Goldthorpe and Lockwood, "Affluence and the British Class Structure," pp. 150-155.

[26] As evidence of the degree of "privatization" within the sample it may be noted that on the question of the two or three people with whom spare time was most often spent, 7 per cent of the couples could not mention even one person in this connection and 21 per cent only mention one between them. The average number referred to husband and wife *together* was under three. Again in the case of visits made by and to the wives, the range of persons involved appears much narrower than that suggested in most studies of the "traditional" worker. Only 3 per cent of the wives mentioned seeing more than 6 people in this way during the past week, and 51 per cent mentioned only one person or none at all.

pattern to some degree reflects decisions made in constructing the sample.[27] Nonetheless, even allowing for this and for the fact that our respondents were males in the younger age groups, there can be little doubt on these figures that their level of Labour voting was, to say the very least, not lower than that which has been indicated for manual workers generally on the basis of national surveys;[28] and this, it may be remarked, was at the election in which the effects of working-class affluence were supposed to have told most heavily against the Labour Party. In fact, our data show that to a very large extent our affluent workers have been quite stable in their support of Labour: 69 per cent have been regular Labour voters from 1945 onwards or from whenever they first voted as opposed to 12 per cent being regular Conservative supporters. Moreover, among the remainder – the uncommitted or "switchers" – there was no trend whatsoever towards greater Conservative voting in course of the 1950s. Finally when our respondents were asked how they intended to vote at the forthcoming general election (1964), the division between the two main parties was again 69 per cent Labour, 12 per cent Conservative. Thus, while the data we are able to produce from our sample may be insufficient in themselves to refute conclusively the thesis which links working-class affluence with a political shift to the right, they are at all events conspicuously at odds with this and show, at least, that such a shift certainly does not occur in any necessary and automatic way.

Furthermore, that no simple relationship exists between affluence and vote is also indicated by our more detailed analyses. It is true that within our sample there is a tendency for the degree of Conservative voting to rise slightly with the level of both the husband's and the family's income. Again, the percentage of Conservative voters in the 1959 election was higher among those who reported that their standard of living had risen during the last ten years than it was among those who reported no such rise. However, in both of these cases, it turns out that the relationship in question is much reduced – and sometimes even eliminated – if one holds constant various other factors to which we shall shortly turn. The same limitation, it may be added, also applies to the relationship between Conservative voting and house ownership to which several writers have attached particular significance.[29] And moreover, in this case, the association was not in fact a particularly stable one: 15 per

[27] The Labour vote in the five main occupational groups was as follows: craftsmen, 76 per cent; setters, 52 per cent; process workers, 77 per cent; machinists, 76 per cent; assemblers 68 per cent. Similar variation occurs in all other voting data referred to subsequently.

[28] See, for example, the data presented in Robert R. Alford, *Party and Society*, London: John Murray, 1963, ch. 6 and Appendix B.

[29] See, for example, Mark Abrams *et al.*, *Must Labour Lose?*, London: Penguin Books, 1960, pp. 42-43.

cent of the present owner-occupiers in our sample had been regular Conservative voters as against 7 per cent of those who were not owner-occupiers; but only 12 per cent of the former group compared with 11 per cent of the latter were intending to vote Conservative at the next election.

It would then seem fairly clear that the voting patterns of the workers we studied cannot be satisfactorily explained as any kind of straightforward reaction to their affluent condition. The evidence cannot be made to fit such an interpretation. Instead, our findings would suggest a view which, sociologically, makes far more sense. It is that in seeking to understand the voting behaviour of the men in our sample, major emphasis must be placed not on variables relating to their income, possessions, or standard of living generally, but rather on the similarities and differences in their social experiences and social relationships within the main milieux of their daily existence. In other words, one must not jump directly from economic circumstances to political action but should focus one's attention, rather, on the social reality which lies, as it were, behind these circumstances and which at the same time makes the political action meaningful.

Consider, for example, the salient fact that, notwithstanding their affluence, the percentage of men in our sample voting Labour is, if anything, higher than one would expect on the basis of national survey data. In the explanation of this, we would suggest, the most relevant considerations include the following: (i) that the men in question are all manual wage workers employed in large-scale industrial enterprises; (ii) that, as such, they are mostly members of trade unions;[30] (iii) that, in the vast majority of cases (96 per cent), they have been manual wage workers of one kind or another for most of their working lives; and (iv) that, again in the majority of cases, they were brought up in working-class families (68 per cent) and have married the daughters of such families (63 per cent). Given, then, the typical pattern of past experience and prevailing social relationships which these characteristics imply — and which affluence can scarcely affect — a high Labour vote is no longer very surprising. We can understand it as resulting from a complex of mutually reinforcing traditions and group pressures, exercising their influence at work, in the family and in the local community.

This interpretation, moreover, can be extended and confirmed if we now turn again to the Conservative minority. Our data reveal, as would be predicted, that these Conservative supporters, apart of course from all being wage workers, do not share to the same extent as the rest of the sample the working-class characteristics which have just been set out. Most notably, they are more likely than the Labour voters to be men

[30] Overall, 87 per cent of the sample were union members. All the setters and machinists belonged to a union and so too did 88 per cent of the craftsmen, 78 per cent of the process workers and 79 per cent of the assemblers.

who have remained outside the union movement (22 per cent against 11 per cent) or who have become union members only in course of their present employment (67 per cent against 39 per cent); and they would also appear generally more likely to have some connection in one way or another with white-collar society — through coming from a white-collar family or having married into such a family, through having held a white-collar job or having a wife with such a job.[31] It is, then, factors such as these which can modify — sometimes considerably — the relationship between Conservative voting and the economic variables to which we earlier referred. For example, of the non-unionists in the sample, 20 per cent intended voting Conservative in 1964 as compared with only 11 per cent of the union members; and within these two categories no association between income and vote is any longer apparent. Similarly, if we divide up the sample according to the degree of individuals' "white-collar affiliation," we find that 21 per cent of those in the "high" group are intending Conservative voters as against 10 per cent in the "intermediate" group and only 7 per cent in the "low" group.[32] And once more, income level appears to have no effect on vote when this further factor is held constant. In these ways too, therefore, it becomes evident that the link between affluence and vote is, at most, an indirect and uncertain one. The Conservative voters in our sample illustrate this point no less than the affluent supporters of Labour.

Finally in this section, we turn from the social correlates of party choice to a consideration of the voting behaviour of our respondents from their own point of view. In our interviews, we asked all those who had formed a fairly stable attachment to a party the reason for this; and the analysis of replies we received, in the case of the Labour majority in particular, is an important supplement to the foregoing discussion.

To begin with, the emphasis which we previously gave to certain class characteristics in understanding the high Labour vote in our sample is quite strongly confirmed by Labour supporters' own explanation of their position. By far the most frequent kind of reason given for an attachment to the Labour Party was one phrased in terms of class and of class and family custom: the Labour Party was the party which "stands for the working class," which "looks after ordinary working people like us" or, simply, the party which "working-class people vote for." In fact, 70

[31] Of the Conservative voters, 45 per cent had white-collar connections in at least two of these ways — through both their parents or parents-in-law and through their own or their wives' occupational experience. The corresponding figure for the Labour voters was 23 per cent. (These figures and those in the text relate to intended vote, 1964.)

[32] The "high" group comprized men with white-collar connections through both their parents or parents-in-law and through their own or their wives' occupational experience; those in the "intermediate" group had connections in one or other of these ways; and those in the "low" group had no such connections.

per cent of the 147 regular Labour supporters supplied answers giving reasons in this vein. In this way, therefore, these men would appear to differ little from the mass of Labour voters in the country as a whole. Abrams, for example, has reported on the basis of a national survey, carried out in 1960, that Labour is regarded by the large majority of its adherents as being an essentially "class" party.[33] To this extent, then, there is again evidence that affluence has, in itself, done little as yet to erode the class basis of Labour support.

At the same time, though, it is worth noting that the only other kind of explanation which Labour voters at all frequently provided was one which indicated an attachment to the party of a somewhat less affective and more calculative nature. Just under a quarter (24 per cent) gave reasons for their support in terms of particular material advantages which they expected to gain from certain aspects of Labour's policy — in relation, for instance, to social services or the management of the economy. Such a position is not, of course, in any way inconsistent with a sharp awareness of "class" interests: nonetheless, where an outlook of this kind prevails, the tie to the Labour Party is one which could quite conceivably be broken — even if only temporarily — given circumstances which make Conservative policy appear the more attractive in economic terms. And there are other data from our interviews which suggest this same possibility.[34]

However, it should be added here that it was among the Conservative voters that calculative attitudes of the sort in question were most strongly in evidence. Exactly half of the 24 "stable" Conservative voters stated that they supported this party because they believed that they personally were better off economically under Conservative government or because they felt that the Conservatives had the better men and policies for creating general prosperity. On the other hand, instances of a more traditionalistic attachment to the Conservatives of a "deferential" kind were rare; and more relevantly from the point of view of the *embourgeoisement* thesis, we were able to find no evidence at all of the "socially aspiring" Conservative — that is, of the manual worker who votes Conservative because of the higher status which he feels this action serves to symbolize. In this connection, it should be remembered that the Conservative supporters in our sample, to a greater extent than the Labour voters, were likely to be cross-pressured — with white-collar

[33] Op. cit., pp. 12-14.

[34] For example, in reply to a question on whether it would make any difference which party won the next election, a third of the intending Labour voters felt that it would not. And when attention was in this way directed to proximate and current issues, even those who felt that the election result would make a difference tended to see this largely in terms of social welfare and other economic "pay-offs" which they might expect from a Labour victory, rather than in terms of "the working class in power" or the implementation of socialist ideas.

relationships and experience set in opposition to their present role and status as industrial workers. In their case, thus, a largely instrumental view of politics is perhaps to be more expected than any tendency to regard party choice as an attribute of class or status group membership.

Our conclusion to this last section may, we believe, usefully serve as our conclusion to this paper as a whole. The point emerging from the foregoing discussion which carries most general significance is, in our view, the following: that the dynamics of working-class politics cannot be regarded as forming part of any inexorable process of social change deriving from continually rising standards of living. Certainly, the sequence, assumed in much previous discussion, of affluence – *embourgeoisement* – Conservative voting is generally unsupported by our findings. The acquisition by manual workers and their families of relatively high incomes and living standards does not, on our evidence, lead to widespread changes in their social values and life-styles in the direction of "middle-classness"; neither would it appear to be conducive to a political shift to the right, or in any way incompatible with a continuing high level of support for Labour. "Middle-classness" is not, after all, simply a matter of money; and politics has never been reducible to a mere epiphenomenon of economic conditions. The position of a group within a system of social stratification is not decisively determined by the income or possessions of its members, but rather by their characteristic life-chances and experiences and by the nature of their relationships with other groups. And it is in this context that their politics must be understood – a context which changes much more slowly than the relative levels of wages and salaries or patterns of consumption.

Our affluent workers remain, in spite of their affluence, men who live by selling their labour power to their employers in return for wages; and, in all probability, they will still be so at the end of their working days. Again, although they and their families enjoy a standard of living comparable to that of many white-collar families, their social worlds are still to a large extent separate from those of the latter, except where bridges of kinship, or to a lesser degree of neighbourhood, can span the social distance between them. Nor is there much indication that affluence has encouraged the desire to *seek* acceptance in new social milieux at higher status levels. Thus, we would suggest, there is, as yet at least, little basis for expecting any particular change in the political attitudes and behaviour of these workers, apart perhaps from the spread of the more calculative – more rational – outlook to which we have referred.

We do not, of course, seek in this way to rule out the possibility that at some future date, when working-class affluence is more general and of longer standing, it may prove to have political implications of major importance. But in this case, we would argue, what still remains entirely uncertain is what these implications will be. The assumption that they will necessarily favour the Right, and social and political stability, has no firm basis: it may equally well be that by 1990 a latter-day John Millar will be again invoking the affluent worker as the source of social dissent and of political radicalism.

7   JEAN FLOUD

Social-Class Factors in Educational Achievement

The aptitudes and abilities of individuals are rarely specific, so that as long as there is equality of educational opportunity and freedom of vocational choice and of movement between occupations, they may be expected to find their way into positions which will stretch their capacities and enable them to make their maximum contribution to the needs of society. It is true that freedom of movement is one thing and getting the right person into the right place another; but the former is a precondition of the latter. The best contribution that the educational system can make to the economic problem is to send forward recruits to the labour force, potentially mobile, with or without further education as may be necessary, within the widest possible range of occupations, whether by guidance, direction, or merely in response to the prevailing pattern of economic incentive.

To state the problem thus abstractly is to understate the difficulties. It is safe to say that the greater the degree of industrialisation, the more are young people limited in their choice of employment by their educational attainments and the more difficult is it for adults to move outside the range of occupations for which their formal educational attainments

Reprinted by permission of the author from A. H. Halsey, ed., *Ability and Educational Opportunity* (Paris: Organisation for Economic Co-operation and Development, 1961), pp. 34-37, 93-107.
Jean Floud, educated in London, was associated with the pioneering mobility research guided by D. V. Glass, and has become a specialist in the sociology of education. Mrs. Floud is now at Nuffield College, Oxford University.

equip them. Quite apart, therefore, from the primary difficulty of ensuring that ability translates itself into the appropriate educational achievement, it is important to devise educational arrangements which will not gratuitously reinforce this endemic tendency to rigidity in the supply of labour in a modern economy.

We may begin with the fundamental problem, which we may express in this way: how may differences in educational performance be reduced to differences of natural endowment? Some pupils will always do better than others, but it is desirable that the order of inequality should be, as it were, a natural one, unmarred by factitious and irrelevant social differences. No matter that such an objective is "only an ideal" and must in practice remain for ever unattainable; the important thing is that it should guide policy and that we should actively seek to approach it.

In all modern western societies, the phenomenon of *social class* is a prime source of, so to speak, "unnatural" inequalities in education; that is to say, of inequalities which do not rest on differences of endowment.[1] It is the purpose of this paper to explore the manifold ways in which it makes its obstructive influence felt, and to suggest practical measures for the consideration of policy-makers and administrators who, because they believe in the natural right of individuals to education, or because they want "talent" to find its own level in the labour market, are anxious to bring ability, educational opportunity and performance into something like perfect relationship.

Social class interferes with this relationship in a number of ways: at any given level of ability, it is both cause and consequence of inequalities of educational opportunity, in the sense of unequal chances of access to educational institutions or facilities; or, again at a given level of ability, it may influence the volume and direction of pupils' energies and, hence, their educational output; or, finally and more radically, it may affect the very structure of ability itself. It follows that it is susceptible of investigation and amenable to policy in very varying degrees. Until 1945, roughly speaking, the problem of social class in education was seen, by social investigators and policy makers alike, primarily as a *barrier to opportunity*. The problem was an institutional one: how to secure equality of access for children of comparable ability, regardless of their social origins, to institutions of secondary and higher education designed for, and still used in the main by, the offspring of the superior social classes. In so far as social class was seen to influence educational *performance* the problem was conceived of as a material one: how to mitigate the handicaps of poverty, malnutrition and overcrowding by using the schools as social

---

[1] Other important sources of such inequalities readily suggest themselves: e.g. sex, geographical locality, ethnic or religious affiliation. To the extent that they are related to the more complex phenomenon of social class they are touched upon in this paper: some of the others are dealt with elsewhere in the conference.

agencies – by distributing free milk and meals to necessitous children and developing the school medical services. Only in the post-war period has the continuing attempt to democratise secondary and higher education in unfamiliar conditions of full employment and widespread prosperity confronted us with the need to formulate the problem more subtly and to see social class as a profound influence on the *educability* of children.

Here we are not concerned with snobbery in education – with invidious social differences in school or overt social bias in selection procedures – but with the existence of fundamental differences as between the social classes in ways of life, values, attitudes and aspirations, as well as in material circumstances. So far as education is concerned, these class differences, which reflect a social distribution of probabilities in the life experiences of children of different social origins, can be translated as probabilities that they will respond differently to school, even at the same level of measured intelligence. The important thing to know is, first, what are the probabilities of response to schooling as we now organise it or offer it, and second, within what limits can we change or redistribute these probabilities given defined social, political or economic aims and certain resources. I will try to elucidate these points and illustrate them as well as I can, in the main from British experience.

SOCIAL CLASS AND EDUCATIONAL OPPORTUNITY

The educational systems of most European countries have grown up in the image of out-moded social class systems. That is to say, they reflect a stage of economic and social development in which education was a corollary, rather than a determinant, of social class position. Various types of independent and publicly-maintained schools have grown up to serve the different social classes and have developed distinctive and restrictive relations with the universities and with the occupational structure. These relations have been modified by the democratising tendencies of recent years. Both in France and in England, for example, the social composition of the traditionally middle-class grammar-type secondary schools has been transformed since 1945.[2] In both countries the way has been opened up for working-class children into the universities and the liberal professions, as well as into the higher ranks of industry and commerce; the social role of the secondary schools as agents of interchange between the classes (social mobility) has become of considerable importance.

But in neither country was the school system designed for the purpose of selecting and promoting talent; and there are a number of difficulties

[2] See Christiane Peyre, "L'Origine sociale des élèves de l'enseignement secondaire en France," pages 6-34 in *Ecole et Société*, ed. Pierre Naville, Paris, 1959; Jean Floud, A. H. Halsey, and F. M. Martin, *Social Class and Educational Opportunity*, London, 1956.

in adapting its aims and organisation to the new task of occupational and social selection thrust upon it by the twin pressures of national economic need and parental anxieties on behalf of their children's future in the labour market. There is no parity of industrial or social status among secondary schools of different types. Only a minority of schools in either country retains pupils for advanced work to the age of eighteen or over, and has a direct connection with the universities and other institutions of full-time further education. These are selective schools, either because they charge fees, or because public provision of this type of schooling is limited and places must be competed for, and are awarded to the most able candidates.

The selective schools are the prime source of recruits for all non-manual occupations and they have a virtual monopoly of entry to the high-ranking professional and managerial occupations. That the supply of trained talent should thus be, to all intents and purposes, dependent on separately organised schools of high social and educational status, catering for a selected minority of able pupils, in itself makes for rigidity.

For historical reasons the provision of selective school places varies considerably as between localities and these differences are associated with differences in the social composition of local population.[3] Broadly speaking, the higher the proportion of non-manual workers in the local population, the larger the proportion of the 11-year old age group admitted to grammar schools. The relationship of the provision of places to the distribution of ability is loose to the point of arbitrariness. Age groups of children at the 11-plus in different localities may show similar proportions with I.Q.'s of 130 + but marked discrepancies in the pro-portions admitted to grammar school. Since these discrepancies are related to the social composition of the age group the effect is to make inequality of opportunity cumulative, with the bizarre result that the less rigorous the selection (the larger the proportion admitted to grammar schools) the greater the rate of success (the larger the proportion of those admitted staying at school for advanced work and proceeding to universities).

The very need to select for entry to secondary schools organised separately makes for rigidity. The supply of places in the selective secondary schools is bound to be relatively inelastic, and quite apart from short-run and localised changes in demand brought about, for instance, by migration, the task of keeping pace with long-term demo-graphic fluctuations is a very formidable one. The result is that relative "class chances" of access to selective schools and the universities to which they lead are not easily equalised or even greatly improved in relation to each other.

[3] In England the provision ranges from 10 per cent to 50 per cent of the age-group; a comparable degree of geographical inequality is illustrated for France with the aid of a more complex index by Christiane Peyre, *op. cit.*

In France, a leap in the numbers of working-class children entering the secondary schools, which resulted in the quadrupling of their proportionate strength in the annual entry between 1936-7 and 1943-4, has been followed by a relative slackening in their contribution, which after 1946 remained stable at about 12 per cent in face of a greatly increased total intake to the schools.[4] Data for England and Wales are fuller than for France, and the difficulties better illustrated from the experience of attempts over half a century to democratise the traditionally selective system of secondary and higher education. That the social composition of the secondary grammar schools has been severely modified by the progressive opening of all places to competition, can be seen from the following rough comparison of the occupations followed by the fathers of boys entering them before and after the Second World War.

TABLE 1. SOCIAL ORIGINS OF BOYS ENTERING SECONDARY GRAMMAR SCHOOLS BEFORE AND AFTER 1944. ENGLAND AND WALES

| | In percentage | |
Occupations of Fathers	1930-1941	1946-1951
Professional and managerial	40	26
Clerical and other non-manual	20	18
Manual	40	56

Source: Pre-war figures from D. V. Glass (ed.), *Social Mobility in Britain*, London, Kegan Paul, 1954, Table VII p. 129. Post-war figures from 15-18 ("The Crowther Report") Vol. II, H.M.S.O. 1960, Table X, p. 130.

Comparable information is not available for the universities, but the changes there too have been marked, although on a smaller scale.

However, although the proportion of grammar school pupils and of university students coming from working-class homes has grown considerably, the percentage of all children at this social level who pass into the grammar schools and universities remains small; and changes in the relative "class-chances" for admission to these institutions have been much less striking than might appear from the changes that have taken place in their social composition. The figures in Table 2 illustrate these points.

The post-war increase by 50 per cent in the proportionate attendance at selective secondary schools and universities is shown in Column 3. From Columns 1 and 2, however, it appears that while the proportion of the relevant age-cohorts of working-class boys passing into the grammar schools has increased by 50 per cent since the war, the figure is still very low — rather less than one in six as compared with nearly one in two of children from non-manual homes. At the university level, the chances of working-class boys are virtually unchanged, although those of boys

[4] See Christiane Peyre, *op. cit.*

TABLE 2. CHANGES IN THE SOCIAL DISTRIBUTION OF EDUCATIONAL OPPORTUNITY. SECONDARY AND UNIVERSITY EDUCATION OF BOYS REACHING THE AGE OF ELEVEN BEFORE AND AFTER THE SECOND WORLD WAR, IN ENGLAND AND WALES

| | | Percentage Attending | | |
		Working-Class[1]	Other[2]	All
1931-40	Independent Efficient or Grammar[3]	9.8	38.9	14.7
	University	1.7	8.5	3.7
1946-51	Independent Efficient or Grammar[3]	14.5	48.5	23.0
	University	1.6[4]	19.2[4]	5.6[5]

Source: Figures for national samples of boys reaching the age of eleven, 1931-40, derived from D. V. Glass (ed.) op. cit. Tables 1 & 2, pp. 18-19; those for the 1946-51 group from 15-18 ("The Crowther Report") op. cit.; Tables 3a & 9, pp. 122 & 130 respectively. I am indebted to my colleague, Simon Pratt (Ford Unit for Research in the Economics and Administration of Education, University of London Institute of Education) for the corrected percentages of those attending universities.

[1] i.e. Sons of fathers following manual occupations, whether skilled, semi- or unskilled.

[2] i.e. Sons of fathers following non-manual occupations, whether professional, managerial or other "white-collar."

[3] Independent secondary grammar schools (both private proprietary and "public" endowed schools) inspected by the Ministry and certified "efficient."

[4] The class distributions in Columns 1 and 2 are based on the findings of the National Service survey reported by the Crowther Committee (15-18, Vol. II, H.M.S.O., 1960, Table 3a, p. 121). The chances of working-class boys are probably over-estimated and those of other boys under-estimated in the figures given there, owing to differences of practice as between independent and other schools with regard to deferment of military service. The Report states (p. 109) "Deferment operated heavily throughout all types of school other than the independent efficient schools." The figures in Columns 1 and 2 have been arbitrarily corrected to reduce the error from this source.

[5] The overall chance of a boy going to a university is calculated as the number of men of all ages entering universities in the given years, divided by the size of the age-group most likely to correspond — i.e. an average of those reaching the age of 18-20 in those years. Students commencing first diploma courses (about 4.5 per cent of all students) have been excluded. But the figure of 5.6 per cent overall is nevertheless likely to be on the high side, since no account could be taken of the 10 per cent of all students in England and Wales who are recorded in the reports of the University Grants Committee, without distinction of sex, as living outside the United Kingdom. England and Wales are more likely to have a net import than export of men students. However, it is likely that any error is proportionally reflected in the figures in Columns 1 and 2.

from other families have more than doubled. Only one working-class boy in fifty proceeded to the universities in the post-war period, as compared with one in five of boys from other families.

It should be made clear that these trends cannot be accounted for by overt social bias in the selection process. There is conclusive evidence[5] to show that awards of places in grammar schools and universities are made today (as they were not before 1945) to children of all classes on equal intellectual terms; that is to say that the social distribution of available places closely reflects the social distribution of measured intelligence. It is nevertheless not the case that the differences in over-all "class chances," revealed in Table 2 can be attributed simply to social class differences in measured intelligence, well attested though these be. They must be accounted for in part by the pressure of population in the post-war years, and in part by the wide local variations in grammar school provision, associated with variations in the social composition of the population. That social class differences in ability as measured by intelligence tests are by no means alone responsible for the existing social class inequalities of educational opportunity, is convincingly demonstrated in the section of "the Crowther Report," dealing with the distribution of latent ability.

The following table, compiled from data provided in the Report, shows the social differences in opportunity which prevail in England even as between children at the same general level of ability.

TABLE 3. SOCIAL CLASS DIFFERENCES IN THE SCHOOLING OF ARMY RECRUITS (1956-58) AT TWO LEVELS OF ABILITY

Secondary Schooling	Father's Occupation									
	Professional and Managerial		Clerical and Other Non-Manual		Skilled Manual		Semi-skilled Manual		Unskilled Manual	
	Group		Group		Group		Group		Group	
	1	2	1	2	1	2	1	2	1	2
	%	%	%	%	%	%	%	%	%	%
Independent or grammar	89.4	58.6	86.8	32.4	76.0	22.1	77.0	18.0	55.0	14.0
Technical	6.8	10.5	7.5	14.2	10.8	11.0	9.0	11.3	22.2	12.3
All selective	96.2	69.1	94.3	46.6	86.8	53.1	86.0	29.3	77.2	26.3

Source: Compiled from Table 2a, 15-18 ("The Crowther Report") Vol. II, H.M.S.O., 1960, p. 120.

In the second order of ability, 58.6 per cent of the Army recruits in the sample whose fathers were of the professional and managerial class had attended grammar or independent schools. At the same level of ability,

[5] Cf. Jean Floud, A. H. Halsey, and F. M. Martin, *op. cit.*

only 22 per cent of the sons of skilled workers had done so – and it is not the case, as might be hoped, that more of them had attended technical schools instead. Even in the first order of ability, the social differences in schooling are marked. It seems that the post-war movement of educational reform has brought the abler sons of the skilled working-class into the grammar and technical schools. But ability and opportunity are still in imperfect relationship, with social class as the intervening variable.

ABILITY, SOCIAL CLASS AND EDUCATIONAL PERFORMANCE

We come now to the second important aspect of the relations between social class and education – its influence, at any given level of ability, on the volume and direction of pupils' energies and consequently on their output or performance in school.

It must be admitted at the outset that although the relations between ability, social class and educational performance are known in broad terms they have not yet been precisely worked out. In the first place, we do not yet know how the relations hold as the variables fluctuate. Mc-Clelland remarks pertinently in the course of an attack on the supposed linearity of the relationship of intelligence-test scores to school performance:[6] "Let us admit that morons cannot do good school work, but what evidence is there that intelligence is not a threshold type of variable; that once a person has a certain minimal level of intelligence, his performance beyond that point is uncorrelated with his ability?" And he urges "the desirability of plotting carefully the relationship of ability-test scores to performance criteria *over the entire range* in order to check for threshold, deceleration, or other curvi-linear relationships." We evidently need a thorough investigation of the relationships between these three variables throughout the whole range of each.

In the second place, insofar as we have established these relations, we do not as yet know what they might mean. What are the differences of family environment underlying the closer dependence of school performance on home background than on I.Q.? The influence on performance of two features of the family – its size and socio-economic status – has been repeatedly and conclusively demonstrated. A brief discussion of these will illustrate the state of our knowledge.

Class as a Socio-Economic Handicap

There is a well-known positive relationship between socio-economic status, as judged by father's occupation, and intelligence-test scores; but there is a significantly closer relationship between father's occupation and success in school. This may express anything from the crude impact

[6] D. McClelland, *et al.*, *Talent and Society*, New York: Van Nostrand, 1959, pp. 12-14.

of gross material or economic handicap to imponderable, cultural determinants of motivation.

Absolute poverty needs no discussion. Fees cannot be paid, nor can adolescent earnings be foregone by the family; malnutrition and overcrowding in the home are obvious impediments to learning. General social reform is the only answer to these conditions; they cannot be lived down in school. However, they need not be exacerbated by allowing the traditional association of poor homes with poor schools to persist; and they may be mitigated in the case of the small minority of talented children who survive their circumstances or rise above them, if scholarships and maintenance allowances are generously awarded. Even with such a programme of educational aid, however, the authorities must be prepared for wastage of talent, in the shape of underachievement in the primary schools and a more or less substantial "refusal-rate" in respect of places offered in secondary schools and universities to the able children of impoverished families.

Relative poverty or material hardship is less easy to define and deal with, mainly because the question of incentives enters in once a certain crippling level of absolute poverty is left behind. Income probably behaves as a threshold variable; at a certain low level it acts as a direct impediment to a child's educational chances, even where parents are favourably disposed; at a certain high level it liberates, making it possible for parents to implement without difficulty their interest in their children's education. At any level between these extremes, however, it does not act as an independent variable at all. It follows that in circumstances such as those prevailing in Britain, where absolute poverty, at any rate among the families of young children, is at a minimum, but where an income of any size is obtained by the fathers of only a fraction of any age-group, the attitudes of parents and children towards education are of prime importance in the under-development of talent and should be deliberately cultivated if an improved educational harvest is desired.

La Famille Éducogène

Parental attitudes are the principal ingredient in the sub-culture which a social class represents from the point of view of the school. They are at once symbol and source of social differences in the educational performance of children at the same general level of ability.

The French have coined the apt phrase "la famille éducogène" to describe families providing for their children an educative environment including, in particular, supporting social and intellectual pressures in the same direction as those exerted by the schools. For obvious reasons, such families are proportionally more numerous at the top of the social scale, and it is possible also that they are qualitatively superior as well; but the notion is to some extent relative.

At any given social level, "la famille éducogène" as so far identified by investigators, need not be more prosperous, though it tends to be smaller than average; it is likely that the parents will have had some education beyond the compulsory minimum; the mother before marriage may have followed an occupation superior to that of the father; and the climate of opinion in the home will be educationally favourable by such elementary criteria as willingness to visit the school and talk with teachers, and a knowledgeable approach to educational facilities. The children of such families will tend to be more successful on average, both as regards competition for entry to selected schools and universities, and as regards propensity to stay the course once admitted.

The following table illustrates these points. It is true that such figures are open to the objection that they merely reflect differences of intelligence among parents which are adequate to account for the different success rates of their children in the secondary selection examination. But investigations which have taken intelligence as well as family environment into consideration in trying to account for differences in school performance, show the closer dependence of the latter on family environment.[7]

These findings must cause one to take another look at the correlation between socio-economic status and school performance. It may be differently expressed as a social distribution of "familles éducogènes" — by saying that such families are proportionally more numerous with each step up the social scale. The question then arises: what factors make for a change in this distribution? (Under what conditions can we expect a weakening of the correlation between socio-economic status and school performance?). Before turning to this question we must briefly note the bearing of family size on educational performance.

Family Size and Educational Performance

It is a well established fact that children from small families *at all social levels* tend, on the average, to perform better both in intelligence tests and at school. There seems to be little doubt that, as a recent investigator put it, "the presence of a large number of siblings (or some factor related to it) is an adverse element as far as educational attainment is concerned, quite apart from the low intelligence usually associated with large families."[8] This relationship obviously has its economic aspect even in the Welfare State. It has also been suggested, more subtly, that the child of a large family learns the verbal skills, so decisive both in intelligence tests and in school performance, less effectively from his peers than does the child of a small family from adults, and carries

[7] E. Fraser, *Home Environment and the School*, University of London Press, 1960. See also A. Girard, "Mobilité sociale et dimension de famille; enquête dans les lycées et les facultés," *Population*, 1951, pp. 103-124.

[8] E. Fraser, *op. cit.*

TABLE 4. AWARDS OF PLACES IN SECONDARY GRAMMAR SCHOOLS IN
RELATION TO VARIOUS FEATURES OF CHILDREN'S HOME BACKGROUND
IN AN ENGLISH LOCALITY, 1952

Features of Home Background	Awards of Grammar School Places to Children of Fathers Following Various Occupations							
	Skilled Manual		Unskilled Manual		Non-Manual		All 11-Year Olds, 1952	
	No. of Children	% Award	No. of Children	% Award	No. of Children	% Award	No. of Children	% Award
1. *Income* of chief wage earner rated:								
High[1]	378	19	81	9	208	34	667	22
Low	213	16	215	13	194	31	622	20
2. *Father's education:*								
a) Secondary:								
Selective	82	21	23	13	205	42	310	34
Other	541	16	286	12	231	24	1,058	17
b) Further:								
Some	160	26	27	22	223	38	410	40
None	472	14	286	11	244	28	1,002	16
3. *Parents' attitudes towards education:*								
a) Discussed child's education with primary teacher:								
Yes	268	27	95	22	287	38	650	31
No	364	10	217	7	179	20	760	12
b) Preference expressed for:								
Grammar school	304	29	135	21	322	47	761	31
Modern school	328	6	178	4	145	19	651	8
c) School leaving age preferred:								
18+	145	35	44	27	188	49	377	41
16-17	250	16	102	17	188	28	540	21
15 (compulsory minimum)	226	6	159	3	81	7	466	5
4. *Family Size:*								
1-2 children	277	21	122	17	255	35	654	26
3-4 children	245	12	126	11	169	31	540	18
5+ children	108	17	64	2	42	21	214	13

Source: Jean Floud, A. H. Halsey, and F. M. Martin, *Social Class and Educational Opportunity*, London, 1956, pp. 104-7.
[1] The definition of "high" income varied according to social class status:
Non-manual: £10 per week or over.   Manual: £7.10 per week or over.

the handicap at least until the age of eleven.[9] But there must be more to the matter than this. Quite apart from class differences in strength of the influence of family size on children's verbal development, which have not been investigated but are probably considerable, there is some evidence to the effect that the educational disadvantages of a large family are less marked for the children of Catholic parents, even at the bottom of the social scale.[10] If generally true, this would cast doubt on the notion that the significance of a small family for educational performance should be sought in some distinctive quality of educational value in the environment it provides. It would lend colour to the suggestion that for children at a given social level, relative size of family is, generally speaking, symptomatic of parental attitudes and family pressures favourable to a child's educational progress — the best index, in fact, of "la famille éducogène" in all cases where religious principles do not prohibit the expression of these favourable attitudes in family limitation.

We thus arrive at the suggestion that once the grosser material handicaps are eliminated and parents' attitudes come into their own as independent variables, the size of the family, rather than its socio-economic status, emerges as potentially the most important single indication of the educative quality of home environment. However, a frontal attack on the problem of the determinants of family size at different social levels is notoriously difficult. We must be content in the short run to examine some of the more accessible differences of family culture, of which size is for the time being a general indication, and of which parents' attitudes towards their children's education and subsequent occupations are a particular manifestation.[11]

SOCIAL CLASS AND THE DEMAND FOR EDUCATION

Here we return to the question raised above of the conditions under which the correlation between socio-economic status and success in school may be weakened by the spread of "la famille éducogène." Parents' attitudes towards education are, in the short run, class-typed. What is the effect of social policy on these attitudes? Do "middle-class" educational attitudes spread hand-in-hand with "middle-class" prosperity? To some extent this will happen, especially since the spread of prosperity is bound up with a scale and pace of economic development which itself generates a public thirst for educational qualifications. Affluence

[9] J. D. Nisbet, *Family Environment: A Direct Effect of Family Size on Intelligence*, London, 1953.

[10] Jean Floud, A. H. Halsey, and F. M. Martin, *op. cit.*

[11] For some indication of the position in the United States, see J. A. Kahl, "Educational and Occupational Aspirations of 'Common Man' Boys," *Harvard Educational Review*, Summer, 1953.

does not breed "la famille éducogène," but it provides both incentives and the means for such families to become widespread. Evidence has already been gathered of a post-war transformation of the attitudes of parents in England to their children's education. The Crowther Committee, in its recent report, urges the Government to ride on the crest of this wave of public interest and to raise the school-leaving age to sixteen, noting that parents do not in general allow their children to receive less education than they themselves have had, so that the process of extending educational opportunity is cumulative from one generation to the next.

However, even under conditions in which the demand for education is rising generally, social-class influences may continue to distort the pattern of *effective* demand. Thus, the rising demand from working-class families for a selective and extended education for their children, their success in competition for places in the grammar schools in which this demand can be met, and the upthrust of advanced courses in the secondary modern schools catering overwhelmingly for working-class children, are common-places of the English educational scene. Yet the fact remains that there is quite severe class-based wastage and early-leaving from these grammar schools.[12] Table 5 illustrates this:

TABLE 5. CONTRASTS IN THE OCCUPATIONAL COMPOSITION
OF THE GRAMMAR SCHOOL-LEAVERS UP TO, AND OVER, 16

School Composition		
Parental Occupational Group	*Leavers Up to 16* %	*Leavers at 17 and 18* %
Professional and managerial	17	39
Clerical and other non-manual	17	20
Skilled manual	51	34
Semi-skilled manual	9	5
Unskilled manual	6	2
Total = 100%	863	579

Source: 15-18 ("The Crowther Report") Volume II, H.M.S.O. 1960, p. 132.

HOMES AND SCHOOLS AND THE
PROBLEM OF EDUCABILITY

The social as distinct from the purely academic character of the process of attrition at the secondary stage which is illustrated in Table 5 is well established. Thus, for instance, it has been strikingly demonstrated

[12] For relevant evidence of a comparable situation see A. Girard, "L'Enquête nationale sur l'orientation et la sélection des enfants d'âge scolaire," *Population*, 4, 1954.

that changes in the rank order of children on entry to the English grammar school are not random but are systematically related to their social class origins, so that the proportion of children in the top one-third of the performance hierarchy who are drawn from working-class families falls from about two-thirds on entry to around one-third at the end of the seven-year school course.[13]

It is important to realise, however, that social selection disguised as academic selection is a process at work in all schools. By the time children reach the threshold of secondary education at the age of eleven, those drawn from certain social groups have as a whole already begun to outstrip scholastically those from families at the other end of the scale, and the same process is continued among those selected for grammar schools during their time there.

It is not merely that children from the higher social classes are more intelligent than others (in the sense that on average they score better in tests of intelligence). Table 5 reflects the further striking fact that improvement in school performance between 11 and 16 within the highly select group of grammar school pupils, which raises many from the bottom group on entry to the top group on completion of the course, is most common among the children of professional and managerial workers; while the corresponding deterioration which causes many placed in the top group on selection to fall to the lower group on completion is most common among the children of semi- and unskilled workers.[14]

This seems to indicate a problem of social assimilation. The grammar schools grew up to serve the middle-classes, and although before 1945 a highly selected minority of able working-class children was satisfactorily assimilated, the much larger post-war contingents have proved difficult. But American experience, essentially similar, but less well-defined in the context of a non-selective school system, makes it clear that the problem is not specific but general, and must be thought of in broader terms.

We select the most likely candidates for success in the way of life that our schools represent, and we know something, although not as much as we need to know, about the kind of families which produce children who are, as it were, apt for success in schools as we now organise them. But when we are confronted with children of proven initial capacity, as measured by whatever standards we use in selecting them, who in the event fail "to give teacher what he wants," we are brought up against our ignorance of the fundamental conditions of success in our schools. We need to ask ourselves, what exactly does teacher want, and how far are his demands justifiable, given certain educational, social, political or economic assumptions and aims?

[13] *Early Leaving*, H.M.S.O., 1954.
[14] *Ibid*.

"What teacher wants" can be thought of quite explicitly in terms of curriculum content and classroom skills — Latin, say, or verbal and arithmetical facility. But it must also be thought of in more subtle terms if we are to understand the processes of social selection in education. Teachers may take for granted and find it reasonable to demand of all children the social equipment with which the average middle-class child tends to come to school; a certain capacity to assume responsibility, a relative independence of mind and breadth of interests. They may demand assumptions about life on the part of their pupils which are in fact "middle-class" assumptions; such as that life is one long progress towards ever deferred gratifications; that the present is always at a discount and the future at a premium; that one must have always a career rather than a job; that the popular pleasures purveyed by the mass-media are at best worthless and at worst sinful.

Schools, in fact, make all sorts of tacit social and cultural demands on children to which they are not all equipped to respond, and it is worth making the point that the tendency for the gap between the demands and assumptions of the school and the skills and assumptions that the children bring with them is widening. This is partly because the social composition of our secondary schools is becoming increasingly representative of the population at large and they contain a substantial minority, in some areas a majority, of pupils from working-class homes. It is also because the effect of current competitive pressures is to load examination syllabi and push minimum standards of acceptable performance ever higher. Every year the dice are loaded more and more heavily against children from underprivileged homes and in favour of those who come with an initial set of cultural advantages in the shape of parental supports and pressures, which are in the same direction as those which the school expects them to be. The children from culturally impoverished homes can spend today less and less time on the pursuits which might conceivably mitigate the effects of their impoverished background, and the schools have at least two jobs to do in present circumstances. They have not merely to instruct their pupils up to an ever rising standard of competence; they have also to tackle for an increasing proportion of their pupils all sorts of educational tasks normally undertaken in a middle-class home by parents with at least some degree of education analogous to, or comparable with, that to which the child aspires or is entitled by virtue of his ability.

If to equalise opportunity in the interests of maximising the flow of talent is the aim of policy, then the implications of our growing understanding of the relations between home and school are very radical — much more radical than was foreseen when governments first began to remedy material defects in children's homes by distributing free milk and meals. As family environments change demographically, economically and culturally, together with the structure of opportunities in the labour market, the organisation of education must respond to the same pressures so that full advantage can be taken of the changing patterns of demand.

The necessary measures may be primarily political and administrative in character — it may be a question of re-organising schooling along "comprehensive" or "common school" lines, if it can be shown that this will make for a longer average school life and greater fluidity in the supply of labour. But other measures may be indicated. Thus, recent work on social-class differences in linguistic capacity indicates that the handicap which reflects itself in the poorer average educational performance of working-class children is deeply rooted in the social structure of working-class community and family life.[15] In groups of working-class children, particularly those from semi- and unskilled families, scores on verbal tests are grossly depressed in relation to scores at the higher levels of non-verbal tests. It seems that the very nature of his ability is profoundly influenced by the social environment of the child; and that the linguistic handicap of working-class children becomes a more general intellectual handicap at the secondary stage of education. Successful learning may, therefore, be dependent on different educational measures for children of different backgrounds. Bernstein[16] infers the proposition, for instance, that the more humble the origins of pupils the smaller the optimum number in class. One might also infer the need for financial re-allocation as between primary and secondary education so as to make extremely small classes the rule in the early stages of primary education rather than, as is now customary, at the advanced stages of secondary education. A truly radical and single-minded policy might also find a use for boarding-schools.

However, here is not the place to do more than indicate the radical implications of the policy of equality of opportunity in the present state of sociological knowledge. Suffice it to say that it involves us in the need for a most elaborate inspection of what actually goes on in schools, of what the assumptions and values are that have been embodied in their organisation, of what tacit as well as explicit demands they make on pupils. At the same time, we need a very much deeper knowledge than we have now of the social and cultural environment of children of different social origins, and of the extent to which they are correspondingly more or less capable of responding to the intellectual and social demands with which school confronts them.

[15] Cf. B. Bernstein, "Social Structure, Language and Learning," *Educational Research*, III, 3, June 1961, pp. 163-176.
[16] *Ibid.*

Selective
Bibliography

Anderson, Perry and Robin Blackburn (eds.), *Towards Socialism* (Ithaca, New York: Cornell University Press, 1966).
A collection of critiques of British stratification from a left-wing perspective.

Beer, Samuel M., *British Politics in the Collectivist Age* (New York: Alfred A. Knopf, 1965).
An analysis of the effects of stratification on voting and other political phenomena.

Bernstein, Basil, "Language and Social Class," *British Journal of Sociology*, XI (1960); and "Social Structure, Language and Learning," *Educational Research* III (June, 1961).
Two preliminary reports on his studies of the language deficiencies of lower-class children.

Douglas, J. W. B., *The Home and the School* (New York: Hillary House, 1964).
A longitudinal study of all children born in a given week in 1946 — from their early family experiences up to entry into secondary school. A new volume carrying them through the first job is promised. The effect of social class variables on life chances is the central theme.

Frankenberg, Ronald, *British Communities* (Baltimore: Penguin Books, 1966).
A theoretical interpretation of the many studies of communities — from villages to urban housing estates.

Glass, D. V., et al., *Social Mobility in Britain* (New York: Free Press, 1955).
A pioneering effort which includes analysis of a sample of 10,000 men, with emphasis on father-son mobility patterns, and also a series of smaller, more specialized studies.

Hoggart, Richard, *The Uses of Literacy* (Fair Lawn, New Jersey: Essential Books, 1957).
The first part contains a reconstruction of traditional working-class culture based on his own youth, and powerfully portrays the tone of such a life.

Klein, Josephine, *Samples from English Cultures* (New York: Humanities Press, 2 vols., 1965).
Summary and interpretation of many community studies from the viewpoint of the life cycle and social psychology of the respondents.

Little, Alan and John Westergaard, "The Trend of Class Differentials in Educational Opportunity in England and Wales," *British Journal of Sociology*, XV (1964).
A statistical summary of the available evidence on changes in social class biases in education.

Lockwood, David, *Black-coated Worker: A Study in Class Consciousness* (Fair Lawn, New Jersey: Essential Books, 1958).
A historical study of the development of the occupation of clerks in Britain, and an analysis of their current role in the class system.

Millar, Robert, *The New Classes* (London: Longmans Green, 1966).
A journalistic account of the contemporary scene.

III

Japan
Oriental Industrialism

In 1868 Japan established a national government devoted to the rapid modernization of her feudal society, then three centuries old. This new regime was created by a dissident group from within the old elite determined to strengthen the nation and protect it from the encroachments of the European powers which were dismembering China. From a society which had been hiding from the world, Japan became a nation determined to interact with the world and absorb the new technology that created power.

The suddenness of this about-face startled both her own people and outside observers. Japan had been known as the quaint hermit of the Orient, a land of lovely scenery, strange customs, and medieval spirit. Almost overnight she became a bustling and energetic nation with a rapid rate of industrial development. Her success was often considered rather mysterious, since it seemed to violate many generalizations about the difficulties of modernization. Why was she so different from China, Indonesia, and India?

However, as understanding of the details of Japan's modernization has deepened, the rapidity of her transformation has lost much of its mystery. The key to understanding has been new knowledge about the

Written by John W. Bennett and the editor.

154

earlier feudal regime. The Tokugawa family had governed Japan since 1603 when the warriors of this house succeeded in defeating rival military groups. In order to insure peace after centuries of intermittent local wars, the Tokugawa instituted a centralized feudalism which had most of the effects, if not the institutionalized forms, of a true national government. Various devices insured the loyalty and obedience of the local lords and magnates; centralized methods of taxation and communications were established; propaganda stressed the nation and its special traditions; and the beginnings of formal education were organized. By 1868 urban life was flowering, merchant houses were gaining wealth and indirect control over the economy, and some 40 per cent of the male population was effectively literate.

The Tokugawa had earlier established a typical feudal or estate system of stratification. The Imperial household and the old landowning nobility had the highest formal status, followed by the military men or *samurai* knights. Peasants were classified as next in prestige and honor after the *samurai*; they in turn were followed by artisans and merchants. The *heimin* (common people) were essentially unclassified.

By the end of Tokugawa rule this system of estates no longer corresponded to the realities of wealth and power. The *samurai* were for practical purposes the true ruling class; the merchants had greater power than the peasants and artisans, even though they were generally forbidden by sumptuary regulations from displaying their wealth. The peasants reacted against their real status of exploited workers by staging a series of local revolts. The growing urbanization had transformed the old agrarian structure to the point that Japan in the middle of the 19th century resembled, in broad outline, France on the eve of the Revolution. The traditional rules of status were no longer congruent with the facts of life.

Underlying the macro system of traditional estates and *de facto* classes was a micro social system of remarkable complexity and order. The borrowings from China had emphasized the role of the family and the hierarchical positions of its members: men dominant over women, and older siblings over younger. This image of familism was syncretized with feudal conceptions of *noblesse oblige* and paternalistic lord-vassal relations to solidify the concepts of obedience, loyalty and solidarity. Practically every functional group in Japanese society, from teams of common laborers to squads of *samurai*, was organized on these hierarchical and familistic lines. Every man knew his place and was motivated to perform competently in his position by constant emphasis on loyalty to superiors and the need for group excellence. Hierarchy was not used to perpetuate privileged incompetence. While this portrait is somewhat idealized, the resulting system was, from the Western perspective, a remarkable synthesis of nepotism and achievement.

For such a system to function smoothly, a considerable degree of suppression of personal impulse and desire was required. The Japanese socialized their young people in a family structure which, as we have noted, mirrored the national polity, and was its foundation rock. The children were taught obedience and self-control, and learned to expect rewards from effective performance. The typical adult personality struck outsiders as tense and dominated by subtleties of etiquette, but well suited to assume the burdensome tasks of national reconstruction. Japan's rapid transformation is not so surprising once these facts are understood; it was the most adequately prepared of all the non-Western countries to move toward industrialism.

The initiation of "industrial nationhood" can follow different political paths. The Japanese were equipped, by their social system and national polity, to undertake the technical tasks that are common to all industrial societies, but that did not mean that they would immediately adopt the open-society format common to the Western nations. Indeed, authoritarian control over the new directions of social change was continually emphasized; the central aim was not private consumption, but rather national strength. The purpose of industrialization was to fortify the wealth and power of Japan, although it provided personal rewards to the worthy. Two popular slogans summarize the underlying values: *fūkoku kyōhei* (prosperous country, strong military); *risshin shussei* (make something of yourself).

Thus the stratification system of Meiji Japan after 1868 was but an adaptation of a structure with a long history. The *samurai* families (the best educated people in the nation) moved from warrior positions to management jobs in government and business. The commercial groups emerged from sumptuary restraints and asserted their economic power. The peasants and laboring masses accepted a subordinate role.

But these lines of stratification were much blurred by the interpersonal relations of hierarchical loyalty within functional groups. Indeed, paternalism grew stronger in early modern Japan. The Meiji settlement eliminated feudalism as a legal scheme, but did not erase its traditions of familial-paternalistic social relations. These continued as essential means of providing the discipline needed for rapid modernization, and were upheld as expressions of *Nippon damashii* — the true Japanese spirit. These interpersonal and communal-like bonds created ambiguity in the system of class stratification until the 1920's.

At that time there was a brief period of relaxation of the stern cultural conservatism that had been in effect, and many underlying economic trends had the opportunity to surface in various social expressions. An urban middle class emerged; the proletariat began to organize and assert itself; agrarian movements for land reform appeared; in short, interest groups with class attributes became visible. But these movements in the direction of an open-class society resembling that of the West were temporarily suppressed by the militaristic reaction of the early 1930's which once again set Japan on a conservative course, reasserting feudalistic traits. This policy led directly to World War II and to Japan's total defeat — the first defeat in her entire history.

The American Occupation after the war again permitted — indeed, deliberately fostered — liberal trends. Many reforms took place, such as the modification of economic monopoly through sales of stock shares of big firms to the public; support for labor unions; the breakup of many paternalistic patterns in the labor market and the substitution of legal rules for job rights and social security benefits; changes in family law which gave women the right to initiate divorce; enfranchisement of women; the transformation of public education into a liberal-democratic instrument instead of a servant of the Japanese spirit of obedience; the de-mythologizing of the Emperor and the switch to constitutional monarchy. These changes all had the effect of shaking up the old social system; the remaining feudal elements were destroyed, and the *samurai* ethic was completely liquidated (it had been discredited by the defeat itself).

Contemporary Japan has a stratification system in which the classes are divided roughly as follows: the political and industrial elite; the bureaucratic "salaryman"; the small-scale artisans and storekeepers (still very prevalent in a Japan where the supermarket has not yet invaded the local neighborhood); the new masses, composed of urban factory workers and the many farmers (more than half) who are part-time industrial workers; the poorer country people.

Education is the mechanism for selecting and training individuals for their roles in this system. As Herbert Passin shows in his essay, reprinted below, the Japanese quickly adopted European methods of schooling and grafted them onto existing Tokugawa procedures. The blend was efficient and modern, yet thoroughly Japanese in spirit. Education became "the ladder of success"; a person could not achieve without an appropriate diploma (and the social connections that went with it). The old social strata were absorbed into the new order via educational selection.

Upward mobility is mostly governed by the ability to pass examinations. Although sons (and increasingly, daughters) of high-level families have advantages that make it easier for them to pass, nevertheless many sons of humble status do very well in school and thus rise to exalted positions. Social mobility rates in Japan are high — probably higher than in Great Britain, and possibly higher than in the United States.[1]

However, the Japanese style of mobility retains particular characteristics. Once a person has achieved a certain examination status, he usually

[1] See Thomas Fox and S. M. Miller, "Occupational Stratification and Mobility," *Studies in Comparative International Development*, Vol. I (1965), No. 1. Also see the article by Tominaga reproduced below.

enters a homogeneous group which controls and limits competition by mechanisms of solidarity. For example, it is exceedingly difficult to get into a university, but once there, most students graduate; the class moves up as a unit. Or, the group of men who enter a business firm at the same time and at the same level become a solidary peer group who help one another on the job, and spend recreational time together off the job. Loyalty to this group and to the boss tends to inhibit movement from one firm to another. The solidarity mechanisms are described in the selection by Ezra Vogel on the salaryman; he also gives chilling detail on the rigors of the examination system.

Statistical evidence shows that inter-firm mobility is not completely avoided; indeed, among smaller firms it is quite common. The analysis of Ken'ichi Tominaga is based on a sample survey in 1960, and indicates rates and processes of both inter-generational and intra-generational mobility.

The article by Shizuo Matsushima gives further information on employment practices and their effect on labor-management relations. He shows how the Japanese system has given labor unions a special characteristic: solidarity with the firm leads to economic conservatism, at the same time that the national organization of unions leads to political radicalism.

Japan has successfully transformed herself into a modern industrial nation. The average level of living is still low by European and American standards, but very high by Asian standards. The economy is dynamic: it grows rapidly, and it produces, as well as consumes, advanced technology. The educational system is efficiently tied to the needs of the labor market. The age of mass consumption has begun.

The new social strata in Japan increasingly resemble those in the open society familiar to Westerners; thus structurally, Japan's uniqueness has faded away. Only in the subtler areas of interpersonal relations does the special style of Japan continue to dominate; here the traditional culture flourishes. Etiquette, formality of manners stressing shades of distinction in status and honor, esthetic sensitivity to physical objects and human feelings, family solidarity — the old ways have blended with the new macrostructure and continue to shape behavior.

Education and Career

In 1947, under the influence of the American Occupation, the entire educational system was reorganized, both in structure and curriculum. In the first place, Japan shifted from a multi-channel to a single-channel structure, each level qualifying students for the next higher level. The separate tracks were consolidated at each level. (A separate although rather limited junior college system on the American model was later added.)

Compulsory education was increased to nine years of schooling, and a 6-3-3-4 structure was adopted (six years of elementary school; three years of lower secondary, corresponding to the American junior high school; three years of upper secondary, corresponding to the American senior high school; and four years of university).

Coeducation, which was formerly limited to the elementary school, was now "recognized" by law, and a common curriculum for boys and girls became the pattern for all schools. In spite of the opposition of many parents, afraid that their daughters would be corrupted and the traditional family system undermined, coeducation has been widely accepted and now dominates the school system. Women's education has been placed on the same footing as that for men; they can attend the same schools and go on to the same universities. Today, women number about 13 per cent of the total university population (excluding the "junior colleges" where they number over 60 per cent). In the leading universities they usually constitute less than 5 per cent of the student body. However, there is a marked tendency for them to cluster in certain departments and fields as, for example, literature or English literature in particular, where they often outnumber men by far.

All boys and girls attend lower secondary school, and over 60 per cent

Reprinted and condensed with permission of the author and publisher from Herbert Passin, *Society and Education in Japan* (New York: Teachers College Press), © 1967, Teachers College, Columbia University.

Herbert Passin attended the University of Illinois and the University of Chicago. An anthropologist, sociologist and journalist of wide experience and interests, he has done field work with Mexican Indians, North American farmers, Japanese rural and urban communities, and in India. He is Professor of Sociology at Columbia University, and a representative of the Ford Foundation in Asia.

go on to senior high school (64 per cent in 1962). The government
prediction is that the percentage will rise to 72 by the year 1970.

In order to meet the increased demand, the number of universities
jumped from 49 in 1942 to over 245 in 1955 (565, if we include the new
junior colleges with two or three years of schooling). The growth of the
university population may be seen in the following tabulation:

University Attendance (University and Graduate School)

	Students	Teachers	Schools
1877	235	91	1
1882	563	123	1
1897	1,974	191	2
1907	6,272	503	3
1917	7,291	924	4
1927	34,633	4,643	37
1937	49,546	6,334	45
1947	87,898	8,259	49
1952	399,513	36,978	220
1957	642,106	55,345	231
1960	711,618	61,021	245

It is tempting to see in these figures a ninefold increase in the university students. But if one looks at the total "higher education" population, which included the *semmongakkō* as well as the university, the
increase, although dramatic, will be somewhat less spectacular:[1]

	University Students	Students in Higher Education
1936	70,304	159,889
1946	82,861	278,527
1952		501,912

Nevertheless, even though a good part of the increase was simply an
upgrading within the category of "higher education," the upgrading as
well as the increase has intensified the competition for the limited number
of prestige jobs. Before the reforms the university student was a rare bird;
today he is one of a vast throng jostling for attention and prestige. In
the same way, the scarcity value of the professor has also declined with
the enormous increase in university-faculty members.

So radical a change in the educational system has profound implications for Japanese life and society. One obvious effect is to keep young
people out of the labor force for a prolonged period, which means that
they must be supported during that time by their parents and that they
very likely entertain higher expectations than early labor-force entrants

[1] The *semmongakkō* were special technical schools at a somewhat lower level
of training than universities. They were absorbed into the university system in
the post-war reforms of 1947.

before the war. The level of qualification requirements constantly rises, so that jobs that formerly required only an elementary school certificate now require lower secondary, or even upper secondary, education; white-collar positions, formerly available to middle school or *semmongakkō* graduates, now increasingly require a university degree.

Although we cannot disentangle the specific effects of coeducation from all the other postwar changes affecting women, certainly they are considerable. Not only have women entered the labor force in much larger numbers and at much higher levels of skill and pay than ever before, but they are moving rapidly from an automatic acceptance of the traditional role of Japanese women. A woman who has gone through higher education in competition with boys and who has come to associate with them daily has a different outlook on such matters as dating, absolute obedience to husbands, companionship in marriage, and the inherent inferiority of women from that of her mother — whose schooling and school life were entirely different.

Since upper secondary education is now so widely available, the point of competitive stress in the system has shifted from the middle school-higher school to the high school-university transition. But the "examination hell" remains as live a subject as in the past. Reports such as the following are frequent:[2]

> A youth despondent over his failure to pass a college entrance examination committed suicide by electrocuting himself on a high-tension wire. . . . The youth carried a note in his pocket which said he felt he could no longer live in this world because he was too weak-minded.

Whether the examination system is in fact responsible for the high suicide rate among Japanese youth, it is certainly widely believed to be so. Finland and Austria have comparable total suicide rates, but in the fifteen to twenty-four age group Japan outstrips them by far.

Selected Suicide Rates[a]

	All Ages[b]		Age Group[c] 15-24	
	Male	Female	Male	Female
Japan (1955)	31.6	19.0	60.8	36.7
Finland (1956)	37.0	9.0	18.1	—
Austria (1956)	32.4	14.5	17.4	8.1

a From United Nations, *Demographic Yearbook, 1957*, Table 17.
b Per 100,000 population.
c Per 100,000 population of the 15-24 age group.

2 *Japan Times*, July 10, 1962.

In 1955, there were 658,343 applicants for 136,467 announced openings in the universities (4.8:1). Since then the ratio has become somewhat more favorable, although there are still on the average more than five times as many high school graduates as there are university vacancies. Not all of them apply, however, but the rates today are running at about 25 per cent, and they can be expected to increase. University education is being claimed as an inherent right by more and more people, and the demand for full equality of educational opportunity has become a major issue. As of the moment, however, supply is still far from meeting the growing demand. More than one-third of the applicants will not be able to get into any university at all. For the metropolitan areas of Tokyo, Kyoto, and Osaka, the applications outrun vacancies by more than three times, and for the prestige universities, in some years only one out of 10 or 20 applicants will be accepted.[3]

The forced-draft creation of new universities, hastily knocked together from pre-war higher schools, *semmongakkō*, technical schools, and normal schools, has, if anything, intensified the quality gap, and with it, the competition for entry into the better schools. If university education has much less scarcity value than before, the individual student must make up for this by the quality of the school he attends. The result is that in spite of all efforts to equalize quality, the former Imperial universities still outrank the private universities, and the gap between the older universities, whether public or private, and the newly formed institutions is even greater.[4] Tokyo, with one-third of the universities and one-half the student population of the country, still remains the target of the ambitious. This pressure has created a new social phenomenon, the *rōnin* (named for the masterless samurai of the Tokugawa period) — students who, failing to pass the entrance examinations for the first-rank schools, spend years cramming for a retake rather than enter an inferior institution. By now they form a significant proportion of the new entrants to such schools as Tokyo University, thereby cutting down the number of openings available for applicants fresh from senior high school. What we have, a Japanese educator once wrote, is not a 6-3-3-4 system but a

[3] A few examples of the ratio for schools in the Tokyo area in 1955 are: Waseda University (political science and economics), 22.7 : 1; Tokyo University of Foreign Languages, 20.5 : 1; Keiō University (economics), 12.7 : 1; Tokyo Institute of Technology, 11.6 : 1; Hitotsubashi University, 9.6 : 1; and Tokyo University (Literature Faculty), 8.3 : 1.

[4] With the single exception of the newly formed International Christian University whose students rank among the highest. In the 1953 National Scholastic Aptitude Test, for example, scores for the top four were: Tokyo University, 60.63; International Christian University, 55.57; Hitotsubashi University, 55.37; and Osaka University, 55.00. The average for all Japan was 35.50.

6-3-x-3-x-4 system, "x" representing the years spent trying to get through the entrance examinations for the better senior high schools and universities.[5] (Some would add another "x" after the four years of university — for the "university hospital.")

The competition at the senior high school level is not quite so pressing, but there are ominous signs. Efforts to equalize the quality of the schools by distributing good students uniformly through control of examination results and manipulated school districting have not been entirely successful. Many parents find ways to send their children to good schools outside their home districts. The problem has become so serious that good school districts in Tokyo openly levy a special "voluntary contribution" on nonresident pupils. Falsified residential documents are arranged, and in some cases a mother may move into a particular district with her child so that he can go to the good school. According to a survey in 1957, in a class of 62 pupils in one of Tokyo's better high schools, only 27 actually had their residence properly within that school district. Middle-class parents know that certain schools are better than others and offer a much higher probability of entrance into the desirable schools on the next higher level.

These quality differences are explicitly recognized by society. A Tokyo University degree is obviously much more highly regarded than a degree from a new provincial university. And the better companies, which are the main target of the university graduate, maintain either implicit or explicit quotas on the number of entrants to be taken from various schools. The graduate of a good school has a demonstrably better chance to secure a job, and a job with high status, than the graduate of a lower-ranking school.

SCHOOLING AND FAMILY BACKGROUND

In feudal Japan family, class, and personal connections had formed the main pathways to recognized achievement, even though within these limitations personal merit carried some weight. But once the turmoil of the transition period had subsided and the new school system, and also the other reforms, were well on their way — say, within twenty years — new channels of achievement and mobility began to take on institutional

[5] In a recent year, for example, 271,000 of Japan's 1,000,000 high school graduates applied for admission to the 72 national universities. But in addition there ware 100,000 *rōnin* applicants from previous years. According to Shimizu Yoshiro, *Shiken (Examination)*, 1957, of 13,485 applicants to Tokyo University in 1957, 66 per cent had spent from one to three years as *rōnin*, only 34 per cent applying fresh from high school. Of the 2,004 successful applicants, 72 per cent were *rōnin*, and only 28 per cent were straight from high school. (The corresponding percentages for all national universities are 50 fresh from high school and 50 *rōnin*.)

shape. To get ahead in the world it was no longer sufficient simply to come from a good family; one had to go to a good school and do well in it. Education became the new escalator for talent and achievement, and the demand for qualified men far exceeded the capacity of the schools to provide them. But if family origin was no longer sufficient, neither was ability alone. Post-Meiji Japan has perhaps as good a record of opening the way to talent as any other country. But it is not yet — nor is any other country — Michael Young's meritocracy.[6] In principle, complete equality of educational opportunity was established from 1872 onward. In practice, however, the various segments of the population were differentially prepared, sometimes financially and sometimes culturally, to take advantage of it.

Surveys of school attendance in 1873 — the first year of operation of the new school system — show that it was the samurai who responded with greatest alacrity. In a sample of 40 *shijuku* (private academies) in the Tokyo area, 80 per cent of the students were samurai, and only 17 per cent commoners. (The overwhelming majority of the schools were *shijuku* — 1,123 out of 1,189, with 50,595 out of the total school attendance of 55,385). An official survey of school attendance in 1886 clearly shows this differential class utilization of the new opportunities. The percentage of school attendance in two prefectures, according to parents' occupations, was as follows:

	Mie Prefecture	*Saga Prefecture*
Miscellaneous[a]	73.87%	62.48%
Agriculture[b]	52.87	28.86
Industry	54.45	43.45
Commerce	68.74	51.13
Labor[c]	37.47	24.32
Total	53.81	42.02

[a] "Miscellaneous" (*shogyō*) refers to clerical, administrative, teaching, and governmental posts. A good part of the former samurai would be found here, as well as persons of educated family backgrounds.
[b] Mainly peasants.
[c] The "labor force" (*rōryoku*), in other words, the "working class" as it then existed.

The highest rates of utilization are found among the two classes that had the highest rates of school attendance during Tokugawa times, samurai and merchants. The lowest are those for workers — then a relatively new class, mainly formed from peasants, and particularly their noninheriting junior sons. That Mie peasants were much ahead of Saga

[6] Michael Young, *The Rise of the Meritocracy* (Baltimore: Penguin Books, 1961).

peasants reflects Mie's relative advancement during the Tokugawa period over Saga, one of the more backward areas on the island of Kyushu. A breakdown by levels of education shows this even more clearly. While almost 5 per cent of all upper-class Mie children attending school were in schools above the elementary level, the corresponding proportion for labor was 0.15 per cent and for peasants 0.60 per cent.

The reluctance and even outright resistance of peasants during the first decades of the Meiji Period was not mere stupid obstinacy, but rather a combination of lack of understanding with genuine economic problems. School fees continued in force in some parts of the country until the beginning of the twentieth century. Even where schools were entirely free, families often had to weigh the clear loss of the child's present income (or labor) against hazy future gains. To go on to university, a young man who was a potential money earner for his family — or who was at least physically capable of supporting himself — had to be maintained for three years of higher preparatory school and three years of university.

Nevertheless, higher education has spread downward to the lower classes at a tolerably rapid pace. Although demand for higher education has always exceeded supply, the drastic impartiality of the screening process has taken some of the sting away. Examples of wealthy boys unable to enter the great universities and of poor boys able to make the grade have always been visible.

By the end of the Tokugawa era, the samurai class numbered approximately 5 per cent of the total population. Since it was almost completely literate, it was obviously in the best position to take advantage of the new opportunities. In 1878, for example, ten years after the Restoration — and one year after commoners were permitted to enter its preparatory school — eight out of ten students at Tokyo University were still of samurai origin. But ten years later, the proportion had gone down to six out of ten. In the regular university departments, the proportion of students of samurai origin declined from 74 per cent in 1878 to 52 per cent in 1885. But the increase of "commoner" students, which has gone on apace since the beginning of the Meiji Era, has still not meant complete equality of educational access. Relative affluence has acted to some extent as a filter. The bulk of university students have been, by and large, sons of well-to-do families — or at least of families able to support them through school. A survey of Tokyo University students in 1938, for example, shows 71 per cent "entirely dependent on their families," and another 15 per cent "partially dependent." Only 9 per cent reported themselves entirely dependent on their own resources. The comparable nationwide figures show that 43 per cent found it "easy" for their parents to support them in school, 49 per cent found it "possible," and 8 per cent found it "hard." This would imply that the majority came from families at least well enough off to support them in school.

A recent study offers the following international comparison:

	USSR	USA	Japan
University Students:			
Higher-class origin	50%	63%	73%
Lower-class origin	50	37	27

Although Japan seems to have a greater proportion of university students from the higher classes than the Soviet Union, a closer reading of the data suggests another possible interpretation. The chart from which these figures are drawn tells us that the proportion of the total population listed in the "higher-class" group for the Soviet Union is 20 per cent and for Japan 34 per cent. Reading the table a slightly different way, then, we can say that in the Soviet Union the population group that constitutes the upper 20 per cent of the population contributes 50 per cent of the university students, or two and a half times its proportion in the population; while in Japan, the upper 34 per cent contributes 73 per cent of the university population, or slightly more than twice its proportionate weight in the general population. From this point of view, there would appear to be more mobility in higher education in Japan than in the Soviet Union.

SCHOOL AND JOB

In spite of the tremendous national effort, university development was a slow growth. In 1885, seventeen years after the Meiji Restoration, Tokyo Imperial University (established in 1877) was still the only university in the country, and it had only a few hundred students. More young people went abroad for their higher education than were able to obtain it at home. Even as late as 1904, Tokyo Imperial had only produced about 5,000 graduates (the newer Kyoto Imperial, established in 1897, about 100), and between 1912 and 1925, Japan produced a total of only 42,000 graduates.[7] As against these small numbers, the needs in various fields were overwhelming. According to a survey conducted by Tokyo Imperial University in 1904, of 1,700 judicial officers (including judges and procurators), only 300 were university graduates; of 4,300 secondary school teachers, only 300; and of 40,000 physicians and surgeons, only 600 had university training.[8]

The Japanese solution was elitist. Instead of lowering standards and opening the universities to the vast floods of applicants, a harshly com-

---

[7] See Ministry of Education, *Demand and Supply for University Graduates — Japan*, August 1958, Appendix 1, pp. 64-65.

[8] Alfred Stead, ed., *Japan by the Japanese*, A Survey by Its Highest Authorities (London: William Heinemann, 1904), p. 238.

petitive selection process was adopted. The examination system became its symbol.

Once universal education came into full operation, the educational ladder became the skeletal core of the social-achievement ladder. Those with elementary education went into agricultural or manual-labor jobs, middle school graduates into lower-ranking white-collar positions, and university graduates into the higher administrative and executive positions. Although it was not entirely impossible for a person with elementary school education to go up in the ranks, the odds were heavily against his going very far. Enterprises were usually divided into two entirely separate channels, a labor, or production, channel, and an administrative channel. Once a worker entered a firm in the production channel, he was able to move up the ranks through seniority and personal merit, but he could not move over into the administrative channel.

In the larger enterprises, a further distinction was usually made between a lower administrative and a higher executive channel. These two were somewhat less impermeable, but someone who started in the lower channel was not likely to go very high in the executive line. The separation worked the other way as well. Companies would not accept persons with higher education in production or other low-grade jobs.[9] No greater tragedy could be imagined than for educated people to be forced by economic conditions to take inferior jobs, as in the 1920's and 1930's, when "*Tōdai* (Tokyo University) policemen" and lower-grade civil servants came to public notice. And this may have had something to do with the alienation of intellectuals from the regime that developed so rapidly in the 1920's and 1930's.

In government as well, schooling was made a decisive consideration, especially in the higher civil service. For these posts one had to come from a proper university. In some cases the university was specified, in other cases the choice was assured by a two-stage system — first, the examination which established an eligibility list, and then a personal interview, which virtually guaranteed that only graduates of the proper schools would be appointed.

The hierarchical distinctions that grew up among the universities and the *semmongakkō* had immediate consequences for career chances. Many companies took their executive-level entrants only from a particular school or schools; others assigned quotas to different schools. Once accepted in a company, salary scales would be found to vary with the school. The Japan Broadcasting Corporation, for example, before the war used to give Imperial university graduates a starting salary of 80 yen per month, private university graduates 75, and *semmongakkō* graduates 70. In

[9] The best discussion in English of company-recruitment policies is to be found in James Abegglen, *The Japanese Factory* (New York: Free Press of Glencoe, 1958).

1927, to take another example, the Mitsubishi enterprises paid new company entrants starting salaries on the following scale.

	Monthly salary (in yen)
Graduates of:	
Imperial university (engineering)	90
Imperial university (law)	80
Tokyo Commercial University	80
Waseda and Keiō Universities	75
Other private universities	65-70
Semmongakkō	65-70

The Mitsui Mining Company was equally specific in its starting salaries paid to new employees:

	Monthly salary (in yen)
Technical Employees — Graduates of:	
Imperial universities	75
Waseda (science and engineering)	65
Meiji, Senshū, Mukden Universities	60
Higher technical schools	55
Class A engineering schools	1.30 (per day)

	Monthly salary (in yen)
Clerical and Administrative Employees — Graduates of:	
Imperial universities	75
Waseda and Keiō Universities	65
Other private universities	60
Kōbe Higher Commercial School	60
Other higher commercial schools	55
Semmongakkō	55
Class A commercial schools	1.30 (per day)
Middle schools	1.15 (per day)

For the higher and more desirable posts in Japanese life, it was almost essential to have gone to the elite schools. The lesser universities provided entrée into the lower levels of government and lesser businesses.

The universities not only provided training and connections, but lifetime identification with a clique. These cliques, or *batsu* as they are called, are intimate, informal groups based on personal loyalties that span many fields from the university into business, the professional world, government, and politics. A person without a *batsu* faces Japanese society unsupported, with no one to sponsor him or to help him in times of crisis. It is one's *batsu* that opens the closed doors. Characteristically, each *batsu* has its own sphere of influence, which it guards jealously against outsiders and opens only to its intimates. Universities form their own *batsu*, and even individual departments within the university may have *batsu* on their own.

The student must depend on them heavily for securing a job. All important companies in Japan hire university graduates through one of two channels: the school itself or "connections." According to a recent survey of 502 firms, over 40 per cent secure their applicants through the universities, 5 per cent through "connections," and the rest through some combination of the two. More than 80 per cent specify the universities from which the applicants are to be taken. How do these channels work?

In the case of employment through the universities, the company calls on one or more schools to recommend graduates for its entrance examinations. Each school has its employment office, and in some of the larger schools each department also looks after employment matters. Where close relations exist between company and school, it is often the individual professor, the departmental chairman, or the placement officer who personally makes the selections. In any event, the student's application will not be accepted by the firm unless it has the approval of the appropriate university authority. This is where the school or department *batsu* is decisive for the student.

In some companies, however, the school *batsu* can be bypassed. Influential connections (or *ko'ne*, as they are known) — owners, important stockholders, important clients or customers, relatives, high officers, etc. — can open the way for someone who has not graduated from one of the right schools. There are several types of situation in which such family influence and connections can be effective. First, in the case of a family-held enterprise; second, in the smaller, less prestigeful firms (and usually less desirable to the ambitious graduate); and third, in the discretionary area of an impersonal selection system. An example may make this latter clear. In 1961, one of Japan's great newspapers found itself with 3,000 applicants for only 20 openings. The first examination served as a screening device to determine the 100 most promising candidates. In the second stage, the final 20 were selected from the successful 100 on the basis of interviews and recommendations. An acquaintance boasted that he had used his "influence" to secure a job for the son of a friend. When pressed on this, he explained:

> Of course, he had to do well in the first examination and be among the top 100. Up to that point I could do nothing. But there is so little to choose from among those who come through such a rugged competition that the choice has to be made on personal impression, manners, and recommendations. It was at this point that I was able to use my influence.

Influential connection, therefore, does not automatically guarantee employment. Often it only allows the applicant to enter a competition from which he would otherwise have been barred. In general, the larger and more desirable the firm, the less room is there for connections; it is in the smaller firm that they are most important.

Since — at least in the more desirable firms — there are many more applicants than job openings, a drastic screening examination is used to reduce the list. The survivors of the written examination must then undergo a severe oral examination, usually by high officers of the firm, on the basis of which final choices are made. While the first stage of the examination is objective and impersonal, the second opens the way to a variety of subjective considerations: appearance, manner, background, and outlook. In the subtle chemistry of this encounter, all the particularisms and favoritisms have their play.

The number of connections the schools can establish with companies and other outlets for employment depends on their prestige, the quality of their graduates, and the number of alumni they have in important positions. Once a particular university clique is established in an enterprise, it tends to perpetuate itself, both consciously and unconsciously, through the careful selection of executive-level employees.

It is therefore small wonder that the elite positions in Japanese society have been largely dominated by the graduates of the elite universities — Tokyo Imperial, Kyoto Imperial, and Tokyo Commercial Universities (and to a lesser extent the other former imperial universities). How overwhelming this can be may be seen from a few figures: Before the war Tokyo University had about 12 per cent of the total university population; yet in 1935, for example, of 99 successful applicants for higher civil service positions, 81 were from Tokyo University.

A survey completed in 1958 shows the following distribution among the highest-ranking government officials (Classes I, II, and III):[10]

Educational Background:	Class I	Class II	Class III
National university graduate	97.6%	81.6%	57.1%
Private university graduate	0.	5.6	8.9
Semmongakkō graduate	2.4	11.6	23.6
Middle school graduate	0.	0.9	7.0
Other	0.	0.4	3.4
Tokyo university graduate	80.5	67.2	39.9
Number:	(41)	(558)	(2,317)

Source: Calculated from Kakushochō Kachō-kyū Ijō no Gakureki, Shikaku, oyobi Keireki (The Education, Qualifications, and Records of Branch Chiefs and Above in All Departments and Bureaus), mimeographed report of survey by the Japanese Government, June 1959.

10 In the samplings for postwar years given here and on succeeding pages, the assumption is made that people in these high posts today had their university education before the influence of the postwar reforms came to be felt.

Tokyo University had been originally conceived as a training school for officials. Until 1900, when the newer Kyoto Imperial University produced its first crop of candidates, Tokyo held a complete monopoly of higher civil-service posts, and it was indeed the only true university in the country. Fukuzawa's Keiō was permitted to establish a "university department" only in 1890, and even then it was not granted the same status as Tokyo University, nor were its graduates qualified for the higher civil service. Instead, they turned themselves to the newer fields of industry, journalism, banking, insurance, and politics. Ōkuma's Waseda was established as a "college" (*semmongakkō*) in 1881, and it was not accorded university status until 1902.

Within Tokyo University, it was the Law Faculty that provided the main channel into government. Therefore, during the Meiji Period the ambitious and patriotic young man was likely to aim not only for Tokyo University but for its Law Faculty. In fact, during this period, the majority of Tokyo University students were in the Law Faculty, and even as late as 1959 this faculty, with 38 per cent, outnumbered all other faculties.

Until 1915 the majority of graduates entered government service rather than private industry. The turning point came about 1918, when for the first time graduates entering the business world outnumbered those entering government.

Surveys in the business world show much the same story. A listing of 108 top business and political leaders in 1952 shows 60 Tokyo graduates, and 71 in all from national (former Imperial) universities. A survey of 2,592 executives in 283 companies conducted in 1954 shows 38 per cent of them Tokyo graduates, and a total of 63 per cent graduates of the "big three" — Tokyo, Kyoto, and Hitotsubashi (formerly Tokyo Commercial University). A 1959 survey of the background of executives of firms with a capitalization of one billion yen or more, that is, of the largest firms in Japan, gives similar results: 35 per cent from Tokyo, and a total of 52 per cent from the "big three."

Lower-ranking universities had to carve out their own spheres of influence, and in this many of them have been successful, even if they were excluded from the top positions in government and certain leading companies. Particular areas or institutions fell within the sphere of influence of particular universities. In a recent sampling, for example, it was found that Keiō, one of the two leading private universities of Japan, has its dominant influence in insurance companies and department stores; Waseda, the other leading private university, in certain newspapers and the construction industry. Therefore, a student bent on a particular career has to be sure to get into the proper channels. Keiō would open the way to a satisfactory business career, and Waseda to one in journalism; for government, the Foreign Service, leading banks and corporations, he would have to go to Tokyo.

But woe betide the graduates of a college having no company faction
— warns the *Nippon Times* of December 9, 1955 — for these un-
fortunates usually have to be satisfied with jobs in small and medium
enterprises — unless they are lucky enough to find their way into the
movie world, which is the only enterprise in Japan were talent counts
above everything else and the "old school tie" holds no domain.

How different is the situation today? There can be no doubt that the
postwar reforms have made a difference and that many forces are nibbling
away at the pre-war *batsu* system. One can expect that in the course of
time the *batsu* controls will gradually loosen up, that the class of "good
universities" will broaden, that some of the new universities will achieve
higher public standing. The shortage of personnel required for a rapidly
expanding economy will also have some effect. In certain fields, Japan
has unquestionably moved much closer to full equality of opportunity
and students are judged on the basis of their abilities – at least as tested
by examinations – and achievement. Nevertheless, it is still possible
for a committee of professors to characterize the situation as follows:

A particular school has hegemony among the staff in certain offices
or schools, who exclude graduates of other universities irrespective
of their ability. This is a subtle survival of feudalism amidst the
rationalistic forms of bureaucracy. These differences in quality,
certainly in repute, among universities appear to be widening. Two or
three years of *rōnin* life is not regarded as too high a price to gain
entry to the preferred universities. These social and political forces
penetrate the educational system, and they underlie the incessant
clamor for reviving and strengthening the dual system.

SUPPLY AND DEMAND IN
HIGHER EDUCATION

In an ideal world, there would be an exact correspondence between the
demand for higher education and the facilities available for it and between the number of trained graduates and the number of socially useful
and satisfying jobs. When there are substantial discordances, personal
and political problems arise. On the first score, applications for university entrance in Japan have always run well ahead of vacancies, and this
has meant a rigorously competitive system and much personal unhap-
piness. But on the second score at least, the Meiji Period was one of those
euphoric moments in history when every graduate could find a useful,
productive, and remunerative outlet for his training and talents. The
demand for trained people far outran their production by the universities.
But with the growth both of the industrial sector of the economy and
of the university population, two problems began to appear. In the
first place, graduates seeking "good" jobs found themselves in an increasingly competitive situation. In the second place, the universities were

turning out too many in the humanities and too few in the sciences and technology. With their high expectations and the substantial investment in their long years of training (a minimum of seventeen years of schooling, as compared to sixteen required in the United States for a B.A.), the university-educated were particularly vulnerable to economic insecurity.

By the middle of the second decade of the twentieth century, government was no longer able to absorb so high a proportion of graduates, even from Tokyo and Kyoto Universities, as it had before, so that students had to direct themselves toward private employment. In 1900, for example, of 2,247 graduates of Tokyo and Kyoto Imperial Universities, 68 per cent had gone into government positions and 32 per cent into private industry. As late as 1915, 59 per cent of them were still going into government. But by 1918, the proportions had reversed: Only 48 per cent went into government and 52 per cent into private industry. Since then the trend has accelerated to the point that only 10 per cent of the 1959 graduating class of Tokyo University went into government service (plus one per cent into local government); and even among graduates of the Law Faculty, the traditional breeding ground of top bureaucrats, fully 75 per cent went into private enterprise.

By the second decade of the twentieth century the *sarariiman* (salaryman), the educated white-collar worker, had made his appearance in Japan. No longer the bold, self-confident builder of the nation, a contemporary song describes him "crossing the Kanda Bridge at five in the morning, wearing his frayed Western-style clothes and carrying his lunchbox, briskly clip-clopping towards his miserable pittance."

Thus, in spite of the extremely selective, carefully limited, elite character of the system, within a few decades of its establishment it was already producing too many graduates for the economy to absorb satisfactorily. By the 1920's and '30's intellectual unemployment became a serious political problem. In the year 1936, for example, 44 per cent of the university graduates were unable to get jobs.[11] The employment rate for law, economics, and literature graduates dropped below 50 per cent in 1923 and 1930. Discontent and bitterness among the highly educated, combining as they did with the new influences coming from the Russian Revolution, a new wave of enthusiasm for Western democracy as against German authoritarianism, and the penetration of Marxism among students and intellectuals, made the organized protest movement a significant element in Japanese politics. As against the absolute overproduction of educated persons, there was a shortage of technically qualified personnel. In the same year of 1936, in spite of the unemployment among university graduates, according to R. K. Hall, "the technical schools were able to supply only 16.4 per cent of the

[11] Robert K. Hall, *Education for the New Japan* (New Haven: Yale University Press, 1949), p. 228.

17,630 technicians needed in industry."[12] In 1937 the shortage in electrical and mechanical engineering and applied chemistry was even worse.

From 1937 until the end of the Second World War, military conscription and industrial mobilization solved the problem of unemployment. More than half of the students of the country, it has been estimated, were taken into service.[13] But the end of the war brought it back with even greater severity, and it was further exacerbated by the enormous increase in the university population resulting from the American educational reforms. The threat of unemployment and the difficulty of finding satisfactory work, in spite of years of sacrifice and effort, provided an enormous reservoir of support for socialist and anti-conservative movements.

Until the past three or four years, it was by no means certain that every university graduate could find a job, and even less certain that it would be a job he felt would make use of his qualifications. Although the situation has been improving, there are great differences among the different classes of universities in the job success of their graduates. While in 1959, for example, 79 per cent of university graduates found jobs within three months of graduation, only 55 per cent of the junior college graduates were able to do so.[14] Moreover, if we were to distinguish between the prestige universities and the low-ranking ones, we would find a further gap: The chances of securing any job at all were about twice as high for the graduates of the former than of the latter. If we introduced a further distinction in the desirability of jobs, the difference would be even more extreme. The oversupply, however, is selective not only in university ranking, but also in the field of study. In scientific, technical, and social science fields there has been, if anything, a shortage; the surplus has been primarily in the humanities (literature, history, philosophy, and fine arts), such women's fields as "homemaking" and nursing, and to a lesser extent in education.[15]

Even if, as appears to be the case from the most recent statistics, Japan's economic boom is absorbing almost all the university graduates, the competition remains severe, particularly for the desirable companies. The overwhelming majority of the 150,000 or so university graduates

[12] Hall, *op. cit.*, p. 228.

[13] At the start of the war, university students were exempted, but by 1943 special student exemptions in the social sciences and humanities were ended.

[14] Ministry of Education: *Education in 1959*. Annual Report of the Ministry of Education, March 1961, p. 62.

Another 7 per cent of university graduates, and 8 per cent of junior college graduates, continued their education.

[15] Based on data reported in Ronald Anderson, *Japan — Three Epochs of Modern Education*. Washington, U.S. Dept. of Health, Welfare & Education, Bulletin 1959, No. 11, pp. 144-145.

every year must go into private business, and they all aim for the first-class companies. Of Japan's approximately 440,000 companies, only 2,000 can be considered "large," and it is to these that university graduates try to go; if they fail, they then move down to medium- and small-scale enterprises. According to a survey among 1,000 of these 2,000 leading companies, there are on the average about ten applicants per job opening. (In the case of the newspaper mentioned earlier, the ratio was 150:1.) And the competition for desirable government positions is, if anything, even more extreme. The average number of applicants for the senior diplomatic channel of the Foreign Office is about 600; 16 to 18 are chosen, of whom 10 to 14 are from Tokyo University. (In one recent year, there were 1,100 applicants for six openings.) Since this narrow entranceway is already so rigged in favor of the better schools, competition and frustration are extreme.

From late fall through early spring, the fourth-year university student must scramble for a job, applying to many places and undergoing innumerable examinations, some of them more difficult than anything he has taken during his academic career. Every failure is a heartbreak for the student and his family; the level of ambition clicks downward one step. The result is a typically Japanese phenomenon: books with such unpromising titles as *Compulsory Subjects for Company-Entrance Examinations*, or *Job-Getting Policy Encyclopedia*, become best sellers, with sales running into the millions every year.

POLITICS

The Meiji leaders, who began the modernization of the country, were not themselves the product of modernity. They were men of the *ancien régime*, and even of its privileged orders — most of them lower-ranking samurai — who had been educated in the orthodox fief schools or the *shijuku*. Disaffected, or at the very least discontented with the *status quo* and their position within it, they were quickened into political activity by their awareness of the great power of the West, both as a military, colonial threat and as a system of ideas with which traditional Japan would have to come to terms. The dominant slogans of the day, *fukoku kyōhei* (prosperous country, strong military) and *bunmei kaika* (civilization and enlightenment) expressed the consensus that held them together in a tight oligarchy for a good thirty years: a unified modern state; national strength — both economic and military; the selective import of Western technology. In the light of retrospect, it might be argued that this apparent consensus papered over an inherent fault line — one that was later to show itself in the conflict between the conservative nationalists and the liberals — but in the event, it was powerful enough to hold the elite together.

The establishment of a modern school system did not, therefore, in the first instance influence the redistribution of political power. This was already solidly held by an elite formed in the pre-Meiji Period. The early products of the schools fit into the systems they created, manning the newly opened bureaucratic posts and institutions, and moving cautiously into the slowly developing modern economic sector. Most of the graduates of the higher schools were immediately drawn in.

But the very existence of a school system and its entrenchment as the main channel for access to government position, business, and power brought about important changes in the composition of the elite. The samurai, as a legally privileged class, had been on a rapid downgrade and, particularly after the abortive revolt of Saigō Takamori in 1877 (the very year Tokyo University was established), had to face increasingly vigorous competition from the other classes. Although persons of samurai origin remained disproportionately high among the elite and among those with higher education (as they do even today),[16] their absolute dominance continued to diminish in tandem with the rise of the former underprivileged classes. The emergence into the national political community of the former lower orders is a process that has been going on slowly throughout the ninety years of modern Japanese history, and in a sense it can still be said to be going on. The first enfranchised electorate in Japan numbered about 400,000 people (the population at that time, 1890, was about 40,000,000). By means of tax and property qualifications it was held down to the well-educated, the people of means, the wealthier farmers, and the growing class of industrialists and entrepreneurs. Only in 1925 did universal manhood suffrage bring the working class and the peasantry into the national political community. (Full universal suffrage, including women, and down to the age of twenty years, came only with the American Occupation.)

But in spite of this restriction of the electorate, the growth and differentiation of society, governmental institutions, and the economy went on rapidly. New classes — a modern working class and a modern industrialist class, for example — came into existence, and these expanded in numbers and influence at the expense of the older classes. The rise of military power and the political party system transformed politics from a monopoly of the oligarchy into a three-way struggle, in the course of which there were many compromises and coalitions.

The intellectuals and university graduates of the Meiji Period had been essentially a political elite, taking part in the governance of the country. Whether in government itself as members of the bureaucracy, in one of

[16] See the revealing study of the social composition of business, political, and intellectual elites by James Abegglen and Hiroshi Mannari, "Leaders of Modern Japan," *Economic Development and Cultural Change*, 1960.

the important national institutions (such as the Army or the school system), in politics, or in a private capacity, the educated classes felt themselves committed members of a common national effort. But as the Meiji Period began to draw to its close and the great Restoration leaders to leave the scene, the products of the new universities and the school system began to enter the marketplace. Where in an earlier day any educated person could feel that he was making his personal contribution to national affairs, whether or not he held an official position, now a gap began to appear between the bureaucratic and civil elites. For the first time there were modern intellectuals who felt themselves outside the national political community, or even hostile to it. The early Meiji leaders had all been "generalists," cultivated men with a strong sense of national dedication, rather than technical specialists in particular fields. The new university products included increasing numbers of technicians, engineers, and even writers and artists who looked on politics as a condition of life rather than as an arena of activity. A Mori Ōgai could still feel that the intellectual must serve the nation (he was an MD and novelist) but Shimasaki Tōson and others were already arguing the priority of personal vision and morality as against the state. The educated classes began to divide into two broad streams: a bureaucratic elite taking part in public affairs in one form or another; and a civil element, which again consisted of two parts — the holders of stable, respectable, mainline positions who identified themselves with the "Establishment," and a new intelligentsia, disaffected and inclined toward all the great heresies of individualism, radicalism, liberalism, and Westernism.

Entrance into the Establishment was therefore through the educational channels, but the educational system could not completely channel all of its products. Some of them went into opposition and found arenas of activity in nonmainline channels that were growing up: the trade-union and radical movements; Christian institutions (churches, schools, colleges, social work, etc.); foreign-connected institutions; the growing communications and entertainment industries; and free-lance creative work. In the more organized political and social movements, they joined with the leaders arising from within these movements to form a new leadership which in itself became a counter-elite to the elite of the Establishment.

To reach high political, as distinct from bureaucratic, position, therefore, there were channels other than those of the school system. Local bosses with their own areas of control could be elected to the Diet, even if they had very little schooling. Leaders of mass movements or wealthy businessmen could also be elected. Thus the grass-roots politicians often had their own independent bastions of support from which to negotiate with the official cliques. But within the framework of the party, the various *batsu* had to compete among themselves and make effective coalitions to carry on the practical work of politics. And here the bureau-cratic element, with its school-based *batsu*, played a very important part. Internal party life was essentially a question of struggle, compromise, and coalition among factions. The higher the formal level of political power, the more clearly can clique lines be seen. While the party back-benchers in the Diet might come from many different backgrounds, there is increasing homogeneity as one goes up the scale to, say, party executives and cabinets.

In the February 1962 Diet, for example, 35 per cent of the members of the House of Representatives had less than university education. But even among the university graduates, there was considerable scatter, as may be seen in the following tabulation:

	%		N[a]	
	100		461	
Members of the House of Representatives:				
With some university education	64.6		298	
Completed university education	61.8		285	
Government universities		37.3		172
Private universities		22.5		104
Other		1.9		9
(Tokyo University)		(26.4)		(122)

[a] The Diet membership is actually slightly larger, usually about 467, but with deaths, resignations, and incomplete information, this was the best number on which calculations could be made.

Source: Nihon Seikei Shimbunsha, *Kokkai Binran 37* (*Register of the National Diet, 1962*) (Tokyo, 1962), pp. 99-130. Data for the years 1947, 1949, 1953, and 1958 can be found in Appendix, Chart 8, pp. 164-167, Robert Scalapino and Junnosuke Masumi, *Parties and Politics in Contemporary Japan* (Berkeley and Los Angeles: University of California Press, 1962).

However, when the cabinet level is reached, the prestige university grad-uates are clearly dominant. In the first Ikeda Cabinet, for example, formed in 1960, 13 of the 20 members were from the "big three," and 14 in all were from the national universities.

In the second, formed on July 18, 1962, 11 of the 20 were from the "big three," and 12 were from the national universities.

In these two examples, Tokyo University and the prestige national universities are dominant. However, it is entirely possible that with another prime minister having clique affiliation some other university or combination of universities might become dominant. What is signifi-cant is that these cliques have a strong university base. Ike calculates that between 1918 and 1940, of the 156 men who held cabinet posts, about 45 per cent were Tokyo Imperial University graduates.

Opposition politics is less dominated by university-based cliques, as may be seen in the following.

	Liberal-Democratic Party	*Japan Socialist Party*
Diet Members with University Education:	74%	52%
Government universities	46	21
Tokyo University	33	13

Source: Nihon Seiki Shimbunsha, op. cit.

The sources of leadership are more diverse — from trade unions, farmers' organizations, and popular movements — but as against this, the intellectuals among the leadership stand out more conspicuously as a distinct group.

On the surface, Japanese politics today appears about as polarized as it can be. And yet the old school tie still makes it possible for politicians of the left and the right to maintain some kind of communication across the political gap. It has not been unknown for a socialist to leave the podium after blood-and-thunder denunciation and declaration of war unto the death, only to join a conservative friend in a pleasant social gathering. Every close observer has his own favorite example of these cross-party friendships and of how unexpectedly far they can go. It may be that this is one of the forces that make the polarization of Japanese politics somewhat less bitter and irreconcilable than it often appears to be.

Occupational Mobility in Tokyo

INDUSTRIALIZATION AND OCCUPATIONAL MOBILITY

"As work is divided more, suppleness and liberty become greater. The same individual is seen to raise himself from the most humble to the most important occupations."[1]

This is an observation made by Emile Durkheim about French society at the end of the 19th century. What can we say in the light of over half-a-century's experience after Durkheim? Lipset and Bendix recently concluded that high industrialization yields a high rate of social mobility in any country regardless of its political institutions, historical background, or value orientations.[2] Let us examine the Japanese situation in the light of this generalization, which was based on a comparison of statistical studies from many countries.

Ordinarily, the concept of "social mobility" is used to show the movement of individuals in a given occupational structure, but actually mobility is directly linked to changes in the structure itself. In the case of Japan, the rapid industrialization which began in the Meiji and Taisho era (later part of the 19th century and early part of the 20th century) brought drastic changes in its industrial, occupational and class structure. The proportion of those engaged in the primary industries (mainly agriculture) steadily decreased. In 1920 they occupied about 55 per cent of the total population, but by 1960 the percentage had

Reprinted with permission of the author and publisher from "Japanese Society and the Labor Mobility (Nihon Shakai to Rodo Ido)," *The Journal of Economic Behavior*, Volume II, Number 1, 1962. This article appears in Kunio Okada, ed., *Gitjutsukakushin to Ningen no Mondai*, Diamond-sha: Tokyo, 1964.

Ken'ichi Tominaga was born in Tokyo in 1931, and is one of the more active members of the younger generation of research-minded sociologists. He graduated from Tokyo University Graduate School in 1959, and lectures there in both sociology and economics. He specializes on industrial sociology.

[1] Durkheim, E., *The Division of Labor in Society*, New York: Free Press, 1947, p. 329.

[2] Lipset, S. M. & Bendix, R., *Social Mobility in Industrial Society*, Berkeley and Los Angeles: University of California Press, 1959, pp. 11 ff.

decreased to about 33 per cent. Simultaneously, the proportion engaged in general manufacturing increased from 20 to 33 per cent.

Furthermore, there was a change in the composition of the work force which upgraded many men to higher levels, thus altering the profile of the class structure. The middle strata, composed of professional, administrative and clerical workers, expanded rapidly, offering new opportunities for social ascent.

CONTROVERSY ON THE NATURE OF JAPANESE SOCIETY

Until recently, the predominate view held that Japanese society was rigid and immobile, even though there existed a few scholars who held an opposite view, such as Dr. Tohata who once said:

> . . . . there are very few parents who would want their sons to have the same occupation as theirs. It is generally considered that something is strange with those sons who would succeed to their father's job. Isn't this a basic impetus which drives Japanese people to new and curious things? I should think that is where Japanese society derives its restlessness and hustle.

Ruth Benedict expressed the more orthodox opinion when she stressed that the principle of life which has penetrated deep into the Jananese people is the belief, "to each his own place," and she described the hierarchical status system of Japan in detail.[3] Dr. Takeyoshi Kawashima stated that a familial relationship based on the child's feeling of piety to parents was the basic model of Japanese social relationships.[4] Scholars of Japanese business enterprises expanded this idea and said that the main characteristic of Japanese firms lies in their paternalistic management, an extension of familial relationships.

However, Japanese society has been changing rapidly since 1950. The stress on a rigid status structure emphasizing familial loyalty and paternalism is still valid in respect to certain parts of the country, as revealed by field investigations carried out in rural villages in northeastern Japan and in some mining areas. But it would not be appropriate to apply these particular conclusions to Japanese society as a whole. Urban and modern Japan has an open status system with high mobility. When an international comparison became possible based on recent large-scale statistical investigations, it became very clear that the rate of mobility in Japanese society is not very different from that of such "advanced" countries as the United States, England, Germany and Sweden.

First let me cite an example from my own research data of 1958 on

[3] Benedict, R., *The Chrysanthemum and the Sword: Patterns of Japanese Culture*, Boston: Houghton Mifflin, 1946, Chap. 3.

[4] Kawashima, T., *Nihon Shakai no Kazoku-teki Kosei* (Familistic Structure of Japanese Society), Gakusei-shobo, 1948, p. 17.

182   KEN'ICHI TOMINAGA

marriages.[5] If Japanese society still had such familistic and paternalistic characteristics as stated by Dr. Kawashima, marriages would tend to be limited to members of the same social class. But the rate of intra-class marriage, taken from samples of Tokyo, is approximately 60 per cent, a rate which is almost equal to the rate of 58 per cent found by Hollingshead in Elmtown, U.S.A.[6] Thus, almost one-half of Tokyo marriages cross class boundaries.

In regard to the Japanese labor market, there is a particular concept of a "permanent employment system." This implies that the employment contract presupposes a life-long social relationship between employers and employees. Although this subject has long been studied by Japanese labor economists and sociologists[7] as a part of a series of studies on the backwardness of Japanese society, it sprang into journalistic limelight when Abegglen's work, *The Japanese Factory*,[8] was translated into Japanese. Many researchers have testified that management in Japan has been pursuing policies which encourage intra-firm stabilization of labor by means of welfare facilities, retirement pension systems, and the seniority rule in wages and advancement. But no research has yet been published which comprehensively examined to what extent such management policies are actually effective in holding workers. Abegglen's study over-generalizes from a few cases, and a test of its thesis is over-due.

From these preliminary considerations, we can point out the following questions which need to be examined:

(1) Is the mobility rate in Japan as high as it is in the "advanced" Occidental countries? That is, do the facts support the generalization about industrial society made by Lipset and Bendix?

(2) What is the extent of "permanent employment"? Big business in Japan has been pursuing policies which encourage lifelong stabilization of labor. It is also true that labor unions in recent years have put the slogan "Freedom from Discharge" as one of their important demands. However, the existence of "permanent employment" as an ideal is one thing, and the actual state of labor mobility another. These two subjects have been often confused and it is of importance to ask again, "Are Japanese workers actually under a permanent employment system?"

(3) Traditional economic theory assumes the perfect mobility of the labor market as the starting point of its theoretical construction. It has,

[5] Tominaga, K., "Toshi Kazoku no Kaisi-nai Doshitsusei to Kaiso-kan Ishitsusei" (Intra-class homogeneity and inter-class heterogeneity in housewives of urban families), *Shakaigaku Hyoron*, XXXVIII (1960), 50-86.
[6] Hollingshead, A. B., "Cultural Factors in the Selection of Marriage Mates," *American Sociological Review*, XV (1950), 619-27.
[7] For example K. Okochi, M. Sumiya, S. Ujihara, W. Fujita.
[8] Abegglen, J. C., *The Japanese Factory: Aspects of its Social Organization*, New York: Free Press, 1959.

however, been pointed out by many labor economists that this assumption must be revised and made more realistic. Various barriers to movement from one sector to another do exist, and we shall study some of them here.

In the following sections the writer hopes to examine these three points on the basis of data collected from an investigation carried out by Sigeki Nishimura, Saburo Yasuda, and others, including the writer, in November 1960 in the 23 wards of Tokyo.

RESEARCH TOOLS

The respondents in our Social Stratification and Mobility research of 1960 were male adults over twenty years of age living in metropolitan wards of Tokyo; the number of usable questionnaires totalled 1,227. The men were chosen at random from the election rosters; thirty-six per cent of the original list of men in the sample refused to respond. The final sample closely approximates the census distribution of occupations in Tokyo, except for an over-representation of professionals and administrators. Detailed occupational histories of the respondents and their fathers and grandfathers were obtained.

The occupations and industries in which the respondents have worked in the past were categorized by following the guidelines of the Japanese census. However, in order to measure the social distance moved when a person changes occupations, or to compare a respondent and his father, a scale device is necessary. We used the prestige ratings obtained from the 1955 survey of occupational mobility, and from them constructed a matrix of "social distance" from one occupation to another, as shown in Table 1. It shows for example, a distance of 25 points separating professionals from clerical workers, and 54 points separating professionals from forestry workers.

HOW MUCH MOBILITY?

The problem concerning mobility in the labor market has two phases. First, whether or not one can freely choose an occupation without being influenced by his father's occupation; and second, whether or not one who has already started his occupational career can change to the next job uninfluenced by his previous job. The former concerns inter-generational mobility between father and son, and the latter intra-generational mobility of an individual.

It was clear from the 1955 research that inter-generational mobility in Japan is by no means small (except in agriculture). One of the main reasons is that during the past generation the occupational and employment structures have drastically changed, and the demand for labor in modern occupations and modern employment sectors has increased. This process of modernization is much more concentrated in Tokyo

TABLE 1. SOCIAL DISTANCE SCALE BETWEEN OCCUPATIONS

	Occupation														
	2	3	4	5	6	7	8	9	10	11	12	13	14	15	16
1. Professionals	3	7	21	25	27	31	37	38	40	41	42	43	48	54	55
2. Administrators		4	18	22	24	28	34	35	37	38	39	40	45	51	52
3. Engineers			14	18	20	24	30	31	33	34	35	36	41	47	48
4. Protective workers				4	6	10	16	17	19	20	21	22	27	33	34
5. Clerical workers					2	6	12	13	15	16	17	18	23	29	30
6. Owner-farmers						4	10	11	13	14	15	16	21	27	28
7. Small Merchants							6	7	9	10	11	12	17	23	24
8. Transportation & Communication								1	3	4	5	6	11	17	18
9. Supervisory workers, manufacturing									2	3	4	5	10	16	17
10. Service workers										1	2	3	8	14	15
11. General workers, manufacturing											1	2	7	13	14
12. Sales workers												1	6	12	13
13. Outdoor sales													5	11	12
14. Tenants														6	7
15. Forestry															1
16. Unskilled workers															

Source: Social Mobility Survey, 1955. For a report in English see Kunio Odaka and Sigeki Nisihira, "Social Mobility in Japan: A Report on the 1955 Survey," *East Asian Cultural Studies,* IV (March 1965), 83-126.

than elsewhere. Therefore, as far as Tokyo is concerned, the rate of inter-generational occupational mobility is quite high. Let us elaborate this point.

Table 2 shows to what extent the occupational, industrial, and employment structures changed during the period between the respondents' generation and their fathers'. The percentage of those whose fathers were farmers and who moved to urban occupations is extremely high, and as a result, the number of those engaged in clerical work increased by 2.5 times and that of production workers by 1.6 times. In the employment structure, self-employed business owners decreased markedly, and employees, on the other hand, more than doubled in proportion.

A detailed comparison of fathers and sons shows that the rate of occupational succession is very low; *only 15 per cent of the respondents are now engaged in the same occupation as their fathers.* Indeed, every single occupation shows sons in a position different from their fathers in more than 50 per cent of the cases. Not only do they change occupations, but respondents change industries and employment status at an equally high rate. There is one trend worth noting: sons are somewhat more likely to be mobile if their fathers are in small enterprises, and less likely to be mobile if their fathers are in large enterprises.

TABLE 2. STRUCTURAL CHANGE

	Sons	Fathers
Occupational Structure		
Professionals	10%	8%
Administrators	13	10
Clerical Workers	15	6
Merchants	10	17
Sales Workers	7	2
Farmers	1	28
Transportation Workers	4	3
Supervisory Workers, Manufacturing	10	8
General Workers, Manufacturing	23	14
Unskilled Workers	3	1
Protective and Service Workers	5	4
Total	101%	101%
Industrial Structure		
Agriculture	1%	29%
Construction	8	6
Manufacturing	39	21
Sales	20	18
Finance	4	2
Transportation & Communication	7	7
Service	16	11
Government	5	7
Total	100%	101%
Employment Structure		
Owners & Executives	20%	27%
Self-employed Owners	12	44
Family Workers	4	0
Employees in Small-scale Firms	27	6
Employees in Medium-scale Firms	12	3
Employees in Large-scale Firms	24	20
Temporary Employee	1	0
Total	100%	100%

Figure 1 is a chart showing the relationship between the occupations of fathers and sons; it dichotomizes occupations into non-manual work and manual work. The black part shows the rate of mobility from manual to non-manual or vice versa. The proportion of those who moved up into the non-manual level is 42 per cent, which is higher than that in European countries and the United States, as shown by Lipset and Bendix. Of course, we must remember that a part of this represents farm sons who moved to the city and obtained non-manual jobs.

It is also possible to measure the social distance of mobility in terms of the scale of relative prestige, as shown in Table 3. Those whose mobility distance is zero are less than 20 per cent. A little more than 80 per cent experienced either an upward or a downward mobility. On

FIGURE 1. INTER-GENERATIONAL MANUAL–NON-MANUAL MOBILITY

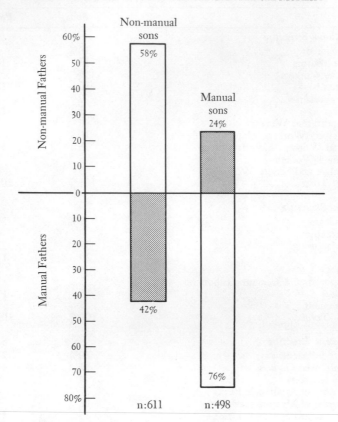

TABLE 3. INTER-GENERATIONAL MOBILITY DISTANCE

Distance of Mobility	Per Cent of Respondents
0	19.4%
1-5	19.2
6-10	13.8
11-15	13.9
16-20	7.9
21-25	10.4
26-30	6.2
31-35	3.8
36-40	3.5
41-45	1.1
46-50	0.1
51-55	0.7
Average distance of mobility: 12.1	

the whole, there are not many cases in which the distance between the occupational positions of fathers and sons is extremely great. By definition, the biggest scale distance is 55; and the smallest is zero; the average distance is 12.1.

Looking at Figure 2, we see the distance moved by administrators was rather high, which means that those who belonged to this category experienced substantial upward social mobility from their fathers. On the other hand, the high score of unskilled workers tells us that these workers generally have experienced substantial downward social mobility from their fathers. Thus, we may conclude that the inter-generational mobility between fathers and sons is considerable, from whatever angle it may be viewed.

Now we turn to movement within a man's career. According to the data acquired in the research, 48 per cent of the respondents remained

FIGURE 2. INTER-GENERATIONAL MOBILITY DISTANCE, BY OCCUPATION OF RESPONDENTS

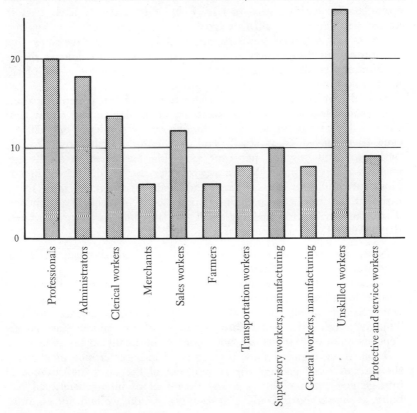

in the same occupations as their first ones, and 64 per cent remained in the same industries. Thus, the intra-generational rates are lower than the inter-generational rates.

Detailed analyses reveal the following trends of movement within careers:

(1) Mobility is not low in all occupations. There is clear distinction between occupations of high mobility and those of low mobility. In the category of professionals, both inward- and outward-mobility are low. The same tendency can be seen in clerical jobs, although not to the same degree. On the other hand, workers in transportation and in unskilled labor have very high inward and outward-mobility, while administrators, supervisory workers in manufacturing, and merchants have a high inward-mobility, but a low outward-mobility. This implies that these occupations can be considered as final goals; it is very rare that people move out of them once they have reached them.

(2) Two points are clearly seen as to position in an establishment cross-classified with its scale or size. First, it is extremely likely that in present-day Japan, an ultimate goal in life is to become a business owner or self-employed businessman. And in fact, the data show that the route from the position of a small factory or shop employee to the position of a small business owner is actually open and forms one of the most typical main channels of upward-mobility.

Secondly, it is another characteristic feature of the present Japanese employment structure that the possibility of moving in and out is least likely in large-scale business firms. Among our respondents, only 20 per cent have moved from small- and medium-scale enterprises to big businesses, and only 28 per cent from big businesses to small- and medium-scale enterprises. When we consider the big differences in employment conditions between large and small businesses, we must recognize that this wall between the two brings about an inequality of chance. Thus, the social factors dividing small and large businesses create a block that inhibits the development of a "perfect" labor market.

Next, let us examine the question of social distance in intragenerational mobility. There are not many chances of mobility between the manual and non-manual categories, as seen in Figure 3. Those who moved from manual to non-manual occupations total 23 per cent, which is only about half of the figure for inter-generational mobility. Thus, it appears that entry into the ranks of the middle class largely depends upon early schooling, not upon advancement on the job.

Table 4 and Figure 4 show the degree of intra-career movement along the scale of social prestige. In 41 per cent of the cases the distance of intra-generational mobility was less than that of inter-generational mobility, as shown above. Looking at each occupation, we find, for example,

FIGURE 3. INTRA-GENERATIONAL MANUAL–NON-MANUAL MOBILITY

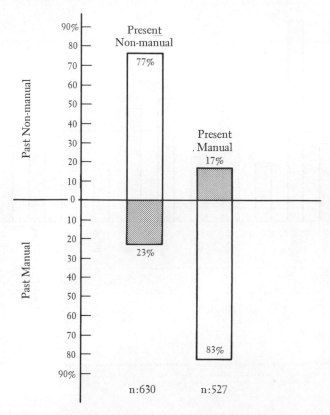

TABLE 4. INTRA-GENERATIONAL MOBILITY DISTANCE

Distance of Mobility	Per Cent of Respondents
0	40.8%
1-5	14.9
6-10	5.1
11-15	10.8
16-20	8.0
21-25	8.8
26-30	2.5
31-35	1.9
36-40	5.0
41-45	1.1
46-50	0.2
51-55	0.7

Average distance of mobility: 9.6

FIGURE 4. INTRA-GENERATIONAL MOBILITY DISTANCE, BY OCCUPATION

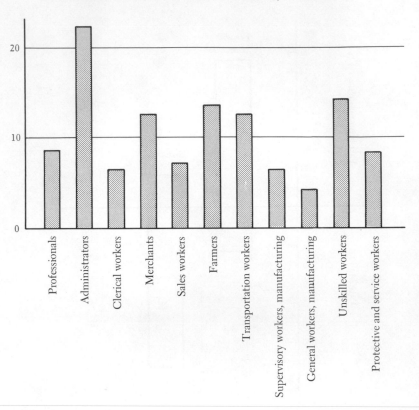

that for clerks and workers in the manufacturing process (both supervisory and general), the distance moved during a man's career was extremely small. But the higher score for administrative occupations tells us again that the road up to this level is open. As to professionals, the inter-generational score is high, and the intra-generational score is low; in other words, this occupation is closed once a career has started because it requires a specific educational background.

Any conclusion drawn from an observation of intra-generational mobility must be very subtle. In every respect it is certain that the degree of intra-generational mobility is not as high as that of inter-generational mobility. However, this does not imply that in every aspect of mobility the Japanese labor market is rigid. As is evident from what we have seen so far, mobility in such a traditional sector as the route from an employee of a small business or family industry to the owner of a small business is high; but on the contrary, for such a modern sector as an employee of big business, clerk or general worker in manufacturing, mobility is relatively low.

CHANGE OF WORK-PLACE AND THE
PROBLEM OF PERMANENT EMPLOYMENT

Abegglen noted the fact that the number of men who leave their work in big business in Japan is extremely low; i.e., the average is 2 or 3 per cent per year, and he found "permanent employment" to be a characteristic feature of the employment system in big Japanese factories. He carefully adds that this cannot be applied to such industries as construction and shipbuilding, and to female workers, who have a much higher rate of turnover.[9]

According to our research data, the average frequency of an employee changing firms is 1.6 times. As Table 5 shows, among employees, 34 per cent of them have never moved from the establishment where they began to work. But 53.2 per cent have changed firms from one to three times during their careers. For owners of businesses with employees, and for self-employed business owners, the average frequency of changing is a little higher.

It is regrettable that we should have at the moment no comparable data for American and European countries. Therefore it is impossible to judge if this rate is higher or lower than the international standard.

The fact that 34 per cent of Japanese employees have never moved to another establishment or job seems to prove the existence of some stability of employment in the Japanese labor market; and it should be particularly noted that this rate is higher for workers in large-scale enterprises than in small-scale ones.

But careful consideration is necessary as to whether it is appropriate to describe the present condition with such a term as "permanent employment"; and whether or not one can conclude that this is a particular characteristic of Japanese industrialization, as some scholars claim. After all, only a portion of the 34 per cent of workers who have not changed jobs can be considered unconditionally as "permanent employees." That figure includes not only those who have experienced a long period of service since the very beginning of their career, but also many beginners who may change their occupations or firms in the future. Indeed, detailed study of the data shows that most changes occur during the first twenty years of service; only after that can men be considered permanently committed. Analysis of the rates of permanence among older men sug-

---

[9] Abegglen, however, refers directly to the data of only two big companies manufacturing electrical machinery, and he does not discuss the trend of the retirement rate. Abegglen, J. C., *op. cit.*, Chap. 2.

TABLE 5. DISTRIBUTION OF FREQUENCIES OF CHANGING ESTABLISHMENTS

	Frequencies of Changes											Total	Average
	0	1	2	3	4	5	6	7	8	9	10		
A	23.5	23.0	21.1	14.1	8.9	4.2	1.9	0.5	1.4	1.4	—	100.0 (213)	2.0
B	22.7	23.4	24.1	13.5	6.4	5.0	2.1	1.4	0.7	—	0.7	100.0 (141)	2.1
C	64.3	21.4	4.8	4.8	2.4	—	2.4	—	—	—	—	100.0 (42)	0.7
D	29.8	22.6	16.8	14.9	7.0	5.7	1.3	1.3	0.6	—	—	100.0 (315)	1.8
E	36.4	19.3	20.0	12.1	5.7	4.3	0.7	0.7	—	0.7	—	100.0 (140)	1.6
F	37.6	21.5	19.4	11.8	3.9	2.2	2.2	1.1	—	—	0.3	100.0 (279)	1.5
Employees	34.0	21.6	18.4	13.2	5.6	4.1	1.5	1.1	0.3	0.1	0.1	100.0 (734)	1.6
Average	30.4	22.5	18.9	13.1	6.4	4.4	2.1	1.1	0.6	0.3	0.2	100.0 (1227)	1.8

A: Business owners & executives.
B: Self-employed business owners (without employees).
C: Family workers.
D: Employees of small-scale firms.
E: Employees of medium-scale firms.
F: Employees of large-scale firms.
Employees: D+E+F.
Average: Among the 1,227 men are included G (temporary employees) and the unemployed (with occupational career).

gests that probably only about 12 per cent of all present employees will in fact stick to the same jobs throughout their careers, assuming that past conditions remain stable enough to predict future trends.

As we saw in Table 5, the bigger the scale of the establishment, the lower the rate of job mobility. Furthermore, clerical, sales and professional workers have low rates of movement. Therefore, such workers in large establishments (especially in manufacturing or government) come closest to the model of "permanent employees."

Comparison of workers with equal terms of service in a single firm, but divided according to the year of entry, shows that the tendency for permanent employment in large firms is a post-war phenomenon. The turnover rates in small firms have not changed much, but in large firms the rates have gone down since the Second World War. This leads us to an interesting theoretical contradiction.

Abegglen sought for the cause of a low turnover rate in big businesses in the traditional and paternalistic social relationships of Japanese culture. Among Japanese social scientists there were some who were fundamentally of the same opinion as Abegglen.[10] However, this explanation is contradictory since immobility is primarily seen in big businesses, and moreover is only a post-war tendency. So their interpretation amounts to the strange conclusion that paternalism is stronger in big business than in small business, and in the post-war period rather than the pre-war period. What is more important, such a viewpoint looks at structural characteristics of Japanese society too statically, and lacks historical insight. The form of permanent employment has not been historically consistent, nor have labor-management policies always sustained immobility. Therefore we cannot support the viewpoint of Abegglen, who tries to link two different societies, the family of feudal merchants in the Tokugawa era and the present big business age. But how are we to explain the present trend toward permanent employment? This is our problem at hand.

A PROVISIONAL GENERALIZATION

The writer takes particular notice of the following points: a high rate of industrialization, in other words, rapid economic growth in process, does not necessarily yield the result of consistent labor mobility in all phases. Basically, the concept of a labor market in a proper sense presupposes a situation which enables people to move toward better opportunities, but it does not imply that there are no restrictions in the direction of mobility. Actually, a man's first occupation establishes many restrictions and it influences his succeeding mobility pattern. Particularly,

[10] The article by Matsushima, S., and Nakano, T., in *Nihon Shakai Yoron* (Outline of Japanese Society), Tokyo Univ. Press, 1958, Chap. 6, is one of the typical examples.

people over middle age are subject to strong restrictions. Thus the market is composed of many heterogeneous parts, and free mobility between occupations, industries and types of firms is not everywhere present. Indeed, only the choice of first occupation seems relatively free of structural restraints.

With the development of technological innovations, with changing quality of skills, and with the realization of generally equal chances of education, those restrictions are generally supposed to decrease. It seems that the general principle by Lipset and Bendix referred to at the beginning of this paper is based on this assumption. Perhaps it would be true as a long-run perspective, but it must be recognized that so far such a phenomenon has not yet appeared all over the Japanese labor market. The fact is, on the contrary, that chances of mobility have been decreasing in the post-war years in large firms.

It seems appropriate to conclude this paper with a simple hypothesis. Unlike what we expect under ordinary laws of a free labor market, workers in the modern sector of industry can enjoy an increase of wages in spite of the existence of large pre-modern, low-wage sectors. The institutional basis for this lies in labor unions. But more fundamentally the modernization of wants on the basis of the changing living standards among modern workers ("wants adjusted to activities," as Marshall said), and the prevalence of a managerial ideology of "welfare in enterprises" must be pointed out. In the pre-modern sector, rather traditional types of wants, activities and ideologies are dominant both among workers and managers. Workers in the modern sector cannot go back to the traditional way of living. The relative lack of mobility between these two sectors in recent years is a consequence of their social bifurcation.

Evidently, both the existence of large differences in working conditions, wants, ideologies and so on, and a lack of labor mobility, forms a chain of cause and effect, thus reinforcing one another. Therefore, unless this reinforcement were broken, there could be no rapid change of the present situation in the near future. However, long-range changes in Japanese society are endemic.

The tentative generalization above helps to interpret the results obtained from our empirical data. As the research data used here are limited, there are, of course, many unsolved problems. This paper is merely one step toward an adequate theory.

The Salary Man

An important element in the new social order is the emergence of a
large "new middle class." The "old middle class" (the small independent
businessman and landowner) has been declining in power and influence
and is gradually being replaced by this "new middle class," the white-
collar employees of the large business corporations and government
bureaucracies.[1] The small independent entrepreneurs who comprise the
old middle class have generally played a central role in small local communities because of their influence and power, but their perspective has
remained focused within this narrow social microcosm. Although some
have profited indirectly from Japan's economic prosperity since 1955,
few members of the old middle class have had the motivation, ability,
and resources to expand their enterprises to take advantage of Japan's
rapid economic growth.[2] They are, rather, being superseded by, or
affiliated with and subordinated to large business corporations which
have the resources and entrepreneurial skill to play the key role in the
recent economic growth. The old middle class has not yet died out by
any means, but the trend of the times has been obvious, and many have
urged their children to become white-collar workers in the large bureaucratic organizations in the cities. The income of the white-collar worker
is less affected by economic fluctuations or by the whims of an arbitrary

Reprinted (and condensed) with permission of the author and publisher from
Japan's New Middle Class by Ezra Vogel (Berkeley and Los Angeles: University
of California Press, 1963).

Ezra Vogel, educated in sociology and psychology at Harvard in the early
nineteen fifties, taught first at Yale, and has now returned to Harvard to teach
sociology and do research on contemporary China.

[1] For a brief account of the distinction between the Japanese "new middle
class" and "old middle class" see Tadashi Fukutake, *Man and Society in Japan*.
Tokyo: Tokyo University Press, 1962.

[2] Cf. John C. Pelzel, "The Small Industrialist in Japan," *Explorations in Entrepreneurial History*, 1954, 7:79-93. Especially since 1955, however, the economic
boom in large companies has assisted the development of certain small industries.
Although the number of small enterprises has decreased compared to before
World War II, the number has remained relatively constant since the war.
Many of these small enterprises have been able to survive by affiliating with a
large company, albeit in a subordinate position.

paternalistic employer than that of the employee in the smaller industries. Because the income of the new middle-class citizen is guaranteed in the form of a regular salary, he has come to be known as the "sarari man" (salary man). This word is not used in Japan to include all who receive a salary, but only white-collar workers in the large bureaucracy of a business firm or government office. Although the two words "salary" and "man" are not ordinarily used together in English, the term "salary man" will be used throughout the present work to convey the Japanese meaning of *sarari man*.

THE DOUBLE STRUCTURE[3]

The salary man's pattern of life stands out in the Japanese context because of the sharp disparity between the large modern organization where he works and the more traditional small- or medium-sized enterprises.[4] Japanese scholars, struck by the coexistence of the modern

[3] Although no precise statistics are available on the growth of the number of salary men, rough estimates can be obtained from the number of white-collar workers who are not self-employed since most white-collar workers (except those in very small enterprises) would be classified as salary men.

	1920	1930	1940	1944	1955	1959
Nonagricultural labor force	12,575,000	14,933,000	18,291,000	19,275,000	23,600,000	27,810,000
White-collar workers	1,496,000	1,517,000	3,524,000	4,842,000	6,100,000	7,300,000

These data are cited in Solomon B. Levine, "Unionization of White-Collar Employees in Japan," unpublished manuscript.

According to the 1960 census, of the 31,549,800 males fifteen years of age and older, only 6,885,500 earned their living from farming, fishing, and lumbering. If one considers professional and technical workers, managers and officials, clerical workers, and protective-service workers as salary men, there were a total of 5,711,200 salary men. *Population Census of Japan*, 1960, II, part iv, Tables 1 and 2.

[4] Although large organizations are associated with the modern sector of the economy, it does not follow that all small- and medium-sized enterprises are associated with traditional occupations. For the distinction between modern and traditional aspects of the economy, see Henry Rosovsky, *Capital Formation in Japan, 1868-1940*, Glencoe, Ill.: The Free Press, 1961. Some more modern small enterprises have already a fairly high salary scale and are competitive for labor with the larger organizations.

Considering the high prestige, power, and income of salary men in government offices before the war, their position has declined since the war compared to salary men in business firms. The starting salary of salary men in government offices is generally about two-thirds of that in private corporations, but the

bureaucratic patterns of large organizations and the more traditional patterns of the small- and middle-sized enterprises have named this phenomenon the "double structure" of Japanese society.

Although some small enterprises have made technological advances and are offering high salaries because of increasing labor shortages, in the typical small enterprise, the worker tends to have a more diffuse relationship with his employer, a relationship that permeates all his life. The employer has some responsibility for looking after the personal needs of his employees, such as providing housing, helping arrange marriage, or giving special assistance in time of trouble. In return, the employee must be available for work at any time, and his personal life is continually subject to the employer's surveillance and approval. What security he has rests on the good will of the employer, which is not always sufficient because the small enterprises are subject to the fluctuations of the market and offer tenuous prospects for long-term security. Although smaller organizations are more paternalistic, workers are not only less satisfied, but there is a greater turnover of labor. At best the paternalism of the small enterprise is restricting and at worst it is a guise under which an opportunistic owner can pay lower wages and exploit his employees by offering a few personal services.

In contrast, the salary man not only receives higher pay and regular wages, but he has regular hours with time off. His promotions occur to some extent automatically on the basis of seniority and skill, and although responsive to wishes of superiors by American standards, he need not be so responsive as workers in smaller enterprises. Because he belongs to a large, stable organization and the firm is committed to him for life,[5] he knows that his job will be more secure against the fluctuations of the business cycle. When he compares himself to the workers in small organizations, he feels proud and satisfied that he is a salary man.

The economic uncertainty and pessimism that persist in Japan amidst the amazing prosperity and industrial development can be explained partly by the mood of the smaller enterprises which fear destruction because they will be unable to survive the economic squeeze if they are forced to offer higher wages and shorter hours. In the context of the pessimism of the smaller traditional enterprises, the salary man represents

---

power of salary men in government remains strong. (For this information I am indebted to Ken'ichi Tominaga.)

[5] The pattern of life-long commitment of the firm to the worker became prominent in large organizations in the early part of this century because of the problem of shortage of skilled workers, but the commitment did not apply to the larger group of unskilled workers. The salary man has the good fortune to have long-term security as a result of this commitment to the skilled workers. (For this background information I am indebted to Professor Kazuo Noda of Rikkyo University.)

for most Japanese the "bright new life." The salary man's career is not a rapid and glorious rise to such great heights that it appears beyond their reach, but a secure path to moderate success. Able and enterprising young men willing to take risks and look out for their own future have the possibility of rising more rapidly, earning more money, and living more luxuriously by working on their own or joining small firms. But most Japanese have no such confidence in their own talents and long-term economic prospects even if they were to have such an opportunity in the short run. For the vast majority of Japanese the life of the salary man seems to represent as high a standard as they can reasonably hope for. The young Japanese girl hopes to marry a salary man even if his salary were lower because his life is steady, he has leisure time, and she can be free of the anxieties and work connected with independent business. Independent shopkeepers, craftsmen, and farmers complain that they cannot compete with salary men in attracting desirable brides. The importance of studying the salary man is not only for understanding this group per se but for understanding the aspirations of other Japanese.

The community where we studied salary men is a section of a Tokyo suburb, selected by Japanese social scientists as typically middle class. From visiting other cities in Japan, from conversing with and reading works of Japanese social scientists, and from having a draft of this manuscript read by Japanese who have lived on all four main islands of Japan, I feel confident that the patterns described here for Mamachi are essentially the same for salary men throughout Japan. Although Japanese are very conscious of variations in regional dialect and custom, Japan is a small country which has been relatively isolated because of its insular position and hence has a much more highly unified culture than most countries.[6]

THE SETTING: MAMACHI

The people of Mamachi think of their neighborhood as *shizuka* (quiet and peaceful), separated from the bustle of Tokyo where most of the husbands work. Until about thirty or forty years ago Mamachi was sparsely settled. Although many new houses have gone up in the last generation, the neighborhood with its narrow paths, large trees, and small gardens still retains an aura of suburban calm.

Virtually all homes in Mamachi are privately-owned, single-storied, unpainted wooden dwellings surrounded by ingenious small gardens, separated from the outside world by high fences. One or two sides of

[6] Editor's note: Vogel's material comes mainly from the result of a year of participant observation in the community; he and his wife and infant son lived in Mamachi (a suburb of Tokyo) and participated as widely as possible in local life. They intensively studied six families, and in addition, interviewed (in Japanese) other families, local officials, and various "experts."

the house, generally facing the sun, have sliding glass doors which can be opened to let in the sun and to air out the house during the day. At night, the sliding wooden doors outside the glass doors will be closed to keep out rain, cold, insects, and prowlers. Construction is generally simple and plain, with thin walls, peaked roofs, small windows, no basement. The homes average perhaps three or four rooms in size, the rooms being separated by sliding paper doors. Many homes have one "Western style" room used for a sitting room or for entertaining guests; it has chairs, a couch and a chest of drawers, and is often decorated in a fashion not too different from American style of a few decades ago. Two or three "Japanese style" rooms covered with soft tatami mats can be used for sitting in the day time and for sleeping at night. In the day time, cushions are brought out to sit on, and a table is set up for meals or for entertaining guests. At night the tables and cushions are put away and bedding is taken out of the large closets and placed over the tatami mats. Other furnishings generally are few and simple: a few chests and bureaus, a television set, a radio, a few pictures, decorations, and perhaps a children's desk and a piano. The kitchen is old-fashioned by American standards. A few people now can afford a mechanized American style kitchen or at least a refrigerator, but most families in Mamachi still have only one or two gas burners and a small wooden ice box which they fill with a piece of ice every few days. The kitchen usually is not furnished very attractively and guests are not invited in. One small room contains a small but high Japanese wooden bath tub where the family spends many an evening taking turns relaxing in very hot water. They have cold running water which is safe to drink, and a few families have a little heater to heat water as it comes out of the tap.

IMPORTANCE OF THE
HUSBAND'S INCOME

In comparison with most families around the world and with rural families in Japan, Mamachi families are unusually dependent on the husband's salary and personal savings. Most Mamachi families do not feel part of a tight-knit group of friends or relatives to whom they can turn in time of financial distress. Perhaps they are too proud to let their relatives know about money difficulties, or doubt their relatives' ability to help, or fear future family quarrels, or feel the family relationship too distant to be comfortable in making the request. Whatever their reasons, most of these families would undergo great sacrifices rather than call on relatives or friends for financial assistance.

In rural Japan, as in rural areas in most countries, a family derives its security from the land and in time of need a family can turn to relatives or other members of the local community for assistance. In most industrialized countries families in great need can expect to receive welfare benefits from the government, but for an industrialized nation, Japan's welfare services are not well developed. Benefits are small and few, and not given automatically to people who meet standardized criteria of "neediness." As a result, families seeking welfare aid are put in the position of having to prostate themselves before welfare officials in order to receive even the minimum of aid. While, for example, even a middle-class family in America would not be very embarrassed by accepting aid for dependent children, social-security payments, compensation for industrial accidents, and the like, the Japanese application procedures are often so humiliating, the chance for receiving aid so uncertain, and the amount of aid so inadequate, that the typical Mamachi family does not expect to seek public help, even in time of need.[7] It is also difficult to obtain loans from banks. Not only are interest rates much higher than in the United States, but banks rarely lend money to individual borrowers, and a borrower may acquire bothersome personal as well as financial obligations. Some families turn to moneylenders, but borrow for only a very short time because interest rates are exorbitant. Although there are several moneylenders in Mamachi and families told us that other families go to moneylenders, no family ever told us that they themselves had used moneylenders. Indeed the stories of people sneaking in to pawn shops sound almost like a criminal escaping the detectives.

The wife of an ordinary middle-class Mamachi family has virtually no chance to earn a living by herself. While some poorer wives are able to take in work like sewing, such jobs are increasingly being done by large industries. Even if a middle-class wife could find such work it would be embarrassing, since few jobs would seem suitable to her status except, perhaps, teaching some housewifely arts at which she was particularly skillful or a special service occupation like hairdressing. Even if another job were available, she would receive a much lower salary than a man in the same position, and perhaps even less than a young girl doing the same job. Ordinarily she would seek work only if widowed, and the income she could earn would probably not be adequate to support herself and her children.

Furthermore, it is difficult for divorced or widowed women to find new husbands or to obtain help from relatives.[8] It is especially difficult for

[7] Some of the Japanese rules regarding welfare sound as if services were more widespread than they are. For a survey of actual welfare conditions see Eiichi Isomura, Takeyoshi Kawashima, and Takashi Koyama, *Kazoku no Fuyoo* (The Maintenance of Needy Families), Tokyo: Kawade Shoboo, 1956.

[8] In 1956, only 6.1 per cent of marriages in Japan were of women who had been married before, but 10 per cent were of men who had been wed before. *Fujin no Genjoo* (The Position of Women), Tokyo: Roodooshoo Fujinshoonen Kyoku, 1959, p. 55. In the United States, between January, 1947, and June, 1954, 19.9 per cent of marriages were of women who had been married before. Paul C. Glick, *American Families*, New York: John Wiley, 1957, p. 141. This

women with children to remarry because men want children of their own and few earn enough money to support large families. But perhaps more important is the tradition of family loyalty. Sons are expected to continue the family name and line of a dead father, and widows are still admired for remaining loyal to their dead husbands. Men feel that a wife who was properly devoted to her first husband would have difficulty transferring that devotion to another man, and a wife who was not properly devoted to her first husband would be less likely to make a good wife for anyone.

The significance of the Japanese salary man lies, therefore, not only in the fact that he is a non-manual worker and an organization man, but in the fact that he has a measure of economic security which most Japanese do not have. In a nonaffluent society where one has no place to turn in time of need, and welfare is provided by neither the government nor the family nor personal connections, the large firm assumes a critical importance because it provides security as well as income.

ORDERLY LIFE OF THE SALARY MAN

The salary men, who dominate Mamachi both in spirit and numbers, range from high-level managers to humble office clerks, from the powerful elite to servile office boys. But whatever the variation, they all tend to live an orderly life, made possible by long-term membership in a large and stable bureaucratic organization. A salary man receives his pay regularly and can predict within a close range his position and salary of five, ten, fifteen, or even twenty years hence. He may not be able to name the department of the company in which he will work, but he can predict with such accuracy when he will become section head that he will be bitterly disappointed if he receives even a small promotion only a year later than he had originally expected. Business fluctuations affect the size of his bonus, but they are likely to have little effect on his salary because the company continues to meet its commitments to him even in time of economic difficulty. A typical salary man never receives an offer from another firm, but even if he were to receive an attractive offer from elsewhere, his long-term interests are best served by remaining in the same firm because his salary and benefits rise sharply with the number of years of service and he knows that he will be dismissed from his own company only for the grossest incompetence or misbehavior.

In addition, he knows that in the event of sickness, accident, or retirement, he unquestionably will receive welfare benefits. The successful independent businessman can provide his own security against sickness

---

difference is too large to be explained only by the difference in the divorce rate.

For a widower it is not only considered advisable but necessary to remarry in order to have someone care for the children. Since the children would remain in the father's line, this is not seen as causing any serious problem.

and injury by his large income and savings; the independent professional must save carefully for such contingencies; the small shopkeeper has almost no hope of being able to cope with such emergencies. The salary man has security, not through his own savings or power, but through the company which, in effect, gives him a guaranteed income and insurance against various kinds of difficulties that he and his family might encounter.

The salary man, then, has security, but his stipend is, after all, rather small in comparison with the successful businessman or even in comparison with the independent professional. Hence, he must carefully control his spending. Perhaps the greatest financial difficulty he will face is the period after retirement. His company will provide some retirement benefits, either in the form of a lump sum or pension, but generally these are small, barely enough for minimum subsistence. The salary man usually is required to retire as early as fifty-five or sixty years of age; afterward, to supplement his company's retirement benefits, he must turn to his savings, supplementary income, or his children, although sometimes his company will help him find a part-time job after retirement. A retired teacher, for example, may get a job as a part-time consultant to a book company. A man with rich relatives or friends may get a part-time job working for them. Some of the less successful may open a small shop. Many have no choice but to live with their children.

The daily life of the salary man is the essence of regularity. Although commuting trains generally run to Tokyo every five or seven minutes, the salary man knows precisely on what train he leaves in the morning. Theoretically, he is expected to work overtime with little or no extra compensation whenever his firm requests it, and he is reluctant to take all the free time to which he is officially entitled. For example, he may be given ten days or two weeks annual vacation, but he ordinarily would not take this much time off. If he were to request his full vacation time, he would be regarded as selfish and disloyal by his co-workers and by his superiors. However, at the same time companies find it increasingly difficult to ask their salary men to work overtime. The salary men have become used to regular hours and regard overtime work without extra compensation as an encroachment on their freedom. They have no objection to working their eight or nine hours a day Monday through Friday and until mid-afternoon on Saturday. But they resent being made to work longer hours.

It is the salary man who makes the sharpest distinction between working time and free time. In contrast to the businessman who mixes business and leisure, to the small shopkeeper who has almost no leisure, and to the independent professional, whose leisure is determined by the absence of patients, the salary man, like his child in school, generally has set hours so that he knows he can plan certain hours of the day and certain days of the week for himself and his family.

In addition to regularity, security, and free time, the companies provide various side benefits which constitute the joy of living. The salary man attends parties, athletic meets, and even trips sponsored by the company. At least once or twice a year, the company treats its employees to an overnight trip to the country, and on other occasions employees take up voluntary collections for company trips.

Foreign observers have described Japanese firms as paternalistic since they look after so many aspects of the employee's life. Yet large firms, in at least one fundamental respect, are much less paternalistic than the traditional small enterprises. In the large firm, privileges are established by routine procedures or rules; they are less determined by a particular relationship to an employer, the whims of superiors, or the fluctuation in the company's financial condition. Rather, they tend to be awarded universally to all members of the organization on the basis of seniority and ability.

FAMILY LIFE

The salary man's contacts are largely restricted to his work associates and to his own immediate family. He lacks the prestige to have important community positions and the money for anything but the simplest entertainment. He spends many evenings at home with the family, and may go on Sunday with the family to the city, perhaps to visit a large park or a department store. For week-day recreation, he and his work associates stop off after work at their favorite bars, tea and coffee houses, or snack bars. Because he expects to be in the same organization all his life, his closest relationships are with work associates and he considers it of utmost importance to keep their friendship.

The salary man is essentially free when he returns home; home is a place to relax. In some cases the salary man, in contrast to other husbands, may even help his wife, albeit not as much as his American counterpart. He may know how to make his own tea and, in extreme cases, he may even know how to cook. He occasionally may help the children with their baths, fold up his own bedding, do a few shopping errands, and go for walks with the children.

However, the wife generally knows little and cares less about her husband's daily activities at the office. She has virtually no opportunity to go out with her husband to meet other men in the company and their wives. The husband's assignments in the company generally are limited, and the problems in which the husband is interested at work have little meaning to the wife. Even if a curious young wife expresses an interest in her husband's work, he has difficulty explaining his work in a way that she can understand and hence he gets little satisfaction in telling her about the details of his work. Because she is so completely separated from the husband's daily world and he knows so little about her community activities, the area of mutual interest tends to be the children and the relatives.

Although the salary man's wife does not understand precisely what her husband does, unless she has unusually high ambitions she is usually satisfied with her husband's position in a large company. From her point of view, the major advantages of her husband's job are the regular hours and wages. She can count on his being home certain hours and she can count on his income. It is possible for the wife to manage household expenses without worrying about how much the income will be next month, or where it will come from. In comparison to the shopkeeper's wife and even to the independent professional, she is happy that she does not have to subject herself to the indignities of long hours of hard work. She can take care of the children and devote herself to them as she wishes. In comparison with the wives on the farm or the shopkeepers' wives, she lives a life of freedom and luxury. She does not have the same desire as her American counterpart to go out and get a job on her own and she does not have the same kind of feelings about being "just a housewife." She is delighted that she can devote herself to her family with so few outside demands.

In planning the children's future it is the salary man and his family who are most dependent on entrance examinations. Unlike the independent professional or the businessman, who can take the children into his own work regardless of the educational institutions the children attended, and unlike the shopkeeper who has lower aspirations for his children, the salary man's children are dependent upon entrance examinations to universities and companies. Hence, they generally place more pressure on their children and spend more time and energy to prepare them for these examinations.

The salary man's family is likely to be limited to parents and children. Association with relatives has nothing to do with business and tends to be based more on mutual liking than on reciprocal obligations. In the businessman's family, there is often a business tie with relatives which keeps the children and the parents together. The son who takes over his father's professional practice is also likely to have close business ties with his parents. Children of shopkeepers help their parents when young, and occasionally one child may succeed to the shop. In the salary man's family, however, there is no such economic bond between parents and children. Because a son's life is more determined by his education and the organization to which he belongs than the size of his inheritance, and the daughter's marriage more dependent on her training and character than the size of the dowry, parents devote themselves to preparing their children properly for work and marriage rather than to accumulating a large inheritance.

Distinctions between the first son and the second son tend to lose significance in the salary man's family. No son succeeds to family headship in any meaningful economic way so that the post-war regulations requiring that inheritance be divided equally among the children poses no problem for the salaried man. Inheritance of family ritual objects generally goes to one son, but a more important problem which leads to a partial preservation of the stem family is the location of elderly parents after retirement. Retirement payments are minimal, and parents usually find it necessary to live with the children if they are to retain the same standard of living after retirement. In addition, elderly couples ordinarily have few opportunities to be integrated into a community except through their children. All children may share the financial responsibility, but the retired parents, and especially a widowed mother, ordinarily continue to live with only one of the children.

The salary man cannot hope to match the style of life of the successful independent businessman. But psychologically he derives a feeling of power by belonging to the large organization. The fact that in Japan a person is so closely identified with the group to which he belongs gives the salary man a backing which enables him in important respects to look down on the businessmen and independent professionals, who have more real power in the local community.

ENTRANCE EXAMINATIONS

No single event, with the possible exception of marriage, determines the course of a young man's life as much as entrance examinations, and nothing, including marriage, requires as many years of planning and hard work. Because all colleges and high schools, and many private junior high schools, grade schools, and even kindergartens use entrance examinations to select only a small proportion of the applicants, and because examinations are open to all,[9] the competition is fierce. Passing examinations to a good school seems as difficult to the Mamachi resident as for a camel to pass through the eye of a needle. There is virtually no limit to how much one can prepare for examinations. The average child studies so hard that Japanese educators speak of the tragedy of their school system which requires students to sacrifice their pleasures, spontaneity, and sparkle for examination success. These arduous preparations constitute a kind of *rite de passage* whereby a young man proves that he has the qualities of ability and endurance necessary for becoming a salary man.

---

[9] This is in contrast to many developing countries where for reason of race, language, ethnic discrimination, or financial requirements, the opportunities are limited to certain groups in the population.

The Japanese commonly refer to entrance examinations as *shiken jigoku* which literally means "examination hell."

The Mamachi youth is willing to endure these tortures because if successful he will be able to join a large successful firm where he can remain for life. To be admitted to such a firm, one must attend a good university, and to attend a good university one must pass the entrance examination. To pass the entrance examination for a good university one must have good training, and to acquire the good training one must pass the entrance examination to a good high school. In the final analysis, success is determined not by intelligence tests, nor by the school record, nor by the teacher's recommendations but by entrance examinations.

Although it seems a tragedy to the participants, there is a certain logic in how the examination system works. Because the firm commits itself to a young man for life and because business in contemporary Japan is highly competitive, the firm must be careful to select men of unusual promise and ability. The number of men a large firm takes in each year is so large and the number of personal connections of company officials so great that it would be impossible to use personal evaluations as the primary basis to select applicants. One need only imagine the problems of large numbers of company employees each urging the company to support his favorite candidate, to understand the convenience and value of a more universalistic basis of judgment. Because there is such wide agreement in Japanese society as to which universities are most desirable, firms consider the university attended as important or even more important than their own examinations for selecting salary men. Not only the university's relative standing, but even its style of life, has considerable stability over time, because of the practice of inbreeding. Nearly all professors at a major university have received their training at the same institution, and it is almost unthinkable for a professor to move from one major university to another. Organizations add to this stability by selecting applicants according to the university's reputation. Young applicants know which universities the firms prefer and choose their university accordingly, thus perpetuating the emphasis on the university attended as a basis for selecting competent young men.

A large company ordinarily hires older workers only when absolutely necessary and even then gives more security and more rapid pay increases to younger employees. Here again, there is a self-fulfilling accuracy to the company's predictions. People who do change companies tend to be opportunistic and less devoted to the company's interests, and the company feels justified in hiring workers directly from college making work experience irrelevant as a criterion.

From the view of the outside observer entrance examinations involve an intensity of affect which cannot be explained only by the desire to obtain a good job. Although the search for security has rational components, as mentioned before, it has been heightened by the many up-heavals in the lifetime of the average adult and by the difficulty which the contemporary urban parent had in finding a long-term livelihood when he was young. For the urban resident, a job in a large corporation is as close as one can come to the security that country relatives have by belonging to a household firmly attached to land and the local com-munity. Just as obtaining land is thought to secure the future of a family even in the next generation, so does a job in a large corporation provide long-range security and insure that one's children can be given a proper position in life.

There are now opportunities in Japanese society for adventurous and talented young men, especially in new fields like electronics, advertising, entertainment, and foreign trade. New small companies in these fields can offer higher salaries than larger organizations, but most young men are unwilling to take this risk of less security; however, those who do not pass the entrance examinations to a good university may have no other choice.

But even if one wants to work in a smaller company, attending a good university makes it easier to get a good job and even to change jobs at a later time. Once a student has passed an entrance examination to a first-rate university, he has no worry about graduating because the university is committed to his success and would dismiss him only for extreme misbehavior or incompetence. Compared to American state uni-versities, which dismiss a large proportion of first-year students, the num-ber of students failed from Japanese universities is negligible. Moreover, students do not transfer from one university to another. Being admitted to a given university becomes, in effect, a basis of ascription which provides fairly clear limits to one's later mobility.

Although students in a good university may still be concerned about being accepted by the best possible organization, the range of differences in status between the corporations or government bureaus they will join is relatively narrow. The room for achievement within the company is also relatively minor compared to whether one attended an outstanding university and whether one was admitted to a large reputable organiza-tion. To a large extent advancement within the firm depends simply on the date of entry into the organization. All new members of a company are admitted on the same day each year, go through the same general training program, and are treated as equals in most matters, such as salary and position. Even when employees begin to get different func-tional assignments, seniority remains relatively more important than skill and ability in determining rank and salary. An employee's standing vis-à-vis outsiders is determined when he enters the firm, and is little affected by the minor differentiations of status within the firm.

Even if some students from a lesser university are admitted to a good company or government office, they still may be at a disadvantage compared to those who attended the better universities. While some say that cliques of graduates of a given high school or university are weaker than before the war, fellow alumni of the same university are known to show preferences for their fellow graduates. It is assumed that those who attended a certain university (and sometimes even a certain department within a university) will feel mutual loyalty and share similar attitudes, making it possible for them to work together harmoniously despite differences of opinion and temperament. Especially in large government bureaus, acceptance in informal circles and even rate of advancement may be affected by the university one attended.

This analysis has focused on the boy and his problem of entering a large organization, but similar considerations apply to girls even though their career is marriage. Girls generally worry less about examinations than boys. Some people even question whether a girl who has attended the most competitive coeducational universities will make a good wife, and many girls prefer not to go to a coeducational school where they would have to study harder to keep up with the boys. But the better girls' schools are regarded as highly desirable, and these schools also require entrance examinations. Marital choice even in urban Japan is still decided in large part on the basis of objective criteria rather than simply on the diffuse relationship between a young man and a young lady, and the university or school attended has become an even more important criterion than ascriptive considerations like family background. Indeed, a boy's family proudly speaks of marrying a girl who attended a well-known girls' school just as her family will speak proudly of a young man who attended a good university. Thus, examinations are crucial to the girl's as well as to the boy's career.

In the view of the Mamachi resident, one's station in life is not predetermined by birth, but it is determined by the time one has his first job. For those who aspire to the new middle class, the opportunities for mobility are highly compressed into one period of life, late adolescence. The intense concentration of pressure for finding one's position in life during this brief time is undoubtedly related to the fact that Japan is the one country in the world where the suicide rate is high in the late teens and early twenties and declines during middle age. Success or failure in finding the right opening at the time of college admission is considered permanent, and failure or fear of failure is disturbing even to the most talented.

PREPARING FOR AND TAKING EXAMINATIONS

Mamachi residents are careful in their selection of schools, and the range and variety of possible choices are enormous. At the apex of educational life are the great national universities, such as Tokyo University, and the well-known public high schools, such as Hibiya and Shinjuku, which students of all social classes can afford to enter if they pass the examinations. Next are the good private universities and the attached private elementary, junior, and senior high schools. Entrance examinations for these schools are almost as difficult as those for the best public institutions but tuition is higher, so that only well-to-do students can attend. Thirdly, there are public and private schools of lesser quality ranging from expensive schools which few salary men can afford, to public and less expensive private schools widely attended by children of salary men. At the bottom of the scale are the local public elementary and junior high schools, the only schools which do not require entrance examinations.

All students are required by law to complete junior high school, but any student who wishes to go beyond must take examinations. (The length of compulsory education is not determined by age but by number of years [nine] of schooling. No student is failed. One might speculate that failing students would arouse the same kind of threat to group solidarity as discharging a man from a firm.) It is assumed that once a student has been admitted to a junior or senior high school or college, he will remain in the same school until he graduates, but it is possible to change school systems at the time of each graduation. Although normally a student takes examinations in order to continue after each successive graduation, certain school systems, known as *escareetaa* (escalator) schools since students can move up within the same system from kindergarten to college, have only nominal examinations for students within the same system. When a child is admitted to an outstanding kindergarten such as those associated with Keio University (private) and Ochanomizu Women's University (public), he is thought to be on the *escareetaa* and established for life. Thus, a heavy premium is placed on getting into the kindergarten of the *escareetaa* schools, and the schools charge higher tuition for kindergarten than for the upper levels. The applicants to the best kindergartens are so numerous that difficult examinations cannot sort out the applicants adequately, and a lottery also is required to select the favored few. Recently, special schools have been opened in Tokyo to prepare three- and four-year-olds for the kindergarten entrance examinations.

Occasionally a Mamachi child takes these difficult kindergarten examinations, but the chance of passing is so slight, private-school costs are so high, and the daily commuting to Tokyo on public transportation is so taxing for mother and child that nearly all Mamachi children go to the local kindergartens and elementary schools. Mamachi families then concentrate on preparing their children for entrance examinations for the better junior and senior high schools and colleges, which are, by and large, in Tokyo.

Junior and senior high-school entrance examinations are not thought to be important for their own sake, but because they permit a child to get the better training that makes it easier to pass an examination to a difficult college. Because college entrance is considered so crucial, many students who fail the examination the first time may choose to wait a year and try the examination again. These students, not attached to any school or university, are called *ronin*, the name formerly used for the lordless samurai. Some persistent young people who have their hopes set on a certain school and whose families can afford to continue supporting them, may attempt the examinations several years before being admitted, in the meantime attending special preparatory schools.

Examinations, by and large, measure educational achievement. Because they must be given to large numbers, they consist mostly of objective factual questions of the multiple-choice variety. At the kindergarten level they may test the child's knowledge of the Japanese syllabary, perhaps a few characters, and elementary arithmetic. Junior-high and high-school examinations generally test science, Japanese language and literature, mathematics, history, and English. College examinations are similar but require more technical and specialized knowledge, especially in foreign languages.

A student ordinarily begins to prepare seriously about a year or two before the examinations that take place in January or February before the new school year begins in April. He studies several hours after school every day, and in the summer vacation preceding the February exams, he spends most of the day and sometimes part of the night in study. He often gives up movies, hobbies, and other recreation during this year of preparation. Athletes usually are advised to drop their sports activities, and music and dance lessons ordinarily are suspended.

In the year preceding the examination the mother spends much time investigating expenses, entrance requirements, and the schools' records in successfully placing their graduates. She visits schools, reads advice columns and books, and gathers information from friends. In addition, she spends much time consulting with her child's teacher and other parents in order to assess her own child's abilities. Naturally she wants her child to get into the best possible school, but this requires strategy and risk-taking. A child can take as many as three or four examinations if they are not offered on the same date, but it is seldom possible to take more. If a child fails all these, he may be out of luck. In addition, the process of taking examinations is tiring for the student and his mother, and they frequently require money payments. If a student tries to take three or four examinations during the same season, he may be so exhausted and discouraged from the first ones that he will not perform well on the later ones. Hence it is important for the mother to assess her child's abilities accurately and have the child take the most appropriate examinations.

The mother does most of the ground work but she must make sure that the father and the child approve her choices. The child's veto of a school is usually final, for while the mother often persuades a child to accept her choice, without his co-operation and hard work, the mother can have little hope of success. The mother does not want to risk being solely responsible for the choice of schools in case the child fails, and she is likely to consult with the father. Indeed, the family is likely to have frequent and sometimes heated discussions during the period of decision-making.

By late January these initial decisions are made, and the process of application begins. A candidate can apply only during an allotted two or three days. The mother applies in person, taking health certificates, school records, and the entrance fees. At almost every school on the first day of applications, there will be a few mothers who have waited in line overnight with their small snack and cushions, so that they will be among the first to apply. These mothers know that schools state that arrival time makes no difference. But apparently they hope that they may impress the school administration with their seriousness of purpose, that the low number on the application blank may be lucky, or that their child may be called for the examination early in the day and hence be somewhat fresher in taking the examinations. Their early arrival simply may reflect anxiety and excitement and a desire to get the application process over with. While most Mamachi mothers think it somewhat foolish to wait overnight, nevertheless many start out on the first train leaving Mamachi, at about four o'clock in the morning, on the day when applications are due. Even then, there may be a long line when they arrive, and those who have enough courage to come later in the day may have a wait of several hours before filling out the application. A mother who is going through the application procedure for the first time or who is applying for her only son is more likely to be among the first in line. If a woman is a "beteran" (veteran) she may be confident enough to come much later.[10] Sometimes it is necessary for the children to go along with the mother for applications, but for a college application the child probably will go by himself. This same standing in line may be done three or four times, depending on the number of applications a person is making.

If a personal interview is required at the elementary and junior high school age, the mother and child will be concerned about the impres-

[10] One is struck by the similarities between the mother's attitudes about giving birth and about having her child take an examination. In both, there exists a great amount of folklore and advice constituting a special subculture passed down from veteran to newcomer. In the examination, however, one's odds for success are much lower, and the amount of effort required is much greater.

sions they make. It may be desirable to bring along letters of introduction from people who have important positions or some personal connection with the faculty, administration, or Parent-Teachers Association. Although a mother and child carefully plan what to say during this interview, it is not uncommon for the child to be frightened and to have difficulty expressing himself in the interview. Even if the mother and child consider the examination more crucial than the interview, they approach the interview as if it were of the greatest importance.

The month or so before and during examinations is commonly known as "examination season." The child studies very long hours, and if the family can afford it, a tutor comes to the house regularly. The child's household responsibilities are taken over by his brothers and sisters who are warned not to interrupt his study. In extreme cases the mother may bring him meals on a tray, sharpen his pencils, and stand ready to serve his every need. His father may come home from work early to help with the studying if the tutor is not available. The family is collectively on tiptoe for fear of disturbing the young scholar. They become almost hypochondriacal, and the slightest sign of a cold is taken seriously as a possible hindrance to examination success. Community activities and social visiting come to a complete halt, so absorbed are the families in their children's preparation. On street corners, at the neighborhood shops, in business offices, and at the dinner table, conversation revolves about the one topic of most immediate concern to all — examinations.

During the weeks around examinations, mothers of applicants try to avoid meeting other mothers and friends. Usually they leave their homes only for necessary shopping or to make arrangements for school applications. If they should meet an acquaintance accidentally, they attempt to steer conversation away from the delicate question of their child's examinations. Since a family will be embarrassed if it becomes known that their child has been refused by a school, the mothers usually do not identify the schools to which they are applying. If it is obvious to the other party, they explain that they do not expect to succeed for they have not prepared properly and they really are trying to get into another school (to which they are almost certain to be admitted). Sometimes a family denies that their child is taking a certain examination only to be discovered on the scene of the exam by the very friend who questioned them. Children also watch closely to see who is missing from school on an examination day to ascertain which schoolmates are taking which exams. On the whole, children are more open and direct in talking about examination plans than their parents, and they often report their findings to their mothers.

Mothers accompany children to all but the college examinations to give them moral support. If the father can take off from work or if the examination is early enough in the day, he may accompany the child in place of the mother. There is a waiting room close to the examination room where parents can sit while the children are taking the examination. A number of mothers reported that they were unable to sleep on the night before the examination. By the end of a series of two or three examinations over a period of eight to ten days, mothers as well as children are so exhausted that they often have to go to bed for a few days.

There is a hiatus of several days before the results of the examinations are announced. If a child takes examinations for two or three different schools, he may hear the results of the first examination before he takes the last. Since the report of the first examination is the first real indication for the family of the child's standing, the results have an exaggerated importance. The mother whose child has passed the first examination generally is jubilant. Conversely families with a failure are extremely gloomy and pessimistic. Tensions increase as families await the results. Most people will not telephone or communicate with examination families until after the results have been announced. A few mothers and children cannot resist talking about the examinations, and worries are at least shared and discussed within the family and among some friends and relatives. Some mothers have said that there is such an ominous weighty feeling during this time that they would almost prefer to hear negative results rather than continue the uncertainty.

The dramatic climax comes with the announcement of the results. Usually grades are not mailed, but the names or code names of successful candidates are posted at the school. Sometimes the names of successful candidates for well-known schools and universities are announced on the radio. Even if a family has heard the results on the radio they also check the posted list to assure themselves that there has not been an error.

The date the list is posted usually is known long in advance, but the time of day often is indefinite. Crowds gather as much as twenty-four hours before the auspicious hour. Frequently parents will go because children might have difficulty controlling their emotions in public. Even the father may take off a day or two from work at this time to check the examination results or to be of moral support to the mother and children. People concerned about controlling their emotions go to see the bulletin board during the night. Some, attempting to be casual, wait several hours after posting to check the results.

If a child has succeeded, he and his parents are only too glad to tell the results, although they will attempt to show the proper reserve. They may whisper the result saying "please don't tell anybody else," but their smiles are irrepressible and there can be no doubt about their satisfaction. If a mother looks troubled, friends do not ask the results. Indeed, the mother of an unsuccessful candidate may cry and sleep for several days before going out to face friends. Although to my knowledge there has been no suicide in Mamachi in recent years as a result of examinations, stories of juvenile suicide as a result of examination failure are widely publicized in the mass media and well known by all those taking examinations.

Because there are so many schools in the Tokyo area and because suburban children attend so many different schools, it is rare for more than two or three students from the same grade school to continue to pass examinations for the same junior high school, high school, and college. Even if two friends should intend to take examinations for the same school in order to continue together in junior high school or high school, if one passes and the other fails, the one who succeeds will not let friendship stand in the way of attending the better school. While at first they may attempt to keep up the friendships while attending different schools, the difference in status leads to embarrassment, and the ties generally become less meaningful.

When confronted with the question of why examination pressure is so intense, many Japanese respondents answered that it is because Japan is a small crowded country with few opportunities for success. This answer unquestionably highlights a factor of crucial importance, but it does not explain everything. There are many universities in Japan which are not difficult to enter, and there are opportunities for success aside from examinations. There are other crowded countries where opportunity is limited but examination pressure much less severe. Implicit in this response is the feeling that one's opportunity to achieve security and social mobility is highly compressed into one brief period of life, and many explicitly recognize that the best way for a commoner to rise on the social ladder is to enter a famous university. At least two other social systems, the family and the school, seem important for understanding the full force of this pressure. The importance of these two systems, like the life-time commitment to a firm, are further manifestations of a striking characteristic pervading Japanese social structure: the high degree of integration and solidarity within a given group.

In most modern societies, the task of educating the youth is performed not in the home but in the school system. For these salaried families, however, education is performed by the school *and* the home. In a sense, parents become assistant teachers, checking frequently with the regular teachers about the work the parents should be doing to help educate and train their children. Therefore to a large extent the parent-child relationship is the relationship of teacher and student. The mother must supervise her child, give him assignments, check the work, and impose necessary sanctions to see that he performs the work adequately. Whereas, in some industrialized societies, the mother-child relationship is more strictly limited to primary socialization and to providing affection, among these salaried families it must also take on in addition a task orientation in which the mother and the child prepare for examinations.

ACHIEVEMENT WITHOUT RIVALRY

The prominence of examinations in the life of Mamachi salaried families reflects an acceptance of the principle that success should be determined by competence as judged by a universal standard. The path of success is not determined primarily by birth or connections but by superior capacity as demonstrated by performance. While Japan is sometimes described as a particularistic society, at the time of examinations particularistic relations clearly give way to these universalistic standards. One of the dangers of open competition, however, it that rivalry may prove disruptive to groups.

Yet the extent of disruption is very limited in groups to which Mamachi residents belong because within the group competition is carefully controlled. Once a child is admitted to a school, grades are not given great importance, and there is a strong feeling of group solidarity which serves to inhibit competitiveness between the students.[11] Once in the firm, one's success has been assured, and rivalry is kept in bounds by the primacy of seniority which is non-competitive and the common interest in the success of the firm. Since schools and firms do not drop members for poor achievement records, there is no feeling that one's remaining in the group depends on another's leaving.

Even in taking entrance examinations, a person plays down competition with friends. A person ordinarily hopes that all in his group of friends will be among those who pass. Even if friends are separated and pursue different paths as a result of examinations, there usually is no feeling of acrimony. In a sense, the one who did not get in feels that the position he hoped for was filled not by his friend but by a stranger.

Achievement patterns also do not disrupt family solidarity. In the United States, for example, where achievement is defined as an individual matter, the child who goes beyond his parents in achievement level often feels that his parents have difficulty understanding the kind of world in which he lives. Among the Mamachi families, however, the child's success is more directly a family success. The mother continually keeps close to the child and his work. Even if the child does not need his family's introductions, he will require the family's help in preparing for the examinations. While disparities between achievement of siblings may create some problems, brothers and sisters are also so involved in each other's success and share in the community respect awarded to a family

---

[11] This pattern appears to begin at an early age. Miss Kazuko Yoshinaga who taught in middle-class kindergartens in both Japan and the United States reported that in kindergartens American children are much more openly competitive than Japanese children. Even about matters of age and size, Japanese kindergarten children rarely engage in comparisons and are less interested in who is bigger and older.

that examinations serve usually to unite siblings as well as other members of the nuclear family.

Under conditions of competing with strangers the achievement pressures are least controlled. Just as considerations of politeness do not prevent the shoving of strangers getting on a subway, so competitiveness is accepted as natural at the time of entrance examinations. In this way, the entrance-examination system operates to preserve the distinction between friends and strangers because blatant competition is concentrated at the time of admission when one competes with strangers. Once admitted, competition is subordinated to loyalty and friendship within the group. Thus the phenomenon of entrance examinations operates to maintain universalistic standards in such a way that it minimizes the threat to group solidarity. The cost to the individual is the anxiety and pressure which he must endure at the crucial point of admission.

ORDER AMIDST RAPID SOCIAL CHANGE

Having examined Mamachi families in some detail, we may now be able to understand how certain features found in Mamachi contributed to the amazing success of Japan in the modernizing process.

Although the contemporary Japanese social structure is in many ways different from the social structures of Europe and America, it is not simply a holdover from traditional patterns. The closed and legalized class system of the Tokugawa period has become an open class system. A predominantly rural nation has, in the last few decades, changed to an urban nation in which less than one-fourth of the male population earn their living from farming, fishing, and forestry. The landowner-tenant relationship has been weakened or destroyed by land reform. The *ie* (stem family of the male line) is being replaced by the nuclear family. In the city, small firms have been giving way to large organizations and government bureaus, and the old paternalism is fast weakening.

In spite of all this change, the picture that emerges from this study of Mamachi, as of other studies of Japanese society, presents a relatively orderly and controlled life. This is particularly striking when compared to the massive disorganization in Europe and America during the industrial revolution and to the revolutionary disruptions in the Chinese family. Although Japanese themselves have been conscious of the strains of adjusting to rapid change, they have not experienced the massive social disorganization so characteristic of many Western cities and of developing countries during the rapid migrations of the cities. The divorce rate in the United States is now five times as high as in 1885, but in Japan it is one-third as high as in 1885. Although the crime rate has gone up slightly, it has not risen sharply enough to indicate any process of widespread disorganization. The process of migration to the cities has been amazingly steady,[12] and the amount of job-changing has been relatively moderate. Unquestionably such rapid change has caused considerable strain in every Japanese individual and group, yet the disruption has remained within bounds, and a high degree of social order has been maintained throughout the transition to a modern society. It is important to consider features of Japanese social structure which have helped to maintain order at the time of the transition to urban industrial society and at the present time when the society has already achieved a high level of modernization.

In other studies, a number of features of Japanese society have already been shown to be important for the ease of Japan's modernization: a high degree of common national culture on the eve of modernization, political unity and stability, the high valuation placed on hard work and productivity, and the planning and organization of the Meiji leaders. Other features have emerged from the present study which are important to consider in the light of their contribution to this orderly process.

The Kinship System

The Japanese stem-family system, whereby one son received the inheritance and continued living with his parents while other sons went elsewhere, facilitated a smooth transition from rural to urban society. The Japanese family lines have had a continuity over generations which perhaps is unsurpassed by any other country. Even under European feudalism, land worked by a family without an heir might revert to the crown to be reassigned, but in Japan the family would itself adopt an heir. Because the family line remained in a single household, it provided a stable unit for village organization. Not only did the kinship system lend stability to rural organization, but it permitted independence for the family which moved to the city.

The movement of second and third sons to the city made it possible for the family to avoid the dissipation of family wealth through multiple inheritance that occurred, for example, in China. It also avoided the confusion that many Chinese families experienced deciding how much each son would receive. The *ie* system required that the parents select a single heir, and since they made this decision while the children were fairly young, they avoided the prolonged adolescence and the tension of the Irish family where the heir was selected at a much later stage. The fact that parents and village elders were instrumental in placing the young children in the city reinforced the authority of the older generation and prevented uncontrolled movement of young people to the city whenever they might feel dissatisfied with their elders' decisions.

The sons who moved to the city knew that they would not receive any

[12] Cf. Irene Taeuber, "Family, Migration and Industrialization in Japan," *American Sociological Review*, 1951, 16:149-157.

inheritance from their parents, and that they would be accepted back into the rural areas only temporarily in time of emergency. The young sons going to the urban areas therefore were fully committed to finding long-term work. They were willing to undergo long apprenticeships and to acquire skills useful at a later stage of life. Again this is in contrast to the migration in many countries where the migrating sons hoped to acquire money quickly and then return to their original home. Even if such migrants remained in the city indefinitely, they seldom had the perseverance to acquire the skills that would compare with the young Japanese migrant.

The younger sons who moved to the city essentially were free of family traditions. The care of elderly parents and the preservation of family property and traditions were left to the elder son who remained at the farm. The younger son came to the city at a time of life when he was able to learn new urban patterns, and there was no strong kinship or provincial association in the city which interfered with his rapid adaptation. Even close supervision from paternalistic employers in the city usually did not interfere with the essential autonomy of the nuclear family of parents and children.

The Group Control of Mobility

Although there has been considerable mobility in Japan in the past century, it has been a movement from one tightly-knit group to another through prescribed channels. This control over mobility has depended in large part on the fact that the labor supply consistently has exceeded the number of positions available.[13] Yet, with the exception of the period of the world depression in the 1930's, there has been a steady expansion of employment opportunities. As a result, people have felt optimistic enough about getting some kind of work in the city to be willing to exert themselves to obtain these limited opportunities. This has taken the form of laying careful groundwork in placing the second or third son who migrated to the city. The constant labor surplus has also permitted employers to take great care in hiring. Because groups have remained fairly tightly-knit, firms have been reluctant to take in people who are not properly sponsored. The widespread requirement of personal introductions has made it possible for local community leaders to maintain control over the emigration to the city. A person from the rural areas who has wanted a job in the city has had to go through channels in his local community in order to get a proper placement in the city.

---

[13] Indeed, many characteristics of Japanese social structure seem to follow from the surplus of labor: the fact that large organizations have more men than can efficiently be used, that women have no work, that well-to-do boys do not take part-time work in vacations for fear of taking jobs from poorer boys, and that the desire to gain security in place of work is so strong.

Even in the cities today, although the crucial factor in gaining admittance to a good school or a large enterprise is the score on the entrance examination, introductions are also desirable. This insures that the child has the proper sponsorship of his family, his community, and his previous school and serves as a powerful sanction for an individual to avoid incurring the disapproval of his own group. Since the person who manages the introduction is in the position of a guarantor for the behavior of the person he introduces, he ordinarily introduces only young people whose families have shown proper allegiance in their original community. Who is hired and under what conditions still depends on market conditions relating to the individual's competence and the labor supply even though carefully controlled by one's original and new groups.

Although firmly attached to the new group once a person moves, his original group remains his refuge in times of difficulty. If, for example, a boy is discharged by an employer or if the employer goes out of business and is unable to offer support, the boy must then turn back to his family and to the person who originally helped him find the job in order to obtain a new situation. If a girl has marital difficulties, she must go back to her original family for assistance in finding a new livelihood. Until recently, the same pattern held true even for an older woman who had trouble in marriage or for an older man who had trouble in his work. If the parents who had originally been responsible for making the placement had died, then the person who inherited the family headship would assume the same responsibility. Today, with such group responsibility somewhat diminished, the passing of years and the death of the person who made the placement may mark an effective end of the attachment to the previous group. However, immediately after the war, many people returning from overseas made claims for help on families from whom they had been separated for a generation or two, and, weakened as the claims were with the passage of time, help was often grudgingly given.

Hence, a person must remain on good terms with the group from which he originally came, even after he has been placed elsewhere. To burn one's bridges destroys security in case of difficulty in the new group. To some extent the person sent back to his original group is always regarded as a *yakkaimono* (a dependent and a nuisance), but as long as he has maintained good relationships with his group and has performed diligently in the group in which he was placed, every effort will be made to provide him with new opportunities and to give him proper care in the meantime.

To maintain good relationships with one's previous group one must also perform well in one's present group. If a girl goes back to her parental home as a result of marital difficulties, her family wants to know if she has done everything possible to make the marriage a success. To some extent, she is always regarded as responsible for marital difficulties, but if the evidence shows she really tried her best, the family and go-betweens will make every effort to find her a new opportunity. Hence, she wants to have her family's approval when she first marries so they will share the responsibility in case of difficulty. Furthermore, she keeps her family informed of the problems to make sure they will be willing to help her in an emergency. Ordinarily, she will not consider divorce or separation unless she has her family's support or at least some assurance that they will help out. Hence, even to leave her present group requires evidence that she has done everything possible to make it a success. The same is true for the young man in relation to his place of employment.

A good relationship with one's sponsors can also be a help in improving one's present situation. Even in the so-called "paternalistic" small shops and plants many employers have exploited the workers. But if the worker had been placed by an influential go-between or if the family of the worker had power and influence, he could rely upon their intervention to improve conditions. Similarly, if a girl were mistreated in marriage, her original family and go-between could bring pressure to bear to insure better treatment. The large firm or government office offers such good working conditions and job security that there is little likelihood that an employee will have to call on the family for assistance, but his original family remains his secondary security system. For the man employed in a small firm the possibility of returning to his original group remains an important consideration, as it does for a girl in her marriage.

The group control over mobility and the mechanism of returning to one's previous group in case of difficulties has contributed to the stability of the social order not only because the movement itself is orderly, but because it has reinforced the power of the group in controlling its members. It insures that a group will neither be ruined nor drastically altered by unexpected departures, and the system of returning through channels insures that a person who has failed in work or marriage may still be integrated into a tightly-knit group.

Group Control of Alienation and Change

At least until very recently, the basic cleavages in Japanese society have not been between the different social strata within a given group but between one group and another. The relationships among group members have generally been sufficiently close and humane, and the possibilities for the lower strata to shift their allegiance to another group have been so limited, that class solidarity going beyond a given group has been relatively weak. The cleavages within the rural village generally have been between one kin group and another or between two prominent families with their respective followers or between several landlords with their respective tenants. In intervillage relationships, instead of poor people in one village uniting with poor people of another village, all residents of one village have generally united to compete with other villages. Workers in a company have a strong attachment to their firm, and even today unions which link workers across company lines are weak.[14] It is precisely this pattern that has led so many Japanese social scientists to criticize their own society as feudalistic. But this feudalistic loyalty has also functioned to prevent cleavages between social classes and between age groups. Even those who complain about elders or upper class generally remain loyal to their own superiors.

Ordinarily Japanese have not been motivated to change their status radically but to rise within the confines of certain groups or through arrangements made by other members of their group. People ordinarily have not seriously considered giving up their way of life for another. Merchants, for example, have not aspired to give up business for another way of life, nor have artisans aspired to give up their crafts.[15] Even though within the last decade large numbers of farmers have turned over the farming to their wives and children while they work in nearby factories or shops, a family with a plot of land rarely expects to leave the farm.

Although Japanese have not been motivated to effect a radical change in their personal status, they have been very much motivated to effect changes within their group. They have been willing and eager to take on new techniques and develop new organizational practices which would improve their group's position relative to other groups. Many of the early pressures for modernization and rationalization came from members of an *ie* or of a firm who were trying to improve their competitive position.

For the same reason, groups also desired to take in competent employees. A business family which was to adopt a son or son-in-law regarded the competence of the young man to carry on the business as one of the most important considerations for selection. Because the owner of the small enterprise expected to be in business indefinitely and was concerned with the future of the enterprise, he was ordinarily willing to take in able young people, provide them with training, and give them opportunities to use their talent. In any field the able employee was a recognizable asset and was treated accordingly.

The paternalistic link between a tenant and the landlord or the worker and his employer have generally contained the alienation of the

---

[14] Solomon B. Levine, *Industrial Relations in Postwar Japan*, Urbana, Ill.: University of Illinois Press, 1958.

[15] Marion Levy has compared these factors in Japanese development with the different situation in China. "Contrasting Factors in the Modernization of China and Japan," *Economic Development and Cultural Change*, 1954, 2:161-197.

worker.[16] Even after World War I when many tenants and employees were beginning to have a sense of alienation against their superiors, much of it was expressed simply in the form of protesting for better conditions within a given organization. Just when alienation was becoming most severe, the seriousness of the disputes was minimized by the spirit of virulent nationalism which served to unite worker and capitalist in the same effort. Later radical societal changes, especially in the rural areas, were kept in bounds by the control of the Allied Occupation.

As a result of the willingness of groups to make changes in the interest of the group, the containment of alienation by paternalistic patterns and later by nationalistic sentiments, and the introduction of major changes under tight organizational control, it has been possible to have major changes in the society without destroying the power of the local groups. The rural community and the urban business enterprise have remained sufficiently strong to absorb the changes and keep them within bounds. However painful the process of change within groups, massive disorganization and anomie have not developed. Changes have been mediated by group consensus so that the basic social units have remained relatively solid in a time of radical changes in internal organization.

Child-Rearing, Personality, and Values

Child-rearing and certain characteristics of personality structure have lent support to the orderly process of change. The child-training techniques make the individual dependent on the group. Even in modern urban society, the concept of expelling a member from a family (*kandoo suru*) or from a village (*mura hachibu*) continue to evoke strong sentiments, and members are motivated to remain in good standing in their own group. The individual is typically group-dependent and is cautious in departing from the wishes of the group; even in moving to a new group he prefers the formality of *o-zen date* (literally, that the table be all set), whereby all arrangements are made previously and he is invited to move in. The value system which stresses the individual's loyalty to the group has given full support to the fundamental allegiance of the individual to the group and has tended to reinforce the ability of groups to control the process of change.

[16] Cf. John C. Pelzel, *Social Stratification in Japanese Urban Economic Life*, doctoral dissertation, Harvard University, 1949.

Labour-Management Relations

In any discussion of Japan's trade unions, great emphasis is always laid on the fact that the overwhelming majority are organised as "enterprise" unions, that is with the enterprise or place of work as the basic unit of organisation. The Basic Survey of Labour Unions, Japan's most authoritative trade union survey, shows that up to 90% of trade unions are organised on this basis, membership consisting of *all* employees in a given establishment. Unions organised on a national or craft basis, which is the commonest form in other countries, are very rarely found in Japan.

It is inevitable that this characteristic should have had much influence on trade union activities in Japan. Since members do not join a union of their own choice, the unions will always contain a certain proportion of workers whose "trade union consciousness" is undeveloped; thus, if union leaders attempt any very militant action, there is always the danger that members will defect and split the union. Further, since the union is based on the enterprise, both management and union leaders belong to the same firm; in these circumstances, the firm's profitability is bound to be a determining factor in any discussion or negotiations. Union activity has therefore tended to be geared to the pace set by management, for management is not obliged to regard wage levels as a constant when making managerial decisions. This has given rise to wide differences in working conditions and wage levels between different enterprises and unions, and such differences make it even more difficult to carry on concerted negotiations on an industrial or craft union basis.

Attention has often been drawn in Japan to the importance of strengthening the national unions as a means of overcoming this weakness of the Japanese trade union movement, but efforts in this direction have borne little fruit, and the enterprise unions have remained dominant. The national unions thus give an impression of being little more than loose federations of enterprise organisations, serving mainly as political

Reprinted by permission of the author and publisher from *Sociological Review Monograph*, Number 10, September 1966, pp. 69-81.

Shizuo Matsushima, graduated from Tokyo University in 1943, and has been teaching in its Department of Sociology since 1950. He specializes in industrial sociology.

groupings. The rules of the national unions do not preclude the admission of individual members, but it is normal practice for the enterprise union to be considered as the unit both in the case of affiliation to and withdrawal from the national body. In addition, when the national union is involved in a dispute, the final right to agree to any settlement is usually retained by the enterprise unions; there is very little uniformity of opinion among them, so that the national unions must spend a great deal of effort in controlling their constituent enterprise unions.

As a result, although the enterprise unions have been quite ready to obey directives to strike on political issues — the most radical type of union activity — they are very reluctant to take any decisive action on issues likely to involve friction with the management of their own enterprise — issues which, in a sense constitute a trade union's proper field of activity. Japanese trade union activity has thus taken on a distinctive character — extremely left-wing in ideology, but right-wing in the matter of action; this latter tends to take place within lines laid down by the management, except where political issues are involved.

II

What, then, are the factors which have given rise to this peculiarity of Japanese trade union activity? The first point we should keep in mind is that the pattern of personal management — the policy of the enterprise towards its workers — is very different from that found in the majority of other countries; in Japan, very great stress is laid on the security of the workers' livelihood.

This attitude is revealed first of all in the engagement of new employees by the company. Apart from candidates for executive posts, which are publicly advertised and for which a fairly stiff examination has to be passed, a very large number of firms engage employees on the strength of family ties or some other close relationship with men already employed by them. Very many firms have found no difficulty in filling their vacancies from applications received in this way, without any recourse to recruitment on the open market. This method of recruitment, of course, narrows the field of choice and precludes the possibility of selection from a wide range of capable applicants; consequently, there has recently been an increase in the number of firms which, in order to keep up with the pace of technical innovation, have felt the need for workers with a high level of basic knowledge and have therefore abandoned this practice in favour of recruitment by public advertisement. Nevertheless, the method of recruiting through personal connections has the overwhelming advantage that accurate information can be obtained about the applicant's ideology, attitudes and skills, and that it is an easy way of obtaining workers likely to identify themselves with the company's interests. The vast majority of Japanese employers, if asked whether they preferred loyal but inefficient workers to those who were efficient but had no sense of loyalty to the company, would choose the former. For the Japanese firm, placing as it does so much emphasis on loyalty, this method of recruitment through personal connections has been ideal. The majority of employees recruited in this way have been the children or close relatives of men already working for the firm. Since the worker can thus in many cases continue to live in accommodation provided by the company and to use company welfare facilities, even after his retirement, this practice has served to give the worker a substantial degree of security, for, with living costs at their present level, retirement benefits are not sufficient to assure a livelihood to the retired worker.

The characteristic attitude of the Japanese employer to his employees can also be seen in the *terms of employment*. This phrase is normally taken to refer to the purchase by the employer of a certain amount of labour for the length of time he requires it, in return for which he pays wages. In Japan, however, though the relationship is superficially the same, it does not in fact consist in the purchase of labour *only for the length of time such labour is required*. The distinctive feature of the employment relationship in Japan is that a firm (and, particularly, a large firm) makes a practice of recruiting annually from among those who have left middle school, high school or university in that year, and these new recruits will take up employment with the full intention of staying with that same firm until retirement age. Once a company has employed a worker it will not attempt to dismiss him unless circumstances make dismissal quite unavoidable. It would seem, as Abegglen pointed out in *The Japanese Factory — Aspects of Its Social Organisation*, that once a worker has been taken on, the firm relinquishes the right to regard him at any subsequent time as unsuitable for the post. For example, in a factory employing 4,350 workers discussed by Abegglen, he was astonished to find that only five or six men were dismissed each year, and this only when no possible mitigating circumstances remained — cases of persistent absenteeism, or of men who had not appeared at the factory for several weeks.

The relationship between the Japanese firm and its employees is thus a permanent one. This has meant that, compared with other countries, the movement of labour between firms in Japan has been very small and that firms have come to regard their labour costs almost as a component of their fixed costs. Consequently, there has been a lack of the flexibility and elasticity in the labour force that a firm needs to cope with fluctuations in business activity. In order to overcome this weakness and provide some flexibility in the work-force, there has grown the practice (rarely seen in other countries) of employing a section of the workers on a temporary basis, with short contracts of employment which can be renewed at intervals of from one to three months. In addition, since the labour market is closed, with workers once dismissed finding it difficult to obtain new employment in a large company, it is usual for trade unions to fight bitterly against any reduction in the labour force. This resistance serves to strengthen even further the distinctive character of the employment relationship.

The third peculiar feature of the Japanese firm is its wage structure. Typically, wages in Japan include large differentials based on the age and length of service of the worker, while insufficient attention is paid to the quality and quantity of the work itself. When a new worker enters a company, after a short period during which he is becoming accustomed to the work, his efficiency will rise sharply. Then, having reached a certain level, it will level out; then again, with the passage of time, it tends to decrease. Wages, on the other hand, will continue to rise in proportion to the worker's length of service, bearing no relationship to this efficiency curve. This type of wage curve is a distinctive feature of the Japanese wage system.

Payment of wages on an hourly basis is far more common than the piecework system, and the hourly wage is usually a so-called composite wage, with the worker's education, skill, length of service, age and work record all taken into consideration. Of these factors, length of service is given by far the greatest weight. This system of wage calculation, of course, has its advantages, reducing labour turnover and consequently the costs involved in recruiting and training new workers. But by far its more important function lies in the security it offers the worker. Since a worker's living costs are bound to increase as he grows older and his family becomes larger, given a low level of wages, it was inevitable that the wage structure should take this form. But, provided a worker remains permanently with the same employer, his age and length of service will rise together, so that wage increases given in return for his increased contribution to the enterprise (measured in length of service) do in fact parallel the increase in his living costs as he grows older.

Retirement benefit, which occurs far more widely and carries far more weight in Japan than in Europe or the United States, has largely the same character as wages. But not only is an individual's retirement benefit based on his final wage level (where the influence of length of service is already large), but this base figure is then multiplied by the number of years he has worked for the firm, and sometimes yet again by some other factor, depending on the company. The weight given to length of service in the calculation of retirement benefit, therefore, is enormous, even when compared with its part in the calculation of wages. It is very clear, therefore, that wages in Japan are paid in such a way as to make it quite contrary to the worker's interests to leave his employment before he reaches retirement age; this situation reflects the wish of the firm to provide security for the workers it has nurtured and trained.

The fourth factor to reveal the attitude of the Japanese firm to its employees is the provision of welfare services. Of course, to the worker, his wages are by far the biggest factor influencing the security of his daily life, but if the firm provides him with other assistance, in his rôle as a consumer, the real value of his wages will be increased. In Japan, expenditure by companies on this type of welfare benefit is very high. According to a survey made in 1961 by the Japan Employers' Federation, the highest figure for this type of expenditure was in the construction industry, at 8,584 yen per worker per month, followed by mining at 7,909 yen and the ceramic industry at 6,890 yen. The average for all firms included in the survey was 4,554 yen per month, while the average wage was 39,041 yen. Expenditure on welfare benefits thus amounted to about 13% of the monthly wage bill.

These welfare benefits most commonly take the form of grants of money on such occasions as marriage, childbirth, illness, death and so on, and the provision of workers' housing, subsidised shopping facilities, and grants or loans in support of various cultural activities. The very high ratio of welfare benefits paid voluntarily to those which Japanese companies are legally obliged to pay reveals the extent of their concern for their workers' welfare and contrasts sharply with the practice in other countries. Of course, the provision of workers' housing near to the place of work in industries such as mining and construction, which often operate in isolated districts, and in industries where technical progress has brought with it a three-shift system of working, could be said to be a necessary development towards the provision of security for the worker; this housing should thus be regarded as part of the productive facilities of the enterprise. But the present situation, however we look at it, is one of over-service to the worker, and even if we accept the argument that this represents an addition of so many thousand yen to the worker's wage-packet, there is a real problem in the fact that this is not paid over to the worker in cash.

The Japanese worker has always set great store by such fringe benefits received over and above his wages, which have served to cover up Japan's low wages to a certain extent and helped to bring about the companies' attitude of concern and responsibility for the daily life of the worker.

In addition to the examples mentioned above, we could mention such practices as share-ownership schemes, and various special training schemes operated by companies for their employees.

III

The term "familism" has often been used to describe this characteristic
Japanese social relationship. Up to the beginning of the Second World
War, the Japanese family had certain distinctive features as a social
group. First, the individual's interests were subordinated to the welfare
of the family as a whole. Secondly, the members of the family were
organised in a hierarchy — head of the family, eldest son, second son
and so on, and, thirdly, the relationship existing between these members
was not one of domination and submission; the head of the family staked
his honour on assuring the livelihood of its members, who willingly co-
operated with him in his efforts to this end.

This relationship of "familism," through the peculiar development of
capitalism in Japan, is found not only in the family unit, but throughout
Japanese society, in rural communities and elsewhere. The same sort of
relationship exists in labour relations: first, the interests of the individual
are subordinated to those of the enterprise. Secondly, a distinct hierarchy
is formed by the creation of differences in status within the enterprise.
In the third place, although the rights of management are guaranteed
by this hierarchical structure, only very rarely must this authority be
openly exercised, since, in return for the company's emphasis on the
provision of security for the workers, they come to have a very strong
affection for the company. "Managerial Familism" is, I feel, a suitable
term for this relationship.

Familism as an "ideology of management" has been emphasised far
less, however, since the end of the Second World War, when it developed
into what is merely a policy of concern for the security of the workers'
livelihood. There are also very wide differences in the form taken by
this relationship between large and small enterprises. In small firms there
is little wage variation based on length of service and age. Up to the
age of thirty or so, wages rise in much the same way as in the larger
enterprises, but after that the curve rises less steeply and a fairly wide
gap develops between wages in the two types of enterprise. In small
companies retirement benefit is either very small or non-existent, while
welfare benefits, where they exist at all, are usually confined to token
money gifts of congratulation or commiseration, requiring little regular
expenditure.

However, what the small enterprise is unable to provide in material
terms is made up for by the strong personal ties, since the smaller the
enterprise the higher the proportion of family members among its workers. These family members serve as the strategic base from which
management can adjust human relationships within the enterprise, the
other employees being embraced in the "quasi-family" atmosphere. In
many cases the proprietor of a small company will live on or very near

the company's premises and young employees will live in their employer's house — a literal "management family."

In a large firm, however, the ties of personal connection are inevitably slender, being replaced by systematized security in the form of wages, welfare benefits and training schemes. Nevertheless, although the form taken may differ, the attitude of management is essentially the same.

This system of management does, of course, have its shortcomings. Personnel management becomes very inefficient; this leads to confusion in the operation of the enterprise and makes it very difficult to express any of the operations in terms of figures. It is almost impossible to predict results and formulate rational plans for the future — a vital task in any modern enterprise. It is true, of course, that this type of management is gradually changing, in response to the demands of technical progress, and efforts are being made, slowly and gradually, to put personnel administration on a more scientific and ordered basis. However, this process has got no further than a partial reform and systematization of these traditional Japanese practices and it cannot yet be said that it has achieved a real correction of the shortcomings referred to above.

Nevertheless, in spite of these shortcomings, the rapid progress made by Japanese industry over the past few years is undeniable; this type of managerial practice must have had some useful function to perform for it ever to have come into existence. We find that it has, in fact, performed a very useful function by arousing in the worker a feeling of affection for the company that employs him and by involving his daily life very closely with the fortunes of that company.

It might seem that these results have been bought at a very high price, but when we consider the number of working days that might be lost and the even higher wages and better working conditions that might have to be conceded as a result of labour disputes, as well as the fall in productivity that could result from low morale, it can be seen that the price is still very low. This is shown very clearly by an international comparison of labour disputes. According to Ross and Hartmann[1] Japan has the second highest figure — after France — for the ratio of the number of workers participating in strike action to the total number of organised workers. Japan's figure is about the same as that for America, three to four times as high as that for Britain, and ten times as high as that for West Germany. However, if we consider the average number of working days lost per striking worker, excluding 1952, the figure for Japan is from three to five days, about the same as for Britain, and half the figure for West Germany. In America the figure is ten days, two or three times that for Japan. Further, if we divide the total number of days lost through strike action by the total number of organised workers (not the

[1] Ross, A. M. & Hartmann, P. T.: *Changing Patterns of Industrial Conflict*, Wiley, London, 1960, p. 205, 9.

total labour force), the resulting figure – the number of working days
lost per union member – is less than one for every year except 1952. In
other words, fewer working days were lost than there were union
members.

We can summarize this situation thus: in other countries, unions are
very loath to indulge in strike action, but once they do go on strike, they
fight to the bitter end, so that strikes tend to be protracted. In Japan,
on the other hand, strikes occur relatively often, but end quickly, involving no very deep conflict between labour and management.

IV

Let us now consider the reasons for the development of these attitudes
on the part of management, which in their turn have given rise to the
characteristic pattern of Japanese trade union behaviour. Personnel
management as we see it today in Japan is of fairly recent origin; until
about 1920 it was very rare for a company to be the direct employer
of its own workers. Until the Russo-Japanese War of 1904-5, most
recruitment and disposition of the work force was done by experienced
workers – who would be called foremen today; they were also responsible
for training, so that there was no reason for the personnel administration
organisation of the company to develop. Wages were paid on an efficiency
basis, either to each individual, or calculated for a small group of workers
together. The wage system did not therefore provide any security of
livelihood as it does today, nor were welfare services at all highly developed.

Under such conditions, labour was very mobile indeed. According to
Shokkō Jijō,[2] the excellent government survey published in 1905, 12.9%
of machine operators had less than six months' service with their firm,
and 39.6% between six months' and one year's service; so over 50%
had changed their place of employment within the space of a year.
However, from about the time of the First World War, the situation began to change, with workers coming under the direct control of the
company which employed them, and by about 1920 this pattern of very
high labour mobility had almost disappeared. The reason for this change
was not only that a high labour turnover involved companies in heavy
expenditure on recruiting, but that, with the introduction of modern
techniques, the migratory "jack-of-all-trades" type of worker was needed
less and less, his place being taken by large numbers of workers who had
received a training in a fairly narrowly specialised field, and were therefore
better fitted for the new situation with its emphasis on the division of
labour.

From about this period, therefore, the enterprise organisation that we
see today began to be established, with its status differentiation between

2 *The Condition of the Workers*, Vol. 2, p. 11.

staff, first class operators, second class operators and so on. The longer the worker's service with the firm, the better were his working conditions, the stress being shifted from degree of experience — hitherto the most important factor — to length of service, with a corresponding increase in the welfare services provided. Thus working conditions, which had been relatively uniform in the period of high labour mobility, began to show differences from firm to firm and the system of personnel management which we have referred to above came into being.

We are still left, however, with the problem of why, once this development had occurred, there was not a far more thorough bureaucratisation of the system of personnel management, and why employment relations in Japan never took the shape of a true buying and selling of labour power. The explanation lies in the peculiarity of the development of the Japanese labour movement. Of course, as so often happens with origins, it is difficult to say exactly when the Japanese labour movement started. We are told that in 1862 there was a strike in part of the Besshi Copper Mine, or that at the beginning of the Meiji era there were riots at various mines and movements for the amelioration of working conditions in the handicraft industries. But these were for the most part lacking in organisation and somewhat different in character from the labour movement as we know it today — a by-product of the Industrial Revolution, whose participants are true modern workers. Looked at in this way, the strikes at the Amamiya Spinning Company in Kōfu in 1886 and the Temma Spinning Company in Osaka in 1894 can perhaps be regarded as the first labour disputes to take place in firms with modern systems of management, so that we can put the start of the Japanese labour movement in the last years of the nineteenth century.

The war with China in 1894-5 gave a great impetus to the development of capitalism in Japan. The labour force increased rapidly, to 400,000 in 1897 and 600,000 in 1907, while the rise in prices caused by the war and the cuts in wages in the depression immediately afterwards both affected the living standards of the people very seriously. It was in these circumstances that Katayama Sen, Takano Fusatarō and others who had returned from America set up the Shokkō Giyūkai ('Volunteer Workers' Society) in 1897. That year also saw the first public lecture meeting on the subject of labour, with enthusiastic speeches pointing out the need for the workers to organise. As a result, the Machine Operators' Union was formed in 1897, followed in the next year by the Railwaymen's Union and the Printers' Union. Labour disputes also increased, from 32 cases in 1897, involving 3,510 workers, to 43 cases involving 6,293 workers in 1898.

This was the first peak in the history of the early labour movement, but it was not to last long. In 1900 the Public Peace Police Act was passed, with the purpose of suppressing the labour movement; it provided for terms of from one to six months' imprisonment or fines, for anyone guilty of demanding negotiations with employers, or of inciting others to join a union or go on strike. The police were thus given an excuse to interfere directly in labour disputes and, as a result, there began a series of defections by union members; this was a severe blow to the union movement, which had not yet achieved sufficient strength to weather an attack of this sort. In the next year, 1901, the first workers' political party, the Shakai Minshutō (Social Democratic Party) was founded by Abe Isoo, Katayama Sen, Kōtoku Shūsui and others, only to be suppressed on the day of its formation, leaving the workers with no legal means of bettering their condition. Inevitably the labour movement continued to work illegally, but it was everywhere faced with ruthless oppression.

From that time until the First World War, the labour movement was given no chance to breathe, though sporadic disputes did occur. The chance for the second peak in its history came with the foundation in 1912 of the Yūaikai (Friendly Love Society). This society pledged itself to "fight to the death for socialism" and espoused a creed of harmony between labour and capital. Nevertheless, the outbreak of the First World War aided even further the development of capitalism – the work force increasing to 1,700,000 – and the distress caused by inflation led to an explosive increase in the number of labour disputes. In 1919, which saw 63,000 workers taking part in 497 disputes, the Yūaikai changed its name to Dai Nippon Rōdō Sōdōmei Yūaikai (Greater Japan General Federation of Labour – Friendly Love Society) becoming noticeably more militant and in 1920 sponsored Japan's first May Day celebrations. In this period, too, the need began to be felt for a guiding principle for trade unionism and, partly because of the influence of the Russian revolution, the association between the labour movement and socialism began. In 1922 the Japan Communist Party was formed, and by 1926 Japan possessed 488 unions, with a total membership of over 350,000.

This was the state of the labour movement when, in 1925, the Public Peace Preservation Law was enacted. It laid down penalties of up to ten years' imprisonment for anyone organizing or joining any group which advocated the reform of the structure of the state, or the abolition of the system of private property. The maximum penalty for the first of these offences was later increased to one of death. In 1931 the number of persons arrested and interrogated under the provisions of this law was 10,422 and in 1932 the figure reached 14,624, clear evidence of the extent of the oppression. Thus trade union activity in Japan was once more cut off abruptly and entered its Dark Age, which was to last until trade unions were given public recognition after the end of the Second World War.

Two facts emerge clearly from an examination of the history of the trade union movement in Japan. The first is that the establishment of Japan's characteristic type of personnel management coincided with the second peak in the movement's history, and that these management methods were developed by employers, largely to combat the rising tide of union activity. The second fact that we should note is that in prewar Japan the union movement was stifled before it had developed into a movement worthy of the name. The normal course of development is for the working class to mature as capitalism develops, becoming a true proletariat and organising itself into a union movement. In Japan's case, however, the organisation of the workers lagged far behind the development of capital, so that, when union activities really began after the Second World War, employers' management policies and methods were already prepared; they were thus able to seize the initiative in the very areas where the unions should have been most active.

In other countries industrial or craft unions with a highly centralised organisation have been able to monopolize their own specific sector of the labour market, controlling it and turning the relationship of supply and demand to their own advantage in order to improve working conditions. In addition, because of their control over the labour market, the unions have assumed the function of labour exchanges and, where union membership is voluntary, this has been a strong factor in encouraging workers to join the unions. And since financial difficulties arising from illness or unemployment can turn a union member into a strike-breaker, the function of unions as mutual aid societies is also very important. They have therefore undertaken the operation of hospitals and sales organisations, as well as the payment of benefits to their members on the occasion of sickness, death, or unemployment. These activities have served to make the unions more attractive, increasing their appeal to their members.

In Japan, however, by the time the unions came into existence, the characteristic employment relationship of the Japanese enterprise had already developed, leaving the unions no scope for controlling the labour market and acting as employment agencies. The employers had also set up their own facilities to provide for the welfare and security of their workers, leaving the unions no direct point of contact with the daily lives of their members. The basis for the development of industrial or craft unions in Japan was thus very weak, and the unions have ended up by being enclosed within each firm as enterprise unions. In such circumstances, the only basis for united action is on political issues; as a result, the Japanese unions have inevitably tended to give too much weight to political activity. A situation exists, therefore, where unity is possible on political issues, but unattainable on issues which are more properly the concern of the trade union movement. The unions are therefore forced into the situation we have already mentioned, where they can act only after the initiative has been taken by the management.

There are gradual changes in this pattern of labour-management relations. As social and economic conditions alter and technical innovation proceeds, further changes are inevitable in the future, particularly if the unions are able to strengthen their position. But the description we have given presents a fair picture of the peculiar character of labour relations in Japan at the present moment.

Selective Bibliography

Bennett, John W. and Ishino, Iwao, *Paternalism in the Japanese Economy* (Minneapolis: University of Minnesota Press, 1963).
    Ethnographic studies of work groups in the period immediately following World War II that illuminate earlier traditions of paternalism and solidarity.

Beardsley, Richard, et al., *Village Japan* (Chicago: University of Chicago Press, 1959).
    A comprehensive study of a modern rural area.

Dore, R. P., *City Life in Japan* (Berkeley: University of California Press, 1958).
    Although somewhat outdated due to the rapidity of change in Japan, the book is a landmark in the study of urban life; it concentrates on a ward in Tokyo, but views it as part of the larger society.

Halmos, Paul, ed., "Japanese Sociological Studies," *The Sociological Review Monograph*, No. 10, September 1966.
    Selected studies by Japanese social scientists.

Lockwood, William W., ed., *The State and Economic Enterprise in Japan* (1965).

Jansen, Marius, ed., *Japanese Attitudes Toward Modernization* (1966).

Dore, R. P., ed., *Social Change in Contemporary Japan* (1967).
    In this series, published by the Princeton University Press, are the collected papers from the "Conferences on Modern Japan," many written by Japanese social scientists. Most of the main contemporary issues are raised and probed.

Kawai, Kazuo, *Japan's American Interlude* (Chicago: University of Chicago Press, 1960).
    An excellent history of the reforms during the American Occupation, and their effects on Japanese society.

Norman, Sir Herbert E., *Japan's Emergence as a Modern State* (New York: Institute of Pacific Relations, 1940).
    Perhaps the most incisive account of the settlement made by the Meiji restoration with the old feudal powers.

Odaka, Kunio and Nishihira, Sigeki, "Social Mobility in Japan: A Report on the 1955 Survey," *East Asian Cultural Studies*, IV (March 1965), 83-126.
    A detailed analysis of a survey on father-son mobility. See also in the same volume the bibliography by Ken'ichi Tominaga, "The Trends of Studies in Social Stratification and Social Mobility in Japan," 74-82.

Reischauer, Edward, *The United States and Japan* (Cambridge, Mass.: Harvard University Press, 1953).
   A standard history of modern Japan, with emphasis on her relations with the United States. Professor Reischauer has served as United States Ambassador to Japan.

Sansom, Sir George, *Japan: A Short Cultural History* (New York: Appleton-Century, Rev. Ed., 1943).
   An explanation of the continuities in Japanese life that form part of the background of the present society.